Kyung Moon Reading Classic 001

William Faulkner

The Sound and the Fury

Edited and Annotated with Introduction

by Kang, Hee

KYUNG MOON Publishers

감사의 글

먼저 본 편저서의 본문은 다음의 포크너 텍스트들을 참고하였음을 알려둔다.

The Sound and the Fury. Corrected ed.: New York: Random House, 1984.

——. US paperback ed.: New York: Vintage, 1990.

——. New York: Vintage International, 1990.

——. Norton Critical Edition, 2nd ed., David Minter, ed. New York: Norton, 1994.

또한 본문 주석들의 내용은 로스(Stephen M. Ross)와 폴크(Noel Polk)가 편집한 *Reading Faulkner: The Sound and the Fury* (Jackson: UP of Mississippi, 1996)로부터 많은 도움을 받았다.

그리고 이 책이 나오기 위해 소중한 시간과 노력을 아끼지 않은 학부와 대학원 제자들, 김정미, 김경모, 김진복, 김도윤, 허지영, 배우선, 최명화, 김지혜, 남양미, 그리고 마지막까지 교정을 위해 함께 읽어 준 손현지와 박은미, 모두에게 감사의 마음을 보낸다.

1. 캄슨 집안의 가부장들과 현 시점의 가족 구성원

제1세대. Quentin MacLachan Compson(1699-1783)—스코트랜드 출신 출판업자의 아들, 캐롤라이나 주에 정착, 그 후 켄터키 주로 이주. (이후 Compson 표기 생략).

제2세대. Charles Steward—자신의 영국군 연대로부터 부상당한 채 버려짐. 켄터키 주로 돌아와 교사, 도박꾼을 전전하다, 미시시피 강 유역을 미국에서 탈퇴하여 스페인에 합병하는 정치연합에 연루되며, 미국에 대한 반역행위보다 그의 과격한 목소리와 행동이 결국 그를 (미국으로부터) 추방당하게 함.

제3세대. Jason Lycurgus—1811년, 미시시피 주 제퍼슨에 정착, 인디언들과 상거래.

제4세대. Q. M.(Quentin MacLachan) II—미시시피 주지사.

제5세대. Jason Lycurgus II—남북전쟁시, 준장으로 참여(군인으로서 실패), 1900년 사망. 이 시점서부터 캄슨 집안의 가세가 기울기 시작. 남부재건(Reconstruction) 시, 집과 땅/농장 저당 잡힘.

제6세대. (작품의 현시점) Jason III (Mr. Compson)—Caroline Bascomb과 결혼. 제이슨 캄슨은 1912년 사망, 캐롤라인은 1933년 사망.

제7세대. Quentin III, Caddy, Jason IV, Benjy.

제8세대. Miss Quentin (캐디의 딸)—혼돈을 피하기 위해 Miss Quentin으로 표기.

현시점의 캄슨가

제이슨과 캐롤라인 캄슨 부부 사이의 4명의 아이들.

퀸턴 III (1890-1910)

캔디스(캐디) (1892-?); 딸 미스 퀸턴 1910년 11월 출생

제이슨 IV (1894-?)

벤자민(벤지) (1895-?)

깁슨가

로스커스와 딜시(Roskus & Dilsey Gibson) 사이에는 버어시(Versh), 티피(T.P.), 그리고 딸 프로니(Frony)가 있음.

버시가 어린 시절 벤지를 돌봤고, 이후에는 티피가 벤지를 돌보며, 러스터(Luster)는 현시점에서 벤지 돌봄 (러스터는 프로니의 아들).

2. 주요시점

벤지 장

주요시점

시점	돌보는 이	사건과 이미지들
1900년	버어시 (벤지가 13세 때까지)	외할머니 죽음, 강가의 물놀이, 캐디의 드레스 벗어 던지는 사건, 퀀턴과 캐디의 다툼, 그녀의 흙 묻은 속옷, 배나무 사건 등. (혹자는 여기까지의 사건을 1898년의 사건들로 본다.)
		모리에서 벤지로 이름 바꿈, 화난 어머니의 모습과 캐디에게 벤지 업고 다니지 말라는 명령, 서재에서의 장면, 지붕 위의 빗소리, 거울 속의 난롯불, 제이슨이 캐디가 벤지를 위해 만들어 준 종이인형들을 못 쓰게 만들어 싸움.
1906	티피	캐디의 향수 사용. 캐디와 벤지가 딜시에게 그 향수 선물.
		캐디와 찰리의 그네 사건(혹자는 이 그네 사건을 1908-10년의 시점으로 본다).
1908	//	초여름, 벤지 혼자 패터슨 부인에게 모리 삼촌의 편지 심부름.
1908-9		12월 크리스마스 이틀 전, 캐디와 벤지 함께

시점	돌보는 이	사건과 이미지들
		패터슨 부인께 삼촌의 연애편지 심부름, 모리 삼촌의 멍든 눈.
		벤지 이제 13세로 캐디 곁을 떠나 혼자서 자야만 함.
1910	//	캐디의 순결 상실. 퀸턴 학교서 싸움.
(4월25일)	//	캐디 결혼식, 벤지와 티피 술에 만취.
(4-5월)	//	벤지가 버지스 딸을 '공격', 벤지의 거세.
(6월2일)	//	퀸턴의 자살, 댄(개 이름)의 울부짖음.
1912	//	캄슨씨의 죽음, 캄슨씨 장례식 날 캐디의 딸(미스 퀸턴)에 대한 언급들, 가족의 묘지 방문 시작(1912 혹은 1913년).
1915	러스터	딜시 남편 로스커스 사망, 할아버지 혼령 본 러스터, 블루(개)의 울부짖음.
1928 현재 (4월 7일)	//	골프 장면, 러스터의 잃어버린 동전, 제이슨이 구매한 새 차, 벤지의 생일케이크, 미스 퀸턴과 그녀의 빨간색 넥타이의 남자, 둘의 그네 사건 등.

퀸턴 장

시점	사건
	어린 시절의 사건들은 앞의 벤지 장과 동일.
1906	나탈리와의 사건. (혹자는 이 사건이 1900-01년경에 일어났다고도 함.)
1907	캐디의 첫 키스, 성에 눈을 뜨면서 화장 지워진, 죄지은 모습의 캐디.
1909	달턴에게 캐디의 처녀성 상실, 달턴을 두고 나누는 오빠 퀸턴과 캐디와의 대화들, 퀸턴이 칼을 캐디의 목에 들이대는 장면, 순결 문제를 두고 퀸턴과 아버지가 나누는 대화, 퀸턴의 근친상간 (근거 없는) 주장, 아버지의 염세주의적, 여성혐오적인 발언들, 달턴을 향한 퀸턴의 경고.
	가을, 캐디의 성 더욱 문란해지자 캄슨 부인은 제이슨으로 하여금 그녀를 염탐케 함, 퀸턴 하버드에서 가을학기 시작.
1910	3월경, 캄슨 부인은 마을에 돌고 있는 스캔들을 피하고 캐디의 결혼 상대를 고르기 위해 그녀를 데리고 휴양지(French Lick)로 여행, 퀸턴은 그들의 가방을 관으로 생각, 휴양지에서 캐디와 허버트의 만남.
	4월 하순경, 결혼식 준비와 차 드라이브, 퀸턴과 허버트간의 대화, 허버트(와 그의 목소리)를 총으로 죽이는 퀸턴의 상상, 캐디에게 결혼하지 말라는 퀸턴의 독려.
	4월 25일, 임신 2개월의 몸으로 캐디의 결혼식(1911년 이혼).
	6월 2일, 자살을 위한 퀸턴의 하루 동안의 여정—시계와 관련된 일들, 편지들, 가방, 디콘에게 부탁할 일, 두 발목에 채울 다리미 두 개, 강가의 소년들, 이탈리아 소녀와의 만남, 제랄드와의 싸움 등.

3. 각 장의 시점과 화자

제1장(벤지 장). 1928년 4월 7일(토요일)—백치 벤지의 감각을 통해 누이 캐디를 구심점으로 캄슨가의 이야기 서술.

제2장(퀸턴 장). 1910년 6월 2일—퀸턴의 입장에서 서술, 그리고 그의 자살.

제3장(제이슨장). 1928년 4월 6일(금요일)—현재 캄슨가의 가부장 역할을 하고 있는 제이슨의 입장에서 서술.

제4장. 1928년 4월 8일(일요일)—작가가 객관적 입장에서 서술하지만 이야기의 중심에 딜시가 있으며, 그 중심은 점차 제이슨에게로 옮겨감.

작품의 각 장은 자신의 이야기를 서술하고 있는 각 화자가 아침에 일어나서, 저녁에 잠자리에 들 때까지(벤지, 제이슨) 그리고 자살하기 직전까지(퀸턴), 하루 동안 일어나는 사건의 진행을 서술하고 있으며, 그 흐름 속으로 끊임없이 과거의 기억들이 치열하게 끼어들어 상존하고 있음을 보여준다.

각 장의 시점은 성서적 차원에서 작품의 주제의식과 연관하여 그 상징적 중요성을 읽어낼 수 있다. 먼저 벤지 장의 토요일("Holy Saturday")은 예수가 십자가에 못 박힌 다음날로 기독교에서는 인류 역사상 가장 불행한 '암흑의 날'로 의미되기에, 작품에서 벤지 실존의 의미와 그의 서사가 갖는 상징성을 연결하여 생각해 볼 수 있다 (벤지 자신이 그리스도로 비유되기도 한다). 제이슨 장의 금요일 ("Good Friday")은 예수가 십자가에 못 박힌 날로, 예수 희생의 의미와 작품에서 제이슨의 실존이 던지는 삶과 그 경험의 의미를 생각해 보며 그의 서사가 갖는 상징성을 곱씹어볼 수 있다. 마지막 장의 일요일은 부활절("Easter Sunday")로서 예수가 죽음으로부터 부활하는 날로, 이 날의 의미와 작품에서 딜시의 중요성 그리고 캄슨가의 운명을 연결하여 생각해 보아야 할 것이다.

4. 각 장의 사건 개요

벤지 장

* 1928년 4월 7일은 벤지가 아침에 일어나 저녁에 잠자리에 들 때까지 하루 동안의 진행 과정을 서술하고 있는 벤지 장의 현시점이다. 이 장은 주변에서 들려오는 소리나 냄새 등 백치 벤지의 감각들이 누이 캐디에 대한 기억들을 일깨우면서, 과거의 기억들이 끊임없이 현재 속으로 드나들고 있는 그의 하루에 대한 이야기를 서술한다. 벤지장의 스토리는, 그날 밤 카니발 쇼 구경을 가기 위해 러스터가 잃어버린 동전을 찾아 헤매면서, 벤지와 동행하고 있는 둘 간의 하루여정이 벤지 장의 사건과 기억들을 감싸면서 병치 · 서술되고 있다. 백치의 심상을 들여다보는 것도 결코 쉬운 일이 아니지만, 첫 장이기 때문에 더욱 혼란스럽게 느껴지는 벤지 장은 러스터와 함께 아침에 집을 나와 주변 울타리와 인접한 골프장 주위를 돌면서 시작된다. 현시점 속으로 진입하고 있는 벤지 기억들의 행렬은 다음과 같이 간추려 볼 수 있다:

  * 패터슨 부인에게 모리 삼촌의 편지를 전달하면서 관련된 기억들;
  * 캄슨씨의 사망 후 기일을 맞아 가족들 공동묘지로 향하는 모습;
  * 어린 시절 강가의 기억과 함께, 할머니 임종하시던 날의 여러 기억들; 여기서 캐디 결혼식 날에 대한 기억들도 끼여 듦; 그리고 함께 연상되는 집안의 다른 죽음들(퀀턴, Mr. 캄슨, 로스커스);
  * 성에 눈을 뜬 캐디의 기억을 중심으로 이어지면서, 캐디의 향수 사건; 13세 된 벤지와 한 침대에서의 잠자리를 거부하는 캐디;

그리고 캐디와 찰리의 그네 장면에 대한 기억은 현시점의 조카 미스 퀸턴과 그녀의 남자친구와의 그네 장면과 오버랩;

* 버지스 딸 에피소드; 그 사건의 결과로 이어지는 벤지의 거세;
* 벤지의 개명(모리에서 벤자민)에 대한 기억; 그리고 캐디가 벤지를 따뜻하게 보살피던 다른 기억들(캐디와 제이슨의 싸움);
* 캐디의 순결 상실; 미스 퀸턴과 제이슨의 갈등 구도;
* 현시점에서, 잠자리에 들기 전, 잠옷을 갈아입으며 자신의 없어진 신체부위; 미스 퀸턴이 집을 탈출하는 장면; 어린시절 캐디와 함께 잠자리에 들던 기억으로 잠 속으로 빠져드는 벤지.

퀸턴 장

퀸턴 장의 현시점(1910년 6월 2일)은 퀸턴이 하버드 대학에서 막 1년의 학업을 마친 시점이고, 이 날은 그가 자살하는 날이다. 이날 하루 사건의 진행을 간단히 살펴보면,

* 아침에 기숙사 방에서 눈을 뜨면서, 시간과 누이라는 말에 집착하는 퀸턴의 모습과 함께; 아버지께 보내는 봉투 속에 가방열쇠를 넣고 2개의 편지 준비(하나는 아버지께 보낼 노트, 다른 하나는 쉬리브에게 남기는 노트); 보석점(시계점)과 철물점(다리미 2개 구매) 경유; 이 모든 와중에도 그는 끊임없이 시계소리와 자신의 그림자의 진행 과정에 집착하고 있다.
* 전차를 탄 후 흑인들 그리고 딜시와 로스커스를 생각하고; 그가 초등생일 때 시간을 어떻게 세었는지의 기억 속으로 빠져들기도 하고; 벤지가 변화를 감지하는 능력과 그의 이름이 바뀌었을 때, 그리고 시간의 흐름에 무지한 벤지에 대한 기억 등으로 빠져 든다.

* 전차에서 내려 다리 근처로 향하며, 그림자 계속 주시; 강 위에 떠 있는 보트(a shell)를 보며 제랄드 생각(그의 여성 편력), 이어지는 달턴에 대한 생각과 함께, 아버지 캄슨씨의 여성관, 그리고 허버트에게로 생각은 이어지고; 주머니 속 쉬리브에게 줄 편지를 디콘에게 전달; 쉬리브 만나, 철물점에서 산 다리미를 신발이라고 거짓말, 블랜드 부인으로부터 쪽지; 다시 시내로 향하며, 전차에서 내려 근처 강을 따라가며 제랄드와 달턴 생각, 허버트와의 대화도 함께 연상, 캐디의 불명예, 임신, 여성의 성; 강가에서 송어잡이 소년들과의 만남, 캐디의 성적인 몸, 허버트 . . . 이 모든 생각들이 함께 뒤섞여 연결; 이탈리아 소녀와의 만남, 불결한 여성의 성, 나탈리와의 에피소드가 함께 연결되어 이어지고, 급기야 (이탈리아) 소녀의 유괴범으로 몰려 치안판사 앞으로; 소풍 나온 대학친구들과 블랜드 부인 일행 만나 함께 사건 수습; 캐디의 문란한 성과 처녀성 상실의 이미지와 함께 연결되는 1909년 여름 강가 장면(퀸턴, 캐디 목에 칼 들이대는); 달턴과의 대면 장면과 이어지는 제랄드와의 싸움; 이 모든 사건들에 대한 기억의 구심점에는, 언제나 캐디와 관련된 기억들과 여성의 오염되고 불결한 성에 대한 이야기가 끊임없이 자리잡고 있다.
* 어린 시절 동화책 속의 가족 그림에 대한 기억; 해질녘, 강물/인동 덩굴의 내음/어머니/죽음의 이미지들이 아버지와의 대화와 함께 퀀턴 장 마지막 부분을 장식하며; 기숙사로 돌아와 다시 몸단장을 하고 마지막 외출을 준비하는 모습으로 퀀턴 장은 맺는다.

제이슨 장은 앞의 두 장들과 비교해 과거 기억들이 현저히 줄어들면서, 거의 현재 시점에서 빠른 속도로 사건들이 진행되고 있다. 조카(미스 컨턴)와의 아침 소동 후 가게(Earl이 소유)에 출근, 캐디에게서 온 편지를 읽고; 한 세일즈맨을 만나 유태인들에 대한 이야기를 나누며; 캐디에게 전보를 치며 증권시장도 점검; 가게로 다시 돌아와 로레인의 편지 본 후 태움; 가족과 집안이야기, 캐디에 대한 기억(어린 컨턴을 두고 홍정하는 잔인한 제이슨과 캐디의 애타는 모성), 캐디 편지와 딸에게 보낸 수표(money order)를 두고 조카 컨턴과 나누는 대화, 캐디가 보낸 수표와 딸에게 보낸 수표까지 은행에 입금한 후 가게로 돌아와 얼과 언쟁(어머니 캐롤라인을 속인다고); 전보, 투자한 주식의 손실(account closed); 얼 허락받고 급히 집에 숨겨둔 돈 갖고 나오다 조카와 함께 있는 녀석 발견; 둘의 추적 시작, 시골길 들어서며 그들을 놓치고, 걸어서 추적하다 차로 돌아오자 둘이 그의 차 타이어 바람을 빼놓고 도주, 시내까지 걸어가 펌프를 구하고, 가솔린 냄새에 격심한 두통; 시내 돌아와 또 다른 전보, 주가 추락; 저녁식사를 하며 다시 조카랑 싸움; 잠자리 들기 위해 자기 방으로 향하면서 벤지방에서 들려오는 엄청난 코골이 소리와 함께, 모녀(캐디와 미스 컨턴)의 거세를 바라는 제이슨의 욕망, 그리고 (주식에서 잃은 돈의 회복을 위해) 하루를 되돌렸으면 하는 그의 욕망으로 제이슨 장은 마무리된다.

마지막 장은 딜시가 오두막에서 나와 날씨를 점검한 후 아침준비를 하는 모습으로 시작; 나무를 주워 캄슨 집으로 향하며 (앞치마를 입고 불을 지피며), 캐롤라인도 일어나 아침준비, 전날 밤 쇼 구경 갔던 러스터가 늦게 일어나 아침 늦게 시작; 딜시는 러스터를 불러서 이층으로 올라가 벤지를 깨워 옷을 입히라고 말하고, 장작이 타는 모습과 시계소리에 귀를 기울이며 부엌에서 딜시만의 순간을 포착; 그 후 러스터가 벤지를 데리고 내려오자 처음으로 벤지의 모습에 대한 묘사; 딜시는 러스터에게 제이슨도 깨우라고 명하고, 제이슨의 심상치 않는 분위기—방 창문이 깨진데 대한 불평과 함께 러스터와 벤지가 그 짓을 저질렀다고 욕함; 미스 퀜턴이 사라진 것을 안 후, 캐롤라인은 퀜턴이 없어진 것을 그녀의 자살로 짐작; 17세의 미스 퀜턴은 제이슨 금고에서 현금을 (약 7000달러로 추정) 빼내 도주; 딜시, 벤지를 데리고 흑인 교회로; 제이슨의 도난 신고와 보안관과의 대화; 미스 퀜턴에 대한 제이슨의 엄청난 분노와 함께 모든 문제를 자신을 제외한 다른 사람들의 탓으로 돌리며 자신이 속임을 당한데 대해 울분을 토하는 제이슨의 모습; 미스 퀜턴이 함께 도주하고 있는 그 남자가 소속된 쇼 단의 목적지인 못슨을 향해 그들 추적; 둘을 추적하는 도중 미치도록 화가 난 제이슨은 마치 세상이 그가 조카를 추적하는데 음모라도 꾸미고 있다고 생각하며, 교회를 지나면서 신을 저주하기까지 하고; 못슨에 도착하여 쇼 단의 나이든 요리사와의 싸움; 그리고 쇼 책임자로부터 같이 도주했다는 그 녀석의 해고 소식 전해 들음; 집으로 돌아오며, 길가에서 벤지와 러스터가 벌이고 있는 창피한 광경을 두고 보여주는 제이슨의 난폭한 반응과 함께, 평온함과 질서를 되찾은 벤지의 모습으로 이야기는 끝을 맺는다.

차 례

April Seventh, 1928

Through the fence,[1] between the curling flower spaces, I could see them hitting.[2] They were coming toward where the flag was and I went along the fence. Luster was hunting in the grass by the flower tree.[3] They took the flag out, and they were hitting. Then they put the flag back and they went to the table, and he hit and the other hit. Then they went on, and I went along the fence. Luster came away from the flower tree and we went along the fence and they stopped and we stopped and I looked through the fence while Luster was hunting in the grass.

"Here, caddie." He hit. They went away across the pasture. I held to the fence and watched them going away.

---

1) 작품을 열고 있는 벤지의 울타리는 상징적 차원에서 많은 것을 함의하고 있다. 먼저 그것은 울타리 안에 갇혀 있는 벤지 실존의 감금상태를 의미하면서, 누이 캐디가 집을 떠난 후에도 그녀를 기다리며 지키고 서있는 "대문"(the gate)의 의미처럼, 캐디를 구심점으로 현재와 과거의 의식들이 넘나들고 있는 상징적 경계이기도 하다.

2) "I"는 이 장의 서술자 벤지이다. 그는 심각한 저능아로 그의 감각세계와 의식의 흐름이 이 장의 서사구도를 형성해낸다. 벤지는 작품에서 두 번, 패터슨 부인과 제이슨에 의해, 백치("idiot")로 호명된다. 작품의 서사 테크닉을 드러내는 첫 문장으로, 벤지는 집 울타리 너머로 주변의 골프장에서 골퍼들이 공을 치고 있는 모습을 서술하고 있지만, 정작 자신은 골프게임의 의미를 인지하지 못하고 있다.

3) 포크너는 「캄슨 부록」에서 러스터를 14세로 쓰고 있다(혹자는 17세 내지는 18세의 나이로 보기도 함). 현시점에서 벤지를 돌보는 딜시의 손자이자 프로니의 아들이다. 그는 오늘밤 카니발 쇼 구경을 가기 위해 잃어버린 동전을 찾고 있다.

"Listen at you, now." Luster said "Aint you something, thirty three years old, going on that way. After I done went all the way to town to buy you that cake. Hush up that moaning.[4)] Aint you going to help me find that quarter so I can go to the show tonight."

They were hitting little, across the pasture. I went back along the fence to where the flag was. It flapped on the bright grass and the trees.

"Come on." Luster said. "We done looked there. They aint no more coming right now. Les go down to the branch and find that quarter before them niggers finds it."

It was red, flapping on the pasture. Then there was a bird slanting and tilting on it. Luster threw. The flag flapped on the bright grass and the trees. I held to the fence.

"Shut up that moaning." Luster said. "I cant make them come if they aint coming, can I. If you dont hush up, mammy aint going to have no birthday for you. If you dont hush, you know what I going to do. I going to eat that cake all up. Eat them candles, too. Eat all them thirty three candles. Come on, les go down to the branch. I got to find my quarter. Maybe we can find one of they balls.[5)] Here. Here they is. Way over yonder. See." He came to the fence and pointed his arm. "See them. They aint coming back here no more. Come on."

We went along the fence and came to the garden fence, where our shadows were. My shadow was higher than Luster's on the fence. We came to the broken place and went through it.

"Wait a minute." Luster said. "You snagged on that nail again.

---

4) 이 문단은 골퍼들이 캐디(caddie)를 부르지만 눈에 보이지 않는 누이(Caddy)에 대한 상실감으로 벤지는 울음을 멈출 수 없으며, 그러한 벤지를 향해 러스터는 화를 내며 울음을 그치라고 다그친다.

5) 잃어버린 동전을 찾을 수 없는 러스터는 혹 골퍼들이 밖으로 보낸 공을 주워 그들에게 주면 그 대가로 동전 하나를 얻을 수 있을까 하는 생각을 담고 있다. 여기 "ball"의 의미를 남성성기와 연관지어 생각해 볼 때, 벤지의 거세와 연결지을 수 있다.

Cant you never crawl through here without snagging on the nail."

Caddy uncaught me and we crawled through.[6] *Uncle Maury said to not let anybody see us, so we better stoop over, Caddy said. Stoop over, Benjy. Like this, see. We stooped over and crossed the garden, where the flowers rasped and rattled against us. The ground was hard. We climbed the fence, where the pigs were grunting and snuffing. I expect they're sorry because one of them got killed today, Caddy said. The ground was hard, churned and knotted.*

Keep your hands in your pockets, Caddy said. Or they'll get froze. You dont want your hands froze on Christmas, do you.

"It's too cold out there." Versh said. "You dont want to go out doors."

"What is it now." Mother said.

"He want to go out doors." Versh said.

"Let him go." Uncle Maury said.

"It's too cold." Mother said. "He'd better stay in. Benjamin. Stop that, now."

"It wont hurt him." Uncle Maury said.

"You, Benjamin." Mother said. "If you dont be good, you'll have to go to the kitchen."

"Mammy say keep him out the kitchen today." Versh said. "She say she got all that cooking to get done."

"Let him go, Caroline." Uncle Maury said. "You'll worry yourself sick over him."

"I know it." Mother said. "It's a judgment on me. I sometimes wonder."

---

6) 바로 앞 문단과 연결하여, 이 장면은 벤지가 울타리 아래로 기어나갈 때마다 못에 옷이 걸리는 상황을 묘사하는 부분이며, 글씨체가 이탤릭체로 바뀌고 있다. 이러한 글씨체의 변화는 벤지 장에서 벤지의 의식이 현재에서 과거(기억)로, 과거(기억)에서 또 다른 과거로, 그리고 과거에서 다시 현재로, 시점이 끊임없이 바뀌면서 그의 의식이 유동하고 있음을 말해준다. 현시점에서 울타리 못에 옷이 걸리는 상황은 어린 시절 누이와 동행하면서 있었던 비슷한 기억 속으로 시점이 이동하고 있다.

"I know, I know." Uncle Maury said. "You must keep your strength up. I'll make you a toddy."

"It just upsets me that much more." Mother said. "Dont you know it does."

"You'll feel better." Uncle Maury said. "Wrap him up good, boy, and take him out for a while."

Uncle Maury went away. Versh went away.

"Please hush." Mother said. "We're trying get you out as fast as we can. I dont want you to get sick."

Versh put my overshoes and overcoat on and we took my cap and went out. Uncle Maury was putting the bottle away in the sideboard in the diningroom.[7)]

"Keep him out about half an hour, boy." Uncle Maury said. "Keep him in the yard, now."

"Yes, sir." Versh said. "We dont never let him get off the place."

We went out doors. The sun was cold and bright.

"Where you heading for." Versh said. "You dont think you going to town, does you." We went through the rattling leaves. The gate was cold.[8)] "You better keep them hands in your pockets." Versh said. "You get them froze onto that gate, then what you do. Whyn't you wait for them in the house." He put my hands into my pockets. I could hear him rattling in the leaves. I could smell the cold. The gate was cold.

"Here some hickeynuts. Whooey. Git up that tree. Look here at this squirl, Benjy."

I couldn't feel the gate at all, but I could smell the bright cold.

"You better put them hands back in your pockets."

---

7) 모리 삼촌의 술 마시는 문제를 처음으로 암시하고 있다.

8) 벤지의 감각적인 언어는 버시와 함께 대문에서 방과 후 집으로 돌아오는 캐디를 기다리며 대문의 차가움을 전하고 있다. 벤지의 이러한 기다림은 캐디가 집을 떠난 지 오랜 뒤에도 계속된다.

Caddy was walking. Then she was running, her booksatchel swinging and jouncing behind her.

"Hello, Benjy." Caddy said. She opened the gate and came in and stooped down. Caddy smelled like leaves. "Did you come to meet me." she said. "Did you come to meet Caddy. What did you let him get his hands so cold for, Versh."

"I told him to keep them in his pockets." Versh said. "Holding on to that ahun gate."[9)]

"Did you come to meet Caddy." she said, rubbing my hands. "What is it. What are you trying to tell Caddy." Caddy smelled like trees[10)] and like when she says we were asleep.

What are you moaning about, Luster said. You can watch them again when we get to the branch. Here. Here's you a jimson weed. He gave me the flower. We went through the fence, into the lot.

"What is it." Caddy said. "What are you trying to tell Caddy. Did they send him out, Versh."

"Couldn't keep him in." Versh said. "He kept on until they let him go and he come right straight down here, looking through the gate."

"What is it." Caddy said. "Did you think it would be Christmas when I came home from school. Is that what you thought. Christmas is the day after tomorrow. Santy Claus, Benjy. Santy Claus. Come on, let's run to the house and get warm." She took my hand and we ran through the bright rustling leaves. We ran up the steps and out of the bright cold, into the dark cold. Uncle Maury was putting the bottle back in the sideboard. He called Caddy.[11)] Caddy said,

---

9) ahun = iron.

10) 벤지는 캐디가 성에 눈을 뜨기 전 순수(순결)한 캐디를 자연(의 냄새)에 비유하곤 한다. 그녀가 성에 눈을 뜨면서 화장을 하고 향수를 사용하는 모습에서는 "캐디에게서 나무 냄새가 나지 않는다"고 말한다.

11) 캐디와 벤지가 집안으로 들어오자 모리 삼촌이 패터슨 부인에게 보낼 편지 심부름을 시키기 위해 캐디를 옆으로 부르고 있다.

"Take him in to the fire, Versh. Go with Versh." she said. "I'll come in a minute."

We went to the fire. Mother said,

"Is he cold, Versh."

"Nome." Versh said.

"Take his overcoat and overshoes off." Mother said. "How many times do I have to tell you not to bring him into the house with his overshoes on."

"Yessum." Versh said. "Hold still, now." He took my overshoes off and unbuttoned my coat. Caddy said,

"Wait, Versh. Cant he go out again, Mother. I want him to go with me."

"You'd better leave him here." Uncle Maury said. "He's been out enough today."

"I think you'd both better stay in." Mother said. "It's getting colder, Dilsey says."

"Oh, Mother." Caddy said.

"Nonsense." Uncle Maury said. "She's been in school all day. She needs the fresh air. Run along, Candace."

"Let him go, Mother." Caddy said. "Please. You know he'll cry."

"Then why did you mention it before him." Mother said. "Why did you come in here. To give him some excuse to worry me again. You' ve been out enough today. I think you'd better sit down here and play with him."

"Let them go, Caroline." Uncle Maury said. "A little cold wont hurt them. Remember, you've got to keep your strength up."

"I know." Mother said. "Nobody knows how I dread Christmas. Nobody knows. I am not one of those women who can stand things. I wish for Jason's[12)] and the children's sakes I was stronger."

"You must do the best you can and not let them worry you." Uncle

12) Jason = Mr. Compson.

Maury said. "Run along, you two. But dont stay out long, now. Your mother will worry."

"Yes, sir." Caddy said. "Come on, Benjy. We're going out doors again." She buttoned my coat and we went toward the door.

"Are you going to take that baby out without his overshoes." Mother said. "Do you want to make him sick, with the house full of company."

"I forgot." Caddy said. "I thought he had them on."

We went back. You must think." Mother said. *Hold still now* Versh said. He put my overshoes on. "Someday I'll be gone, and you'll have to think for him." *Now stomp* Versh said. "Come here and kiss Mother, Benjamin."

Caddy took me to Mother's chair and Mother took my face in her hands and then she held me against her.

"My poor baby." she said. She let me go. "You and Versh take good care of him, honey."

"Yessum." Caddy said. We went out. Caddy said,

"You needn't go, Versh. I'll keep him for a while."

"All right." Versh said. "I aint going out in that cold for no fun." He went on and we stopped in the hall and Caddy knelt and put her arms around me and her cold bright face against mine. She smelled like trees.

"You're not a poor baby. Are you. Are you. You've got your Caddy. Haven't you got your Caddy."

Cant you shut up that moaning and slobbering, Luster said. Aint you shamed of yourself, making all this racket. We passed the carriage house, where the carriage was. It had a new wheel.

"Git in, now, and set still until your maw come." Dilsey said. She shoved me into the carriage. T. P. held the reins. "Clare I dont see how come Jason wont get a new surrey." Dilsey said. "This thing going to fall to pieces under you all some day. Look at them wheels."

Mother came out, pulling her veil down. She had some flowers.

"Where's Roskus." she said.

"Roskus cant lift his arms, today." Dilsey said. "T. P. can drive all right."

"I'm afraid to." Mother said. "It seems to me you all could furnish me with a driver for the carriage once a week. It's little enough I ask, Lord knows."

"You know just as well as me that Roskus got the rheumatism too bad to do more than he have to, Miss Cahline." Dilsey said. "You come on and get in, now. T. P. can drive you just as good as Roskus."

"I'm afraid to." Mother said. "With the baby."

Dilsey went up the steps. "You calling that thing a baby." she said. She took Mother's arm. "A man big as T. P.[13] Come on, now, if you going."

"I'm afraid to." Mother said. They came down the steps and Dilsey helped Mother in. "Perhaps it'll be the best thing, for all of us." Mother said.

"Aint you shamed, talking that way." Dilsey said. "Dont you know it'll take more than a eighteen year old nigger to make Queenie run away. She older than him and Benjy put together. And dont you start no projecking with Queenie,[14] you hear me. T. P. If you dont drive to suit Miss Cahline, I going to put Roskus on you. He aint too tied up to do that."

"Yessum." T. P. said.

"I just know something will happen." Mother said. "Stop, Benjamin."

"Give him a flower to hold." Dilsey said. "That what he wanting."

---

13) 1912년 벤지("that thing")가 17세 되던 해로, 몸은 성인과 다를 바 없는 벤지를 여전히 아이 취급하는 캄슨 부인을 향해 딜시가 하는 말이다.

14) 브라운(Calvin Brown)은 "projecking"을 "무책임하거나 주제넘은 태도로 시간을 낭비하는" 행위로 정의한다(*A Glossary of Faulkner's South*. New Haven: Yale Up, 1976. p156). 딜시는 티피가 말 퀴니를 데리고 문제를 일으킬 수 있는 어떤 허튼 짓도 하지 말라고 경고하고 있다.

She reached her hand in.

"No, no." Mother said. "You'll have them all scattered."

"You hold them." Dilsey said. "I'll get him one out." She gave me a flower and her hand went away.

"Go on now, fore Quentin see you and have to go too." Dilsey said.

"Where is she." Mother said.

"She down to the house playing with Luster." Dilsey said. "Go on, T. P. Drive that surrey like Roskus told you, now."

"Yessem." T. P. said. "Hum up, Queenie."

"Quentin." Mother said. "Dont let   "

"Course I is." Dilsey said.[15)]

The carriage jolted and crunched on the drive. "I'm afraid to go and leave Quentin." Mother said. "I'd better not go. T. P." We went through the gate, where it didn't jolt anymore.[16)] T. P. hit Queenie with the whip.

"You, T. P." Mother said.

"Got to get her going." T. P. said. "Keep her wake up till we get back to the barn."

"Turn around." Mother said. "I'm afraid to go and leave Quentin."

"Cant turn here." T. P. said. Then it was broader.

"Cant you turn here." Mother said.

"All right." T. P. said. We began to turn.

"You, T. P." Mother said, clutching me.

"I got to turn around some how." T. P. said. "Whoa, Queenie." We

---

15) 여기 퀸턴은 캐디의 딸 미스 퀸턴을 말하며, 2-3세 된 아이에게 무슨 일이 없도록 당부하는 캄슨 부인에게 딜시가 충분히 잘 알고 있다면서 그녀의 말을 중단시키고 있다. 혹 캐디가 찾아와 딸을 데려갈까 하는 캄슨 부인의 우려를 암시하는 부분이다.

16) 이 문단은 캄슨 부인이 타고 가는 마차가 얼마나 흔들리면서 덜컹거리는지를 통해, 캄슨가의 집 주변도로와 그곳을 벗어난 마을 도로 간의 차이를 엿볼 수 있는 부분으로, 캄슨 가세가 기울대로 기울어져 있음을 암시한다.

stopped.

"You'll turn us over." Mother said.

"What you want to do, then." T. P. said.

"I'm afraid for you to try to turn around." Mother said.

"Get up, Queenie." T. P. said. We went on.

"I just know Dilsey will let something happen to Quentin while I'm gone." Mother said. "We must hurry back."

"Hum up, there." T. P. said. He hit Queenie with the whip.

"You, T. P." Mother said, clutching me. I could hear Queenie's feet and the bright shapes went smooth and steady on both sides, the shadows of them flowing across Queenie's back. They went on like the bright tops of wheels. Then those on one side stopped at the tall white post where the soldier was. But on the other side they went on smooth and steady, but a little slower.

"What do you want." [17] Jason said. He had his hands in his pockets and a pencil behind his ear.

"We're going to the cemetery." Mother said.

"All right." Jason said. "I dont aim to stop you, do I. Was that all you wanted with me, just to tell me that."

"I know you wont come." Mother said. "I'd feel safer if you would."

"Safe from what." Jason said. "Father and Quentin cant hurt you." Mother put her handkerchief under her veil. "Stop it, Mother." Jason said. "Do you want to get that damn looney to bawling in the middle of the square. Drive on, T. P."

"Hum up, Queenie." T. P. said.

"It's a judgment on me." Mother said. "But I'll be gone too, soon."

"Here." Jason said.

---

17) 캄슨 부인이 탄 마차는 남편과 큰아들 퀸턴의 묘지를 향하던 중, 마을 광장에 위치한 철물점에서 일하는 제이슨을 찾아와 함께 동행하기를 바라는 어머니를 향해 그가 건네는 말이다.

"Whoa." T. P. said. Jason said,

"Uncle Maury's drawing on you for fifty.[18] What do you want to do about it."

"Why ask me." Mother said. "I dont have any say so. I try not to worry you and Dilsey. I'll be gone soon, and then you "

"Go on, T. P." Jason said.

"Hum up, Queenie." T. P. said. The shapes flowed on. The ones on the other side began again, bright and fast and smooth, like when Caddy says we are going to sleep.

Cry baby, Luster said. Aint you shamed. We went through the barn. The stalls were all open. You aint got no spotted pony to ride now, Luster said. The floor was dry and dusty. The roof was falling. The slanting holes were full of spinning yellow. What do you want to go that way, for. You want to get your head knocked off with one of them balls.

"Keep your hands in your pockets." Caddy said. "Or they'll be froze. You dont want your hands froze on Christmas, do you."

We went around the barn. The big cow and the little one were standing in the door, and we could hear Prince and Queenie and Fancy stomping inside the barn. "If it wasn't so cold, we'd ride Fancy." Caddy said. "But it's too cold to hold on today." Then we could see the branch, where the smoke was blowing. "That's where they are killing the pig." Caddy said. "We can come back by there and see them." We went down the hill.

"You want to carry the letter." Caddy said. "You can carry it." She took the letter out of her pocket and put it in mine. "It's a Christmas present." Caddy said. "Uncle Maury is going to surprise Mrs Patterson with it. We got to give it to her without letting anybody see it. Keep your hands in your pockets good, now." We came to the

18) 모리 삼촌이 누이(캄슨 부인)의 은행계좌로부터 50달러를 빼내 쓰고 있다고 어머니께 제이슨이 말한다.

branch.

"It's froze." Caddy said. "Look." She broke the top of the water and held a piece of it against my face. "Ice. That means how cold it is." She helped me across and we went up the hill. "We cant even tell Mother and Father. You know what I think it is. I think it's a surprise for Mother and Father and Mr Patterson both, because Mr Patterson sent you some candy. Do you remember when Mr Patterson sent you some candy last summer." [19)]

There was a fence. The vine was dry, and the wind rattled in it.

"Only I dont see why Uncle Maury didn't send Versh." Caddy said. "Versh wont tell." Mrs Patterson was looking out the window. "You wait here." Caddy said. "Wait right here, now. I'll be back in a minute. Give me the letter." She took the letter out of my pocket. "Keep your hands in your pockets." She climbed the fence with the letter in her hand and went through the brown, rattling flowers. Mrs Patterson came to the door and opened it and stood there.

Mr Patterson was chopping in the green flowers. He stopped chopping and looked at me. Mrs Patterson came across the garden, running. When I saw her eyes I began to cry. You idiot, Mrs Patterson said, I told him never to send you alone again. Give it to me. Quick. Mr Patterson came fast, with the hoe. Mrs Patterson leaned across the fence, reaching her hand. She was trying to climb the fence. Give it to me, she said, Give it to me. Mr Patterson climbed the fence. He took the letter. Mrs Patterson's dress was caught on the fence. I saw her eyes again and I ran down the hill.

"They aint nothing over yonder but houses." Luster said. "We

---

19) 1908년 여름, 모리 삼촌은 벤지 혼자 패터슨 부인에게 보내는 편지를 전달하게 하는데, 그때 벤지는 호미를 가지고 자신을 쫓아오는 패터슨씨에게 놀라 혼난 적이 있었다. 그 후 패터슨씨는 벤지를 놀라게 한 것을 후회하며 그에게 사탕선물을 보내왔는데, 그 의도는 단순히 사과의 의미도 있을 수 있겠지만, 다른 한편으로는 앞으로 아내에게 보내지는 편지들은 그에게 가져오도록 하기 위한 뇌물성 선물이기도 하다.

going down to the branch."

They were washing down at the branch. One of them was singing. I could smell the clothes flapping, and the smoke blowing across the branch.

"You stay down here." Luster said. "You aint got no business up yonder. Them folks hit you, sho."

"What he want to do."

"He dont know what he want to do." Luster said. "He think he want to go up yonder where they knocking that ball. You sit down here and play with your jimson weed. Look at them chillen playing in the branch, if you got to look at something. How came you cant behave yourself like folks." I sat down on the bank, where they were washing, and the smoke blowing blue.

"Is you all seen anything of a quarter down here." Luster said.

"What quarter."

"The one I had here this morning." Luster said." "I lost it somewhere. It fell through this here hole in my pocket. If I dont find it I cant go to the show tonight."

"Where'd you get a quarter, boy. Find it in white folks' pocket while they aint looking."

"Got it at the getting place." [20] Luster said. "Plenty more where that one come from. Only I got to find that one. Is you all found it yet."

"I aint studying no quarter. I got my own business to tend to."

"Come on here." Luster said. "Help me look for it."

"He wouldn't know a quarter if he was to see it, would he."

"He can help look just the same." Luster said. "You all going to the show tonight."

"Dont talk to me about no show. Time I get done over this here tub

---

20) 러스터는 대화를 나누고 있는 빨래터의 흑인들에게 자신이 그 동전을 어디서 구했는지에 대한 답을 피하고 있다.

I be too tired to life my hand to do nothing."

"I bet you be there." Luster said. "I bet you was there last night. I bet you all be right there when that tent open."

"Be enough niggers there without me. Was last night."

"Nigger's money good as white folks, I reckon."

"White folks gives nigger money because know first white man comes along with a band going to get it all back, so nigger can go to work for some more."

"Aint nobody going make you go to that show."

"Aint yet. Aint thought of it, I reckon."

"What you got against white folks."

"Aint got nothing against them. I goes my way and lets white folks go theirs. I aint studying that show."

"Got a man in it can play a tune on a saw.[21)] Play it like a banjo."

"You go last night." Luster said. "I going tonight. If I can find where I lost that quarter."

"You going take him with you, I reckon."

"Me." Luster said. "You reckon I be found anywhere with him, time he star bellering."

"What does you do when he start bellering."

"I whips him." Luster said. He sat down and rolled up his overalls. They played in the branch.

"You all found any balls yet." Luster said.

"Aint you talking biggity.[22)] I bet you better not let your grandmammy hear you talking like that."

Luster got into the branch, where they were playing. He hunted in the water, along the bank.

"I had it when we was down here this morning." Luster said.

"Where bouts you lose it."

---

21) 작은 톱과 나무(망치)를 이용하여 어떤 사람은 연주할 수 있다고 말한다.

22) biggity = pompous, showing off.

"Right out this here hole in my pocket." Luster said. They hunted in the branch. Then they all stood up quick and stopped, then they splashed and fought in the branch. Luster got it and they squatted in the water, looking up the hill through the bushes.

"Where is they." Luster said.

"Aint in sight yet."

Luster put it in his pocket. They came down the hill.

"Did a ball come down here."

"It ought to be in the water. Didn't any of you boys see it or hear it."

"Aint heard nothing come down here." Luster said. "Heard something hit that tree up yonder. Dont know which way it went."

They looked in the branch.

"Hell. Look along the branch. It came down here. I saw it."

They looked along the branch. Then they went back up the hill.

"Have you got that ball." The boy said.

"What I want with it." Luster said. "I aint seen no ball."

The boy got in the water. He went on. He turned and looked at Luster again. He went on down the branch.

The man said "Caddie" up the hill. The boy got out of the water and went up the hill.

"Now, just listen at you." Luster said. "Hush up."

"What he moaning about now."

"Lawd knows." Luster said. "He just starts like that. He been at it all morning. Cause it his birthday, I reckon."

"How old he."

"He thirty three." Luster said. "Thirty three this morning."

"You mean, he been three years old thirty years."

"I going by what mammy say." Luster said. "I dont know. We going to have thirty three candles on a cake, anyway. Little cake. Wont hardly hold them. Hush up. Come on back here." He came and caught my arm. "You old looney." He said. "You want me to whip you."

"I bet you will."

"I is done it. hush, now." Luster said. "Aint I told you you cant go up there. They'll knock your head clean off with one of them balls. Come on, here." He pulled me back. "Sit down." I sat down and he took off my shoes and rolled up my trousers. "Now, git in that water and play and see can you stop that slobbering and moaning."

I hushed and got in the water *and Roskus came and said to come to supper and Caddy said,*

It's not supper time yet. I'm not going.

She was wet. We were playing in the branch and Caddy squatted down and got her dress wet and Versh said,

"Your mommer going to whip you for getting your dress wet."

"She's not going to do any such thing." Caddy said.

"How do you know." Quentin said.

"That's all right how I know." Caddy said. "How do you know."

"She said she was." Quentin said. "Beside, I'm older than you."

"I'm seven years old." Caddy said. "I guess I know."

"I'm older than that." Quentin said. "I go to school. Dont I, Versh."

"I'm going to school next year." Caddy said. "When it comes. Aint I, Versh."

"You know she whip you when you get your dress wet." Versh said.

"It's not wet." Caddy said. She stood up in the water and looked at her dress. "I'll take it off." She said. "Then it'll dry."

"I bet you wont." Quentin said.

"I bet I will." Caddy said.

"I bet you better not." Quentin said.

Caddy came to Versh and me and turned her back.

"Unbutton it, Versh." she said.

"Dont you do it, Versh." Quentin said.

"Taint none of my dress." Versh said.

"You unbutton it, Versh." Caddy said. "Or I'll tell Dilsey what you did yesterday." So Versh unbuttoned it

"You just take your dress off." Quentin said. Caddy took her dress off and threw it on the bank. "Then she didn't have on anything but her bodice and drawers, and Quentin slapped her and she slipped and fell down in the water. When she got up she began to splash water on Quentin, and Quentin splashed water on Caddy. Some of it splashed on Versh and me and Versh picked me up and put me on the bank. He said he was going to tell on Caddy and Quentin, and then Quentin and Caddy began to splash water at Versh. He got behind a bush.

"I'm going to tell mammy on you all." Versh said.

Quentin climbed up the bank and tried to catch Versh, but Versh ran away and Quentin couldn't. When Quentin came back Versh stopped and hollered that he was going to tell. Caddy told him that if he wouldn't tell, they'd let him come back. So Versh said he wouldn't, and they let him.

"Now I guess you're satisfied." Quentin said. "We'll both get whipped now."

"I dont care." Caddy said. "I'll run away."

"Yes you will." Quentin said.

"I'll run away and never come back." Caddy said. I began to cry. Caddy turned around and said "Hush" So I hushed. Then they played in the branch. Jason was playing too. He was by himself further down the branch. Versh came around the bush and lifted me down into the water again. Caddy was all wet and muddy behind, and I started to cry and she came and squatted in the water.

"Hush now." she said. "I'm not going to run away." So I hushed. Caddy smelled like trees in the rain.

What is the matter with you, Luster said. Cant you get done with that moaning and play in the branch like folks.

Whyn't you take him on home. Didn't they told you not to take him off the place.

He still think they own this pasture, Luster said. Cant nobody see down here from the house, noways.

We can. And folks dont like to look at a looney. Taint no luck in it.

Roskus came and said to come to supper and Caddy said it wasn't supper time yet.

"Yes tis." Roskus said. "Dilsey say for you all to come on to the house. Bring them on, Versh." He went up the hill, where the cow was lowing.

"Maybe we'll be dry by the time we get to the house." Quentin said.

"It was all your fault." Caddy said. "I hope we do get whipped." She put her dress on and Versh buttoned it.

"They wont know you got wet." Versh said. "It dont show on you. Less me and Jason tells."

"Are you going to tell, Jason." Caddy said.

"Tell on who." Jason said.

"He wont tell." Quentin said. "Will you, Jason."

"I bet he dose tell." Caddy said. "He'll tell Damuddy." 23)

"He cant tell her." Quentin said. "She's sick. If we walk slow it'll be too dark for them to see."

"I dont care whether they see or not." Caddy said. "I'm going to tell, myself. You carry him up the hill, Versh."

"Jason wont tell." Quentin said. "You remember that bow and arrow I made you, Jason."

"It's broke now." Jason said.

"Let him tell." Caddy said. "I dont give a cuss. Carry Maury up the hill, Versh." 24) Versh squatted and I got on his back.

See you all at the show tonight, Luster said. Come on, here. We got to find that quarter.

"If we go slow, it'll be dark when we get there." Quentin said.

"I'm not going slow." Caddy said. We went up the hill, but Quentin

---

23) 캄슨 부인의 어머니, 아이들의 외할머니.

24) 벤지는 태어난 후 삼촌의 이름을 따와 모리라고 명명되지만, 자라면서 그가 백치라는 사실을 알았을 때 캄슨 부인은 그를 벤자민(벤지)으로 개명한다.

didn't come. He was down at the branch when we got to where we could smell the pigs. They were grunting and snuffing in the trough in the corner. Jason came behind us, with his hands in his pockets. Roskus was milking the cow in the barn door.

The cows came jumping out of the barn.[25)]

"Go on." T. P. said. "Holler again. I going to holler myself. Whooey." Quentin kicked T. P. again. He kicked T. P. into the trough where the pigs ate and T. P. lay there. "Hot dog." T. P. said. "Didn't he get me then. You see that white man kick me that time. Whooey."

I wasn't crying, but I couldn't stop. I wasn't crying, but the ground wasn't still, and then I was crying. The ground kept sloping up and the cows ran up the hill. T. P. tried to get up. He fell down again and the cows ran down the hill. Quentin held my arm and we went toward the barn. Then the barn wasn't there and we had to wait until it came back. I didn't see it come back. It came behind us and Quentin set me down in the trough where the cows ate. I held on to it. It was going away too, and I held to it. The cows ran down the hill again, across the door. I couldn't stop. Quentin and T. P. came up the hill, fighting T. P. was falling down the hill and Quentin dragged him up the hill. Quentin hit T. P. I couldn't stop.

"Stand up." Quentin said. "You stay right here. Dont you go away until I get back."

"Me and Benjy going back to the wedding." T. P. said. "Whooey."

Quentin hit T. P. again. Then he began to thump T. P. against the

---

25) 이 장면은 캐디의 결혼식 날 감금되어 있던 벤지가 술에 만취된 채 빠져나와 식장으로 걸음을 옮길 때, 캐디에게로 향하는 만취한 벤지의 눈에는 헛간 앞에서 풀을 뜯고 있는 소들이 마치 헛간에서 달려 나오는 듯한 환각으로 서술되고 있다고 말할 수 있다. 하지만 사실 이 한 줄의 이미지는 해석의 여지가 명확하지 않다. 로스와 폴크는 이 장면을 술 취한 벤지가 언덕에서 넘어져 구르면서 그의 눈에 암소들이 빨리 움직이며 뛰고 있는 것처럼 보인다고 지적하기도 하고, 혹자는 술이 취한 벤지와 티피가 마구간의 암소들을 풀어주었다고 말하기도 한다.

wall. T. P. was laughing. Every time Quentin thumped him against the wall he tried to say Whooey, but he couldn't say it for laughing. I quit crying, but I couldn't stop. T. P. fell on me and the barn door went away. It went down the hill and T. P. was fighting by himself and he fell down again. He was still laughing, and I couldn't stop, and I tried to get up and I fell down, and I couldn't stop. Versh said,

"You sho done it now. I'll declare if you aint. Shut up that yelling."

T. P. was still laughing. He flopped on the door and laughed. "Whooey." He said. "Me and Benjy going back to the wedding. Sassprilluh."[26] T. P. said.

"Hush." Versh said. "Where you get it."

"Out the cellar." T. P. said. "Whooey."

"Hush up." Versh said. "Where bouts in the cellar."

"Anywhere." T. P. said. He laughed some more. "Moren a hundred bottles lef. Moren a million. Look out, nigger, I going to holler."

Quentin said, "Lift him up."

Versh lifted me up.

"Drink this, Benjy." Quentin said. The glass was hot. "Hush, now." Quentin said. "Drink it."

"Sassprilluh." T. P. said. "Lemme drink it, Mr Quentin."

"You shut your mouth." Versh said. "Mr Quentin wear you out."

"Hold him, Versh." Quentin said.

They held me. It was hot on my chin and my shirt. "Drink." Quentin said. They held my head. It was hot inside me, and I began again. I was crying now, and something was happening inside me and I cried more, and they held me until it stopped happening. Then I hushed. It was still going around, and then the shapes began. Open the crib, Versh. They were going slow. Spread those empty sacks on

---

26) 루트 맥주(root beer) 같은 알코올 성분이 없는 탄산음료. 하지만 여기 벤지와 티피가 마시고 취한 것은 이 음료라기보다는 캐디 결혼식을 위해 준비되어 있던 샴페인일 확률이 높다. 아이들에게 이 음료와 샴페인 맛은 비슷할 수 있다.

the floor. They were going faster, almost fast enough. Now. Pick up his feet. They went on, smooth and bright. I could hear T. P. laughing. I went on with them, up the bright hill.[27)]

At the top of the hill Versh put me down. "Come on here, Quentin." He called, looking back down the hill. Quentin was still standing there by the branch. He was chunking into the shadows where the branch was.

"Let the old skizzard stay there." Caddy said. "She took my hand and we went on past the barn and through the gate. There was a frog on the brick walk, squatting in the middle of it. Caddy stepped over it and pulled me on.

"Come on, Maury." she said. It still squatted there until Jason poked at it with his toe.

"He'll make a wart on you." Versh said. The frog hopped away.

"Come on, Maury." Caddy said.

"They got company tonight." Versh said.

"How do you know." Caddy said.

"With all them lights on." Versh said. "Light in every window."

"I reckon we can turn all the lights on without company, if we want to." Caddy said.

"I bet it's company." Versh said. "You all better go in the back and slip upstairs."

"I dont care." Caddy said. "I'll walk right in the parlor where they

---

27) "something is happening inside me", 이 문장은 벤지가 마신 샴페인으로 속이 좋지 않은 상태를 암시하는, 아마 토하고 있는 상황으로 볼 수 있다. 이어지는 장면에서 벤지가 그려내고 있는 이미지는 확실하진 않지만, 술에 취해 어지러운 상태로 잠속으로 빠져들고 있는("부드럽고 환한" 이미지는 그가 잠들 때 주로 동반되는 이미지) 몽롱한 상태를 말하는 것일 수 있다. 분명한 것은 벤지 상태가 좋지 않은 점이며, 토하거나 배설 행위를 하는 것으로 볼 수 있는 것은 퀸턴이 버시에게 쉽게 뒤처리를 하기 위해 바닥에 빈 자루들을 펼치라고 하는데 있다. 그리고 상태가 수습된 후 그들과 함께 언덕 위를 오르고 있는 모습이다.

are."

"I bet your pappy whip you if you do." Versh said.

"I dont care." Caddy said. "I'll walk right in the parlor. I'll walk right in the dining room and eat supper."

"Where you sit." Versh said.

"I'd sit in Damuddy's chair." Caddy said. "She eats in bed."

"I'm hungry." Jason said. He passed us and ran on up the walk. He had his hands in his pockets and he fell down. Versh went and picked him up.

"If you keep them hands out your pockets, you could stay on your feet." Versh said. "You cant never get them out in time to catch yourself, fat as you is."

Father was standing by the kitchen steps.

"Where's Quentin." he said.

"He coming up the walk." Versh said. Quentin was coming slow. His shirt was a white blur.

"Oh." Father said. Light fell down the steps, on him.

"Caddy and Quentin threw water on each other." Jason said.

We waited.

"They did." Father said. Quentin came, and Father said, "You can eat supper in the kitchen tonight." He stooped and took me up, and the light came tumbling down the steps on me too, and I could look down at Caddy and Jason and Quentin and Versh. Father turned toward the steps. "You must be quiet, though." he said.

"Why must we be quiet, Father." Caddy said. "Have we got company."

"Yes." Father said.

"I told you they was company." Versh said.

"You did not." Caddy said. "I was the one that said there was. I said I would   "

"Hush." Father said. They hushed and Father opened the door and we crossed the back porch and went in to the kitchen. Dilsey was there, and Father put me in the chair and closed the apron down and pushed it to the table, where supper was. It was steaming up.

"You mind Dilsey, now." Father said. "Dont let them make any more noise than they can help, Dilsey."

"Yes, sir." Dilsey said. Father went away.

"Remember to mind Dilsey, now." he said behind us. I leaned my face over where the supper was. It steamed up on my face.

"Let them mind me tonight, Father." Caddy said.

"I wont." Jason said. "I'm going to mind Dilsey."

"You'll have to, if Father says so." Caddy said. "Let them mind me, Father."

"I wont." Jason said. "I wont mind you."

"Hush." Father said. "You all mind Caddy, then. When they are done, bring them up the back stairs, Dilsey."

"Yes, sir." Dilsey said.

"There." Caddy said. "Now I guess you'll mind me."

"You all hush, now." Dilsey said. "You got to be quiet tonight."

"Why do we have to be quite tonight." Caddy whispered.

"Never you mind." Dilsey said. "You'll know in the Lawd's own time." She brought my bowl. The steam from it came and tickled my face. "Come here, Versh." Dilsey said.

"When is the Lawd's own time, Dilsey." Caddy said.

"It's Sunday." Quentin said. "Dont you know anything."

"Shhhhhh." Dilsey said. "Didn't Mr Jason say for you all to be quiet. Eat your supper, now. Here, Versh. Git his spoon." Versh's hand came with the spoon, into the bowl. The spoon came up to my mouth. The steam tickled into my mouth. Then we quit eating and we looked at each other and we were quiet, and then we heard it again[28)] and I began to cry.

"What was that." Caddy said. She put her hand on my hand.

"That was Mother." Quentin said. The spoon came up and I ate,

---

28) 캄슨 부인이 어머니(아이들의 할머니)의 죽음에 곡하는 것을 아이들이 듣고 있다.

then I cried again.

"Hush." Caddy said. But I didn't hush and she came and put her arms around me. Dilsey went and closed both the doors and then we couldn't hear it.

"Hush, now." Caddy said. I hushed and ate. Quentin wasn't eating, but Jason was.[29)]

"That was Mother." Quentin said. He got up.

"You set right down." Dilsey said. "They got company in there, and you in them muddy clothes. You set down too, Caddy, and get done eating."

"She was crying." Quentin said.

"It was somebody singing." Caddy said. "Wasn't it, Dilsey."

"You all eat your supper, now, like Mr jason said." Dilsey said. "You'll know in the Lawd's own time." Caddy went back to her chair.

"I told you it was a party." she said.

Versh said, "He done et all that."

"Bring his bowl here." Dilsey said. The bowl went away.

"Dilsey." Caddy said. "Quentin's not eating his supper. Hasn't he got to mind me."

"Eat your supper, Quentin." Dilsey said. "You all got to get done and get out of my kitchen."

"I dont want any more supper." Quentin said.

"You've got to eat if I say you have." Caddy said. "Hasn't he, Dilsey."

The bowl steamed up to my face, and Versh's hand dipped the spoon in it and the steam tickled into my mouth.

"I dont want any more." Quentin said. "How can they have a party

---

29) 할머니의 죽음에 대한 퀸턴과 제이슨의 차별적 반응과 함께 둘의 성격을 엿볼 수 있는 부분으로, 그 상황에서 퀸턴은 밥을 먹을 수 없지만, 정작 할머니의 사랑을 가장 많이 받아온 제이슨은 밥을 잘 먹고 있으며, 몇 줄 뒤에 벤지가 다시 쓰고 있듯이, 제이슨은 밥을 다 먹고 난 후에야 비로소 울음을 터뜨린다.

when Damuddy's sick."

"They'll have it down stairs." Caddy said. "She can come to the landing and see it. That's what I'm going to do when I get my nightie on."

"Mother was crying." Quentin said. "Wasn't she crying, Dilsey."

"Dont you come pestering at me, boy." Dilsey said. I got to get supper for all them folks soon as you all get done eating."

After a while even Jason was through eating, and he began to cry.

"Now you got to tune up." Dilsey said.

"He does it every night since Damuddy was sick and he cant sleep with her." Caddy said. "Cry baby."

"I'm going to tell on you." Jason said.

He was crying. "You've already told." Caddy said. "There's not anything else you can tell, now."

"You all needs to go bed." Dilsey said. She came and lifted me down and wiped my face and hands with a warm cloth. "Versh, can you get them up the back stairs quiet. You, Jason, shut up that crying."

"It's too early to go to bed now." Caddy said. "We dont ever have to go to bed this early."

"You is tonight." Dilsey said. "Your paw say for you to come right on up stairs when you et supper. You heard him."

"He said to mind me." Caddy said.

"I'm not going to mind you." Jason said.

"You have to." Caddy said. "Come on, now. You have to do like I say."

"Make them be quiet, Versh." Dilsey said. "You all going to be quiet, aint you."

"What do we have to be so quiet for, tonight." Caddy said.

"Your mommer aint feeling well." Dilsey said. "You all go on with Versh, now."

"I told you Mother was crying." Quentin said. Versh took me up and opened the door onto the back porch. We went out and Versh closed the door black. I could smell Versh and feel him. You all be quiet, now. We're not going up stairs yet. Mr Jason said for you to come right up stairs. He said to mind me. I'm not going to mind you. But he said for all of us to. Didn't he, Quentin. I could feel Versh's head. I could hear us. Didn't he, Versh. Yes, that right. Then I say for us to go out doors a while. Come on. Versh opened the door and we went out.

We went down the steps.

"I expect we'd better go down to Versh's house, so we'll be quiet." Caddy said. Versh put me down and Caddy took my hand we went down the brick walk.

"Come on." Caddy said. "That frog's gone. He's hopped way over to the garden, by now. Maybe we'll see another one." Roskus came with the milk buckets. He went on. Quentin wasn't coming with us. He was sitting on the kitchen steps. We went down to Versh's house. I liked to smell Versh's house. *There was a fire in it and T. P. squatting in his shirt tail in front of it, chunking it into a blaze.*

Then I got up and T. P. dressed me and we went to the kitchen and ate. Dilsey was singing and I began to cry and she stopped.

"Keep him away from the house, now." Dilsey said.

"We cant go that way." T. P. said.

We played in the branch.

"We cant go around yonder." T. P. said. "Dont you know mammy say we cant."

Dilsey was singing in the kitchen and I began to cry.

"Hush." T. P. said. "Come on. Les go down to the barn."

Roskus was milking at the barn. He was milking with one hand, and groaning. Some birds sat on the barn door and watched him. One of them came down and ate with the cows. I watched Roskus milk while T. P. was feeding Queenie and Prince. The calf was in the pig pen. It nuzzled at the wire, bawling.

"T. P." Roskus said. T P. said Sir, in the barn. Fancy held her head over the door, because T. P. hadn't fed her yet. "Git done there."

Roskus said. "You got to do this milking. I cant use my right hand no more."

T. P. came and milked.

"Whyn't you get the doctor." T. P. said.

"Doctor cant do no good." Roskus said. "Not on this place."

"What wrong with this place." T. P. said.

"Taint no luck on this place." Roskus said. "Turn that calf in if you done."

Taint no luck on this place, Roskus said. The fire rose and fell behind him and Versh, sliding on his and Versh's face. Dilsey finished putting me to bed. The bed smelled like T. P. liked it.

"What you know about it." Dilsey said. "What trance you been in."

"Dont need no trance." Roskus said. "Aint the sign of it laying right there on that bed. Aint the sign of it been here for folks to see fifteen years now." [30)]

"Spose it is." Dilsey said. "It aint hurt none of you and yourn, is it. Versh working and Frony married off your hands and T. P. getting big enough to take your place when rheumatism finish getting you."

"They been two, now." Roskus said. "Going to be one more.[31)] I seen the sign, and you is too."

"I heard a squinch owl that night." T. P. said. "Dan wouldn't come and get his supper, neither. Wouldn't come no closer than the barn. Begun howling right after dark. Versh heard him."

"Going to be more than one more." Dilsey said. "Show me the man what aint going to die, bless Jesus."

---

30) 로스커스는 캄슨 집안의 재수 없는 "징표"로 (침대에 누워 있는 15세의) 벤지의 존재를 두고 하는 말이다.

31) 두 죽음은 퀸턴과 할머니의 죽음이다. 여기 예고되고 있는 "또 하나"(의 죽음)는, 캄슨씨의 술 중독 상태가 초래할 불길한 징조나 집을 떠날 캐디의 불행한 운명을 염두에 두고 있다고도 할 수 있지만, 아마도 다가올 캄슨씨의 죽음을 예언하고 있다고 하겠다.

"Dying aint all." Roskus said.

"I knows what you thinking." Dilsey said. "And they aint going to be no luck in saying that name, lessen you going to set up with him while he cries." 32)

"They aint no luck on this place." Roskus said. "I seen it at first but when they changed his name I knowed it."

"Hush your mouth." Dilsey said. She pulled the covers up. It smelled like T. P. "You all shut up now, till he get to sleep."

"I seen the sign." Roskus said.

"Sign T. P. got to do all your work for you." Dilsey said. *Take him and Quentin down to the house and let them play with Luster, where Frony can watch them, T. P., and go and help your paw.*

We finished eating. T. P. took Quentin up and we went down to T. P.'s house. Luster was playing in the dirt. T. P. put Quentin down and she played in the dirt too. Luster had some spools and he and Quentin fought and Quentin had the spools. Luster cried and Frony came and gave Luster a tin can to play with, and then I had the spools and Quentin fought me and I cried.

"Hush." Frony said. "Aint you shamed of yourself. Taking a baby's play pretty." She took the spools from me and gave them back them to Quentin.

"Hush, now." Frony said. "Hush, I tell you."

"Hush up." Frony said. "You needs whipping, that's what you needs." She took Luster and Quentin up. "Come on here." she said. We went to the barn. T. P. was milking the cow. Roskus was sitting on the box.

"What's the matter with him now." Roskus said.

"You have to keep him down here." Frony said. "He frighting

---

32) 여기 로스커스는 캐디의 '타락'과 집을 떠난 것을 말하고 있으며, 딜시는 남편이 캐디의 이름을 입 밖에 내지 않도록 막고 있는데, '캐디' 소리를 듣고 또 울기 시작할 벤지를 염두에 두고 있다.

these babies again. Taking they play things. Stay here with T. P. now, and see can you hush a while."

"Clean that udder good now." Roskus said. "You milked that young cow dry last winter. If you milk this one dry, they aint going to be no more milk."

Dilsey was singing.

"Not around yonder." T. P. said. "Dont you know mammy say you cant go around there."

They were singing.[33)]

"Come on." T. P. said. "Les go play with Quentin and Luster. Come on."

Quentin and Luster were playing in the dirt in front of T. P.'s house. There was a fire in the house, rising and falling, with Roskus sitting black against it.

"That's three, thank the Lawd." Roskus said. "I told you two years ago. They aint no luck on this place."

"Whyn't you get out, then." Dilsey said. She was undressing me. "Your bad luck talk got them Memphis notions into Versh. That ought to satisfy you."

"If that all the bad luck Versh have." Roskus said.

Frony came in.

"You all done." Dilsey said.

"T. P. finishing up." Frony said. "Miss Cahline want you to put Quentin to bed."

"I'm coming just as fast as I can." Dilsey said. "She ought to know by this time I aint got no wings."

"That's what I tell you." Roskus said. "They aint no luck going be on no place where one of they own chillen's name aint never spoke."

"Hush." Dilsey said. "Do you want to get him started."

---

33) 티피는 어른들이 애도의 곡을 하고 있는 장례식장 주변을 벤지가 접근 못하도록 딜시의 명을 받아 실행하고 있다.

"Raising a child not to know its own mammy's name." Roskus said.

"Dont you bother your head about her." Dilsey said. "I raised all of them and I reckon I can raise one more. Hush, now. Let him get to sleep if he will."

"Saying a name." Frony said. "He dont know nobody's name."

"You just say it and see if he dont." Dilsey said. "You say it to him while he sleeping and I bet he hear you."

"He know lot more than folks thinks." Roskus said. "He knowed they time was coming, like that pointer done. He could tell you when hisn coming, if he could talk. Or yours. Or mine."

"You take Luster outen that bed, mammy." Frony said. "That boy conjure him." 34)

"Hush your mouth." Dilsey said. "Aint you got no better sense than that. What you want to listen to Roskus for, anyway. Get in, Benjy."

Dilsey pushed me and I got in the bed, where Luster already was. He was asleep. Dilsey took a long piece of wood and laid it between Luster and me. "Stay on your side now." Dilsey said. "Luster little, and you dont want to hurt him."

You cant go yet, T. P. said. Wait.

We looked around the coner of the house and watched the carriages go away.

"Now." T. P. said. He took Quentin up and we ran down to the corner of the fence and watched them pass. "There he go." T. P. said. "See that one with the glass in it. Look at him. He laying in there. See him." 35)

Come on, Luster said, I going to take this here ball down home,

---

34) 프로니는 아들 러스터가 벤지와 함께 자는 것이 아들에게 어떤 저주라도 내리지 않을까 걱정하고 있다.

35) 묘지를 향하는 유리로 된 운구차에 누워 있는 캄슨씨의 시신을 티피는 벤지에게 보라고 말한다.

where I wont lose it. Naw, sir, you cant have it. If them men sees you with it, they'll say you stole it. Hush up, now. You cant have it. What business you got with it. You cant play no ball.

Frony and T. P. were playing in the dirt by the door. T. P. had lightning bugs in a bottle.

"How did you all get back out." Frony said.

"We've got company." Caddy said. "Father said for us to mind me tonight. I expect you and T. P. will have to mind me too."

"I'm not going to mind you." Jason said. "Frony and T. P. dont have to either."

"They will if I say so." Caddy said. "Maybe I wont say for them to."

"T. P. dont mind nobody." Frony said. "Is they started the funeral yet."

"What's a funeral." Jason said.

"Didn't mammy tell you not to tell them." Versh said.

"Where they moans." Frony said. "They moaned two days on Sis Beulah Clay."

They moaned at Dilsey's house. Dilsey was moaning. When Dilsey moaned Luster said, Hush, and we hushed, and then I began to cry and Blue howled under the kitchen steps. Then Dilsey stopped and we stopped.

"Oh." Caddy said. "That's niggers. White folks dont have funerals."

"Mammy said us not to tell them, Frony." Versh said.

"Tell them what." Caddy said.

Dilsey moaned, and when it got to the place I began to cry and Blue howled under the steps. Luster, Frony said in the window. Take them down to the barn. I cant get no cooking done with all that racket. That hound too. Get them outen here.

I aint going down there, Luster said. I might meet pappy down there. I seen him last night, waving his arms in the barn.

"I like to know why not." Frony said. "White folks dies too. Your grandmammy dead as any nigger can get, I reckon."

"Dogs are dead." Caddy said. "And when Nancy[36] fell in the ditch and Roskus shot her and the buzzards came and undressed her."

The bones rounded out of the ditch, where the dark vines were in the black ditch, into the moonlight, like some of the shapes had stopped. Then they all stopped and it was dark, and when I stopped to start again I could hear Mother, and feet walking fast away, and I could smell it.[37] Then the room came, but my eyes went shut. I didn't stop. I could smell it. T. P. unpinned the bed clothes.

"Hush." he said. "Shhhhhhhh."

But I could smell it. T. P. pulled me up and he put on my clothes fast.

"Hush, Benjy." he said. "We going down to our house. You want to go down to our house, where Frony is. Hush. Shhhhh."

He laced my shoes and put my cap on and we went out. There was a light in the hall. Across the hall we could hear Mother.

"Shhhhhh, Benjy." T. P. said. "We'll be out in a minute."

A door opened and I could smell it more than ever, and a head came out. It wasn't Father. Father was sick there.[38]

"Can you take him out of the house."

---

36) 말 이름. 팬시(Fancy)와 짝이었던 말. 그리고 댄(Dan)은 집안의 개 이름이며, 곧 이어지는 퀸턴의 죽음에 대한 기억들을 벤지가 떠올릴 때 댄의 이름이 여러 번 언급된다.

37) 벤지 마음 속의 "환한 형체"(they)가 갑자기 사라지면서 그를 암흑 속으로 빠뜨리며 아마도 그를 울게 만들고 있다. 그가 "시작하기 위해 멈췄다"는 표현은 잠시 울음을 멈추었다 다시 울기 위해 호흡을 가다듬고 있는 순간을 포착하면서, 그 사이에 어머니의 울음소리를 듣고 있는 부분이다. 여기 어머니는 퀸턴의 죽음을 두고 울고 있으며, 바쁘게 사라지고 있는 누군가의 발소리는 딜시나, 아버지, 아니면 캐롤라인의 상태를 점검하기 위해 온 의사의 발소리일 수 있다. 벤지가 맡고 있는 냄새 또한 의사에게서 나는 약냄새와 관련된 것으로 볼 수 있으며, 동시에 그것은 죽음의 냄새와 연관된 것으로 그의 감각적인 언어사용을 엿볼 수 있다. 그리고 이 모든 것은 티피가 밤중에 벤지를 침대에서 데리고 나와 자기(딜시)네 집으로 데려가기 위해 옷을 입히고 있는 순간에 일어나고 있다.

38) 가족이 모두 퀸턴의 자살을 두고 슬퍼하고 있는 장면과 연결되어, 벤지의 눈에는 아마 술에 취한 아버지의 상태를 두고 "아프다"고 묘사할 가능성이 크다.

"That's where we going." T. P. said. Dilsey came up the stairs.

"Hush." she said. "Hush. Take him down home, T. P. Frony fixing him a bed. You all look after him, now. Hush, Benjy. Go on with T. P."

She went where we could hear Mother.

"Better keep him there." It wasn't Father. He shut the door, but I could still smell it.

We went down stairs. The stairs went down into the dark and T. P. took my hand, and we went out the door, out of the dark. Dan was sitting in the back yard, howling.

"He smell it." T. P said. "Is that the way you found it out."

We went down the steps, where our shadows were.

"I forgot your coat." T. P. said. "You ought to had it. But I aint going back."

Dan howled.

"Hush now." T. P. said. Our Shadows moved, but Dan's shadow didn't move except to howl when he did.

"I cant take you down home, bellering like you is." T. P. said. "You was bad enough before you got that bullfrog voice.[39] Come on."

We went along the brick walk, with our shadows. The pig pen smelled like pigs. The cow stood in the lot, chewing at us. Dan howled.

"You going to wake the whole town up." T. P. said. "Cant you hush."

We saw Fancy, eating by the branch. The moon shone on the water when we got there.

"Naw, sir." T. P. said. "This too close. We cant stop here. Come on. Now, just look at you. Got your whole led wet. Come on, here." Dan howled.

The ditch came up out of the buzzing grass. The bones rounded out

---

39) 황소개구리가 내는 소리. 사춘기를 들어선 벤지가 변성기를 경험하며 내는 목소리를 두고 하는 말이다.

of the black vines.

"Now." T. P. said. "Beller your head off if you want to. You got the whole night and a twenty acre pasture to beller in."

T. P. lay down in the ditch and I sat down, watching the bones where the buzzards ate Nancy, flapping black and slow and heavy out of the ditch.

I had it when we was down here before, Luster said. I showed it to you. Didn't you see it. I took it out of my pocket right here and showed it to you.

"Do you think buzzards are going to undress Damuddy." Caddy said. "You're crazy."

"You're a skizzard." Jason said. He began to cry.

"You're a knobnot." Caddy said. Jason cried. His hands were in his pockets.

"Jason going to be rich man." Versh said. "He holding his money all the time."

Jason cried.

"Now you've got him started." Caddy said. "Hush up, Jason. How can buzzards get in where Damuddy is. Father wouldn't let them. Would you let a buzzard undress you. Hush up, now."

Jason hushed. "Frony said it was a funeral." he said.

"Well it's not." Caddy said. "It's a party.[40)] Frony dont know anything about it. He wants your lightning bugs, T. P. Let him hold it a while."

T. P. gave me the bottle of lightning bugs.

"I bet if we go around to the parlor window we can see something." Caddy said. "Then you'll believe me."

"I already knows." Frony said. "I dont need to see."

"You better hush your mouth, Frony." Versh said. "Mammy going whip you."

---

40) 캐디가 할머니 장례식 철야를 파티라고 오해하며 하는 말이다.

"What is it." Caddy said.

"I knows what I knows." Frony said.

"Come on." Caddy said. "Let's go around to the front."

We started to go.

"T. P. wants his lightning bugs." Frony said.

"Let him hold it a while longer, T. P." Caddy said. "We'll bring it back."

"You all never caught them." Frony said.

"If I say you and T. P. can come too, will you let him hold it." Caddy said.

"Aint nobody said me and T. P. got to mind you." Frony said.

"If I say you dont have to, will you let him hold it." Caddy said.

"All right." Frony said. "Let him hold it, T. P. We going to watch them moaning."

"They aint moaning." Caddy said. "I tell you it's a party. Are they moaning, Versh."

"We aint going to know what they doing, standing here." Versh said.

"Come on." Caddy said. "Frony and T. P. dont have to mind me. But the rest of us do. You better carry him, Versh. It's getting dark."

Versh took me up and we went on around the kitchen.

When we looked around the corner we could see the lights coming up the drive.[41] *T. P. went back to the cellar door and opened it.*

You know what's down there, T. P. said. Soda water.[42] *I seen Mr Jason come up with both hands full of them. Wait here a minute.*

T. P. went and looked in the kitchen door. Dilsey said, What are you peeping in here for. Where's Benjy.

He out here, T. P. said.

---

41) 캐디의 결혼식이 끝난 후 초저녁 즈음, 교회(식장)로부터 리셉션을 위해 집으로 돌아오고 있는 자동차들의 불빛을 묘사하고 있다.

42) 여기 "소다수"는 결혼식 하객들에서 제공되고 있던 샴페인이다.

Go on and watch him, Dilsey said. Keep him out the house now.

Yessum, T. P. said. Is they started yet.

You go on and keep that boy out of sight, Dilsey said. I got all I can tend to.

A snake crawled out from under the house. Jason said he wasn't afraid of snakes and Caddy said he was but she wasn't and Versh said they both were and Caddy said to be quite, like Father said.

You aint got to start bellering now, T. P. said. You want some this sassprilluh.

It tickled my nose and eyes.

If you aint going to drink it, let me get to it, T. P. said. All right, here tis. We better get another bottle while aint nobody bothering us. You be quite, now.

We stopped under the tree by the parlor window. Versh set me down in the wet grass. It was cold. There were lights in all the windows.

"That's where Damuddy is." Caddy said. "She's sick every day now. When she gets well we're going to have a picnic."

"I knows what I knows." Frony said.

The trees were buzzing, and the grass.

"The one next to it is where we have the measles." Caddy said. "Where do you and T. P. have the measles, Frony."

"Has them just wherever we is, I reckon." Frony said.

"They haven't started yet." Caddy said.

They getting ready to start, T. P. said. You stand right here now while I get that box so we can see in the window. Here, les finish drinking this here sassprilluh. It make me feel just like a squinch owl inside.

We drank the sassprilluh and T. P. pushed the bottle through the lattice, under the house, and went away. I could hear them in the parlor and I clawed my hands against the wall.[43] T. P. dragged the box. He fell down, and he began to laugh. He lay there, laughing into the grass. He got up and dragged the box under the window, trying not to laugh.

"I skeered I going to holler." T. P. said. "Git on the box and see is they started."

"They haven't started because the band hasn't come yet."[44] Caddy said.

"They aint going to have no band." Frony said.

"How do you know." Caddy said.

"I knows what I knows." Frony said.

"You dont know anything." Caddy said. She went to the tree. "Push me up, Versh."

"Your paw told you to stay out that tree." Versh said.

"That was a long time ago." Caddy said. "I expect he's forgotten about it. Besides, he said to mind me tonight. Didn't he didn't he say to mind me tonight."

"I'm not going to mind you." Jason said. "Frony and T. P. are not going to either."

"Push me up, Versh." Caddy said.

"All right." Versh said. "You the one going to get whipped. I aint." He went and pushed Caddy up into the tree to the first limb. We watched the muddy bottom of her drawers.[45] Then we couldn't see her. We could hear the tree thrashing.

---

43) 벤지는 거실 안에서 일어나고 있는 결혼식 파티의 소리를 들을 수 있지만 볼 수가 없어, 안으로 들어갈 수 없는 좌절감으로 벽을 할퀴고 있다.

44) 이 부분도 포크너가 작품의 몇 군데서 시점의 변화를 표시하지 않고 지나치는 곳이다. 앞서 캐디가 할머니의 장례식 철야 장면을 파티로 오해하고 있는 장면과 연결되어, 음악 밴드가 아직 도착하지 않아 파티가 시작되지 않고 있다고 말한다. 이는 벤지의 마음속에 캐디의 결혼식과 할머니의 장례식 장면들이 서로 엉켜 하나처럼 기억되고 있는 점을 단적으로 보여준다.

45) 캐디가 (결국 파티가 아닌) 할머니의 죽음을 보기 위해 나무 위를 올라가 집안을 들여다보는 장면으로, 아래서 형제들과 딜시의 아이들이 그녀의 "흙 묻은 속옷"을 올려다보고 있다. 포크너가 작품을 시작할 수 있었던 핵심적인 이미지이기도 하다.

"Mr Jason said if you break that tree he whip you." Versh said.

"I'm going to tell on her too." Jason said.

The tree quit thrashing. We looked up into the still branches.

"What you seeing." Frony whispered.

I saw them. Then I saw Caddy, with flowers in her hair, and a long veil like shining wind. Caddy Caddy

"Hush." T. P. said. "They going to hear you. Get down quick." He pulled me. Caddy. I clawed my hands against the wall Caddy. T. P. pulled me. "Hush." he said. "Hush. Come on here quick." He pulled me on. Caddy "Hush up, Benjy. You want them to hear you. Come on, les drink some more sassprilluh, then we can come back if you hush. We better get one more bottle or we both be hollering. We can say Dan drunk it. Mr Quentin always saying he so smart, we can say he sassprilluh dog, too."

The moonlight came down the cellar stairs. We drank some more sassprilluh.

"You know what I wish." T. P. said. "I wish a bear would walk in that cellar door. You know what I do. I walk right up to him and spit in he eye. Gimme that bottle to stop my mouth before I holler."

T. P fell down. He began to laugh, and the cellar door and the moonlight jumped away and something hit me.

"Hush up." T. P. said, trying not to laugh. "Lawd, they'll all hear us. Get up." T. P said. "Get up, Benjy, quick." He was thrashing about and laughing and I tried to get up. The cellar steps ran up the hill in the moonlight and T. P. fell up the hill, into the moonlight, and I ran against the fence and T. P. ran behind me saying "Hush up hush up." Then he fell into the flowers, laughing, and I ran into the box. But when I tried to climb onto it it jumped away and hit me on the back of the head and my throat made a sound. It made the sound again and I stopped trying to get up, and it made the sound again and I began to cry. But my throat kept on making the sound while T. P. was pulling me. It kept on making it and I couldn't tell if I was crying or not, and T. P. fell down on top of me, laughing, and it kept on making the sound and Quentin kicked T. P. and Caddy put her arms around me, and her shining veil, and I couldn't smell trees anymore and I began to cry.[46)]

Benjy, Caddy said, Benjy. She put her arms around me again, but I went away. "What is it, Benjy." she said. "Is it this hat." She took her hat off and came again, and I went away.

"Benjy." she said. "What is it, Benjy. What has Caddy done."

"He dont like that prissy dress." Jason said. "You think you're grown up, dont you. You think you're better than anybody else, dont you. Prissy."

"You shut your mouth." Caddy said. "You dirty little beast. Benjy."

"Just because you are fourteen, you think you're grown up, dont you." Jason said. "You think you're something. Dont you."

"Hush, Benjy." Caddy said. "You'll disturb Mother. Hush."

But I didn't hush, and when she went away I followed, and she stopped on the stairs and waited and I stopped too.

"What is it, Benjy." Caddy said. "Tell Caddy. She'll do it. Try."

"Candace." Mother said.

"Yessum." Caddy said.

"Why are you teasing him." Mother said. "Bring him here."

We went to Mother's room, where she was lying with the sickness on a cloth on her head.[47)]

"What is the matter now." Mother said. "Benjamin."

---

46) 웨딩드레스를 입고 화장(향수)을 한 캐디의 모습은 평소 벤지가 알고 있는 그녀의 모습이 아닌 것이다. 그리하여 캐디가 자신을 달래는 데도 불구하고 캐디에게서 더 이상 나무 냄새를 맡을 수 없어 그는 울음을 터뜨리고 있다. 연결된 이탤릭체의 문장은 결혼식 날의 생소한 캐디의 모습이 14세 된 캐디가 처음으로 향수를 뿌렸던 그날의 기억으로 되돌아가 그녀를 거절하는 모습과, 또 다른 시점에서 모자를 쓴 생소한 그녀를 거부하고 있는 벤지의 모습이 한 문단에서 함께 연결되고 있다.

47) 어머니 캐롤라인이 아파 머리 위에 장뇌("camphor")로 젖은 천을 올려놓고 몸져누워 있는 방이다. 이 장뇌는 두통이나 어지럼증에 효과가 있는 것으로 소금 냄새와

"Benjy." Caddy said. She came again, but I went away.

"You must have done something to him." Mother said. "Why wont you let him alone, so I can have some peace. Give him the box and please go on and let him alone."

Caddy got the box and set it on the floor and opened it. It was full of stars. When I was still, they were still. When I moved, they glinted and sparkled. I hushed.[48)]

Then I heard Caddy walking and I began again.

"Benjamin." Mother said. "Come here." I went to the door. "You, Benjamin." Mother said.

"What is it now." Father said. "Where are you going."

"Take him downstairs and get someone to watch him, Jason." Mother said. "You know I'm ill, yet you."

Father shut the door behind us.

"T. P." he said.

"Sir." T. P. said downstairs.

"Benjy's coming down." Father said. "Go with T. P."

I went to the bathroom door. I could hear the water.[49)]

"Benjy." T. P. said downstairs.

I could hear the water. I listened to it.

"Benjy." T. P. said downstairs.

I listened to the water.

I couldn't hear the water, and Caddy opened the door.

비슷하다고 알려져 있다.

48) 울음을 그치지 않는 벤지를 달래기 위해 그에게 보석상자를 주라고 어머니는 말하고 있으며, 이어지는 문단에서 그 상자의 귀금속들이 빛에 반사되어 벤지가 움직이면 따라서 광채를 발하고 있는 것을 보며 벤지는 울음을 그친다

49) 여기 벤지는 향수 냄새가 나는 그녀를 욕실로 몰아 누이에게서 그 냄새가 없어지도록 깨끗이 씻고 나오길 기다리는 장면이다. 그리고 몇 줄 뒤에 욕실에서 나온 캐디를 두고 "그녀에게서 나무 냄새가 난다"고 말하며, 캐디는 결국 그 향수를 딜시에게 선물하는 장면으로 이어진다.

"Why, Benjy." she said. She looked at me and I went and she put her arms around me. "Did you find Caddy again." she said. "Did you think Caddy had run away." Caddy smelled like trees.

We went to Caddy's room. She sat down at the mirror. She stopped her hands and looked at me.

"Why, Benjy. What is it." she said. "You mustn't cry. Caddy's not going away. See here." she said. She took up the bottle and took the stopper out and held it to my nose. "Sweet. Smell. Good."

I went away and I didn't hush, and she held the bottle in her hand, looking at me.

"Oh." she said. She put the bottle down and came and put her arms around me. "So that was it. And you were trying to tell Caddy and you couldn't tell her. You wanted to, but you couldn't, could you. Of course Caddy wont. Of course Caddy wont. Just wait till I dress."

Caddy dressed and took up the bottle again and we went down to the kitchen.

"Dilsey." Caddy said. "Benjy's got a present for you." She stopped down and put the bottle in my hand. "Hold it out to Dilsey, now." Caddy held my hand out and Dilsey took the bottle.

"Well I'll declare." Dilsey said. "If my baby aint give Dilsey a bottle of perfume. Just look here, Roskus."

Caddy smelled like trees. "We dont like perfume ourselves." Caddy said.

She smelled like trees.

"Come on, now." Dilsey said. "You too big to sleep with folks You a big boy now. Thirteen years old. Big enough to sleep by yourself in Uncle Maury's room." Dilsey said.[50)]

---

50) 딜시는 13세 된 벤지가 이젠 너무 커서 더 이상 캐디와 함께 잘 수 없음을 시사하면서 모리 삼촌이 사용하던 방에서 혼자 자야 한다고 말한다. 이어지는 문단 역시 작가가 시점의 변화를 표시하지 않은 부분 중 한 곳으로, 모리삼촌과 관련하여 연상되는 이 사건은 이전에 삼촌이 패터슨 부인과의 관계가 들통 나 패터슨씨와의 싸움에서 눈 주

Uncle Maury was sick. His eye was sick, and his mouth. Versh took his supper up to him on the tray.

"Maury says he's going to shoot the scoundrel." Father said. "I told him he'd better not mention it to Patterson before hand." He drank.

"Jason." Mother said.

"Shoot who, father." Quentin said. "What's Uncle Maury going to shoot him for."

"Because he couldn't take a little joke." Father said.

"Jason." Mother said. "How can you. You'd sit right there and see Maury shot down in ambush, and laugh."

"Then Maury'd better stay out of ambush." Father said.

"Shoot who, Father." Quentin said. "Who's Uncle Maury going to shoot."

"Nobody." Father said. "I dont own a pistol."

Mother began to cry. "If you begrudge Maury your food, why aren't you man enough to say so to his face. To ridicule him before the children, behind his back."

"Of course I dont." Father said. "I admire Maury. He is invaluable to my own sense of racial superiority. I wouldn't swap Maury for a matched team. And do you know why, Quentin."

"No, sir." Quentin said.

"*Et ego in arcadia* I have forgotten the latin for hay." [51] Father

---

위와 입 부분을 맞아 멍들은 상처를 두고, 벤지는 삼촌이 "아프다고" 묘사하고 있다.

51) 여기 "Et ego in arcadia"는 라틴 전원시에 잘 알려진 문구로 직역을 하면, "And I in Arcadia" 즉 건초(hay)가 충분한 축복의 땅 "아카디아에 (살고 있는) 나" 정도가 될 것이다(정확한 표현은 "And in Arcadia I had plenty of hay to eat"이다). 그리고 캄슨씨가 아들 퀀턴에게 생각이 안 난다는 "hay"에 대한 라틴어는 "fœum"으로, 은혜/선행/자선의 의미와 관련있다. 따라서 바로 앞에서 캄슨씨가 처남을 두고 암시하고 있는 자신의 입장은 캄슨 집안에 빌붙어 살고 있는 처남 모리는 캄슨씨의 은혜를 입고 있는 처지이며 자신은 은혜/자선을 베푸는 입장이다. 그리고 이 말에 따르면 자선을 베푸는 자는 그 대가로 어떤 보상도 은혜를 입은 자로부터 기대하지 말아야

said. “There, there.” he said. “I was just joking.” He drank and set the glass down and went and put his hand on Mother’s shoulder.

“It’s no joke.” Mother said. “My people are every bit as well born as yours. Just because Maury’s health is bad.”

“Of course.” Father said. “Bad health is the primary reason for all life. Created by disease, within putrefaction, into decay. Versh.”

“Sir.” Versh said behind my chair.

“Take the decanter and fill it.”

“And tell Dilsey to come and take Benjamin up to bed.” Mother said.

“You a big boy.” Dilsey said. “Caddy tired sleeping with you. Hush now, so you can go to sleep.” The room went away, but I didn’t hush, and the room came back and Dilsey came and sat on the bed, looking at me.

“Aint you going to be a good boy and hush.” Dilsey said. “You aint, is you. See can you wait a minute, then.”

She went away. There wasn’t anything in the door. Then Caddy was in it.

“Hush.” Caddy said. “I’m coming”

I hushed and Dilsey turned back the spread and Caddy got in between the spread and the blanket. She didn’t take off her bathrobe.

“Now.” she said. “Here I am.” Dilsey came with a blanket and spread it over her and tucked it around her.

“He be gone in a minute.” Dilsey said. “I leave the light on in your room.”

“All right.” Cadddy said. She snuggled her head beside mine on the pillow. “Goodnight, Dilsey.”

“Goodnight, honey.” Dilsey said. The room went black. *Caddy*

그것이 진정한 자선행위라 할 수 있다. 따라서 캄슨 그늘에서 얻어먹고 사는 모리 삼촌은, 대가로 어떤 보상도 받지 않고 있는 캄슨씨에게는, 후자의 “우월감”을 내세우는 데 없어서는 안 될 존재인 것이다.

smelled like trees.

We looked up into the tree where she was.

"What she seeing, Versh." Frony whispered.

"Shhhhhhh." Caddy said in the tree. Dilsey said,

"You come on here." She came around the corner of the house. "Whyn't you all go on up stairs, like your paw said, stead of slipping out behind my back. Where's Caddy and Quentin."

"I told her not to climb up that tree." Jason said. "I'm going to tell on her."

"Who in what tree." Dilsey said. She came and looked up into the tree. "Caddy." Dilsey said. The branches began to shake again.

"You, Satan." Dilsey said. "Come down from there."

"Hush." Caddy said. "Dont you know Father said to be quite." Her legs came in sight and Dilsey reached up and lifted her out of the tree.

"Aint you got any better sense than to let them come around here." Dilsey said.

"I couldn't do nothing with her." Versh said.

"What you all doing here." Dilsey said. "Who told you to come up to the house."

"She did." Frony said. "She told us to come."

"Who told you you got to do what she say." Dilsey said. "Get on home, now." Frony and T. P. went on. We couldn't see them when they were still going away.

"Out here in the middle of the night." Dilsey said. She took me up and we went to the kitchen.

"Slipping out behind my back." Dilsey said. "When you knowed it's past your bedtime."

"Shhhh, Dilsey." Caddy said. "Dont talk so loud. We've got to be quiet."

"You hush your mouth and get quiet, then." Dilsey said. "Where's Quentin."

"Quentin's mad because we had to mind me tonight." Caddy said.

"He's still got T. P.'s bottle of lightning bugs."

"I reckon T. P. can get along without it." Dilsey said. "You go and find Quentin, Versh. Roskus say he seen him going towards the barn." Versh went on. We couldn't see him.

"They're not doing anything in there." Caddy said. "Just sitting in chairs and looking."

"They dont need no help from you all to do that." Dilsey said. We went around the kitchen.

Where you want to go now, Luster said. You going back to watch them knocking ball again. We done looked for it over there. Here. Wait a minute. You wait right here while I go back and get that ball. I done thought of something.

The kitchen was dark. The trees were black on the sky. Dan came waddling out from under the steps and chewed my ankle. I went around the kitchen, where the moon was. Dan came scuffling along, into the moon.

"Benjy." T. P. said in the house.

The flower tree by the parlor window wasn't dark, but the thick trees were. The grass was buzzing in the moonlight where my shadow walked on the grass.

"You, Benjy." T. P. said in the house. "Where you hiding. You slipping off. I knows it."

Luster came back. Wait, he said. Here. Dont go over there. Miss Quentin and her beau in the swing yonder. you come on this way. Come back here, Benjy.

It was dark under the trees. Dan wouldn't come. He stayed in the moonlight. Then I could see the swing and I began to cry.[52)]

Come away from there, Benjy, Luster said. You know Miss Quentin

---

52) 연인(캐디와 찰리)이 만나는 그네가 있는 나무 아래는 어두웠으며, 그곳에서 둘이 키스를 하고 있는 것을 확인한 벤지는 울기 시작한다. 물론 이 장면은 현시점에서 미스 퀀턴이 빨간 넥타이를 맨 쇼 단의 청년과 그네에서 데이트하는 장면과 겹쳐져 연상되고 있다.

going to get mad.

It was two now, and then one in the swing. Caddy came fast, white in the darkness.

"Benjy." she said. "How did you slip out. Where's Versh."

She put her arms around me and I hushed and held to her dress and tried to pull her away.

"Why, Benjy." she said. "What is it. T. P." she called.

The one in the swing got up and came, and I cried and pulled Caddy's dress.

"Benjy." Caddy said. "It's just Charlie. Dont you know Charlie."

"Where's his nigger." Charlie said. "What do they let him run around loose for."

"Hush, Benjy." Caddy said. "Go away, Charlie. He doesn't like you." Charlie went away and I hushed. I pulled at Caddy's dress.

"Why, Benjy." Caddy said. "Aren't you going to let me stay here and talk to Charlie a while."

"Call that nigger." Charlie said. He came back. I cried louder and pulled at Caddy's dress.

"Go away, Charlie." Caddy said. Charlie came and put his hands on Caddy and I cried more. I cried loud.

"No, no." Caddy said. "No, No."

"He cant talk." Charlie said. "Caddy."

"Are you crazy." Caddy said. She began to breathe fast. "He can see. Dont. Dont." [53] Caddy fought. They both breathed fast. "Please. Please." Caddy whispered.

"Send him away." Charlie said.

"I will." Caddy said. "Let me go."

"Will you send him away." Charlie said.

"Yes." Caddy said. "Let me go." Charlie went away. "Hush."

---

53) 찰리가 다가와 누이의 몸에 손을 대자 더욱 큰소리로 울어대는 벤지와 티피가 보는 앞에서, 찰리는 더욱 노골적으로 캐디를 성적으로 자극하고 있는 장면이다.

Caddy said. "He's gone." I hushed. I could hear her and feel her chest going.

"I'll have to take him to the house." she said. She took my hand. "I'm coming." she whispered.

"Wait." Charlie said. "Call the nigger."

"No." Caddy said. "I'll come back. Come on, Benjy."

"Caddy." Charlie whispered, loud. We went on. "You better come back. Are you coming back." Caddy and I were running. "Caddy." Charlie said. We ran out into the moonlight, toward the kitchen.

"Caddy." Charlie said.

Caddy and I ran. We ran up the kitchen steps, onto the porch, and Caddy knelt down in the dark and held me. I could hear her and feel her chest." "I wont." she said. "I wont anymore, ever. Benjy. Benjy." Then she was crying, and I cried, and we held each other. "Hush." she said. "Hush. I wont anymore." So I hushed and Caddy got up and we went into the kitchen and turned the light on and Caddy took the kitchen soap and washed her mouth at the sink, hard. Caddy smelled like trees.

I kept a telling you to stay away from there, Luster said. They sat up in the swing, quick. Quentin had her hands on her hair. He had a red tie.

You old crazy loon, Quentin said. I'm going to tell Dilsey about the way you let him follow everywhere I go. I'm going to make her whip you good.

"I couldn't stop him." Luster said. "Come on here, Benjy."

"Yes you could." Quentin said. "You didn't try. You were both snooping around after me. Did Grandmother send you all out here to spy on me." She jumped out of the swing. "If you dont take him, right away this minute and keep him away, I'm going to make Jason whip you."

"I cant do nothing with him." Luster said. "You try it if you think you can."

"Shut your mouth." Quentin said. "Are you going to get him

away."

"Ah, let him stay." he said. He had a red tie. The sun was red on it. "Look here, Jack." [54] He struck a match and put it in his mouth. Then he took the match out of his mouth. It was still burning. "Want to try it." he said. I went over there. "Open your mouth." he said. I opened my mouth. Quentin hit the match with her hand and it went away.

"Goddam you." Quentin said. "Do you want to get him started. Dont you know he'll beller all day. I'm going to tell Dilsey on you." She went away running.

"Here, kid." he said. "Hey. Come on back. I aint going to fool with him."

Quentin ran on to the house. She went around the kitchen.

"You played hell then, Jack." he said. "Aint you."

"He cant tell what you saying." Luster said. "He deef and dumb."

"Is." he said. "How long's he been that way."

"Been that way thirty three years today." Luster said. "Born looney. Is you one of them show folks."

"Why." he said.

"I dont ricklick[55] seeing you around here before." Luster said.

"Well, what about it." he said.

"Nothing." Luster said. "I going tonight."

He looked at me.

"You aint the one can play a tune on that saw, is you." Luster said.

"It'll cost you a quarter to find that out." he said. He looked at me. "Why dont they lock him up." he said. "What'd you bring him out here for."

"You aint talking to me." Luster said. "I cant do nothing with him. I just come over here looking for a quarter I lost so I can go to the show tonight. Look like now I aint going to get to go." Luster looked

---

54) 미스 퀸턴의 남자친구(빨간 넥타이)가 벤지를 경멸적으로 부르고 있다.

55) recollect, remember.

on the ground. "You aint got no extra quarter, is you." Luster said.

"No." he said. "I aint."

"I reckon I just have to find that other one, then." Luster said. He put his hand in his pocket. "You dont want to buy no golf ball neither, does you." Luster said.

"What kind of ball." he said.

"Golf ball." Luster said. "I dont want but a quarter."

"What for." he said. "What do I want with it."

"I didn't think you did." Luster said. "Come on here, mulehead." he said. "Come on here and watch them knocking that ball. Here. Here something you can play with along with that jimson weed." Luster picked it up and gave it to me. It was bright.

"Where'd you get that." he said. His tie was red in the sun, walking.

"Found it under this here bush." Luster said. "I thought for a minute it was that quarter I lost."

He came and took it.

"Hush." Luster said. "He going to give it back when he done looking at it."

"Agnes Mabel Becky." [56] he said. He looked toward the house.

"Hush." Luster said. "He fixing to give it back."

He gave it to me and I hushed.

"Who come to see her last night." he said.

"I dont know." Luster said. "They comes every night she can climb down that tree. I dont keep no track of them."

"Damn if one of them didn't leave a track." [57] he said. He looked at the house. Then he went and lay down in the swing. "Go away." he said. "Dont bother me."

---

56) 콘돔 상표명.

57) 그 빨간 넥타이의 사내가 미스 퀸틴이 만나는 녀석들이 꼭 흔적을 남긴다고 말하는 부분으로, 여기 "흔적"(track)은 버려진 콘돔상자를 말한다.

"Come on here." Luster said. "You done played hell now. Time Miss Quentin get done telling on you."

We went to the fence and looked through the curling flower spaces. Luster hunted in the grass.

"I had it right here." he said. I saw the flag flapping, and the sun slanting on the broad grass.

"They'll be some along soon." Luster said. "There some now, but they going away. Come on and help me look for it."

We went along the fence.

"Hush." Luster said. "How can I make them come over here, if they aint coming. Wait. They'll be some in a minute. Look yonder. Here they come."

I went along the fence, to the gate, where the girls passed with their booksatchels.[58] "You, Benjy." Luster said. "Come back here."

You cant do no good looking through the gate, T. P. said. Miss Caddy done gone long ways away. Done got married and left you. You cant do no good, holding to the gate and crying. She cant hear you.

What is it he wants, T. P. Mother said. Cant you play with him and keep him quiet.

He want to go down yonder and look through the gate, T. P. said.

Well, he cannot do it, Mother said. It's raining. You will just have to play with him and keep him quiet. You, Benjamin.

Aint nothing going to quiet him, T. P. said. He think if he down to the gate, Miss Caddy come back.

Nonsense, Mother said.

I could hear them talking. I went out the door and I couldn't hear

---

58) 캐디가 집을 떠난 후에도 벤지는 언제나처럼 방과 후 학교서 돌아오는 캐디를 기다리기 위해 대문가를 향하고 있으며, 길 건너 책가방을 멘 여학생들이 지나가고 있다. 이 장면은 곧 벤지가 한 여학생(버지스 집안의 딸)을 '공격'하여 거세당하는 기억으로 이어진다.

them, and I went down to the gate, where the girls passed with their booksatchels. They looked at me, walking fast, with their heads turned. I tried to say, but they went on, and I went along the fence, trying to say, and they went faster. Then they were running and I came to the corner of the fence and I couldn't go any further, and I held to the fence, looking after them and trying to say.

"You, Benjy." T. P said. "What you doing, slipping out. Dont you know Dilsey whip you."

"You cant do no good, moaning and slobbering through the fence." T. P said. "You done skeered them chillen. Look at them, walking on the other side of the street."

How did he get out, Father said. Did you leave the gate unlatched when you came in, Jason.

Of course not, Jason said. Dont you know I've got better sense than to do that. Do you think I wanted anything like this to happen. This family is bad enough, God knows. I could have told you, all the time. I reckon you'll send him to Jackson,[59] *now. If Mr Burgess dont shoot him first.*

Hush, Father said.

I could have told you, all the time, Jason said.

It was open when I touched it, and I held to it in the twilight. I wasn't crying, and I tried to stop, watching the girls coming along in the twilight. I wasn't crying.

"There he is."

They stopped.

"He cant get out. He wont hurt anybody, anyway. Come on."

"I'm scared to. I'm scared. I'm going to cross the street."

"He cant get out."

I wasn't crying.

"Dont be a fraid cat. Come on."

---

59) 당시 정신장애자 요양소가 미시시피주 잭슨에 소재하였다.

They came on in the twilight. I wasn't crying, and I held to the gate. They came slow.

"I'm scared."

"He wont hurt you. I pass here every day. He just runs along the fence."

They came on. I opened the gate and they stopped, turning. I was trying to say, and I caught her, trying to say, and she screamed and I was trying to say and trying and the bright shapes began to stop and I tried to get out. I tried to get it off of my face, but the bright shapes were agoing again. They were going up the hill to where it fell away and I tried to cry. But when I breathed in, I couldn't breathe out again to cry, and I tried to keep from falling off the hill and I fell off the hill into the bright, whirling shapes.[60)]

Here, looney, Luster said. Here come some. Hush your slobbering and moaning, now.

They came to the flag. He took it out and they hit, then he put the flag back.

"Mister." Luster said.

He looked around. "What." he said.

"Want to buy a golf ball." Luster said.

"Let's see it." he said. He came to the fence and Luster reached the

---

60) 이 문단 역시 벤지의 의식과 이미지가 명료하지 않은 부분이다. 먼저 벤지는 넘지 말아야 할 대문을 열고 나가서 드디어 버지스의 딸에게 "무엇인가를 말하려 하는데," 그것이 무엇인지는—그 여학생에게 강간이나 성적으로 뭔가를 시도하고 있는지, 아니면 그냥 캐디에게 하려고 한 그 어떤 말을 그녀를 향해 말하려 하는 것인지, 아니면 단순히 왜 누이가 집으로 돌아오지 않는지를 그 아이에게 묻고 싶었는지 등—명확하지 않다. 어쨌든, 상황은 그 아이가 놀라 소리치게 되며, 이어지는 장면은 그의 거세 장면으로 해석되고 있다. 벤지는 거세를 위해 수술대 위해 누워 있으며, 그가 얼굴에서 떼어내려 하고 있는 것은 마취 마스크로, 그리고 그가 자주 이미지화하고 있는 "환한 형체"는 수술대 위에 걸려 있는 불빛으로 볼 수 있으면서, 벤지는 마취 상태로 빠져들고 있음을 알 수 있다.

ball through.

"Where'd you get it." he said.

"Found it." Luster said.

"I know that." he said. "Where In somebody's golf bag."

"I found it laying over here in the yard." Luster said. "I'll take a quarter for it."

"What makes you think it's yours." he said.

"I found it." Luster said.

"Then find yourself another one." he said. He put it in his pocket and went away.

"I got to go to that show tonight." Luster said.

"That so." he said. He went to the table. "Fore caddie." he said. He hit.

"I'll declare." Luster said. "You fusses when you dont see them and you fusses when you does. Why cant you hush. Dont you reckon folks gets tired of listening to you all the time. Here. You dropped your jimson weed." He picked it up and gave it back to me. "You needs a new one. You bout wore that one out." We stood at the fence and watched them.

"That white man hard to get along with." Luster said. "You see him take my ball." They went on. We went on along the fence. We came to the garden and we couldn't go any further. I held to the fence and looked through the flower spaces. They went away.

"Now you aint got nothing to moan about." Luster said. "Hush up. I the one got something to moan over, you aint. Here. Whyn't you hold on to that weed. You be bellering about it next." He gave me the flower. "Where you heading now."

Our shadows were on the grass. They got to the trees before we did. Mine got there first. Then we got there, and then the shadows were gone. There was a flower in the bottle. I put the other flower in it.

"Aint you a grown man, now." Luster said. "Playing with two weeds in a bottle. You know what they going to do with you when

Miss Cahline die. They going to send you to Jackson, Where you belong. Mr Jason say so. Where you can hold the bars all day long with the rest of the looneys and slobber. How you like that."

Luster knocked the flowers over with his hand. "That's what they'll do to you at Jackson when you stars bellering."

I tried to pick up the flowers. Luster picked them up, and they went away. I began to cry.

"Beller." Luster said. "Beller. You want something to beller about. All right, then. Caddy." he whispered. "Caddy. Beller now. Caddy."

"Luster." Dilsey said from the kitchen.

The flowers came back.

"Hush." Luster said. "Here they is. Look. It's fixed back just like it was at first. Hush, now."

"You, Luster." Dilsey said.

"Yessum." Luster said. "We coming. You done played hell. Get up." He jerked my arm and I got up. We went out of the trees. Our shadows were gone.

"Hush." Luster said. "Look at all them folks watching you. Hush."

"You bring him on here." Dilsey said. She came down the steps.

"What you done to him now." she said.

"Aint done nothing to him." Luster said. "He just started bellering."

"Yes you is." Dilsey said. "You done something to him. Where you been."

"Over yonder under them cedars." Luster said.

"Getting Quentin all riled up." Dilsey said. "What cant you keep him away from her. Dont you know she dont like him where she at."

"Got as much time for him as I is." Luster said. "He aint none of my uncle."

"Dont you sass me, nigger boy." Dilsey said.

"I aint done nothing to him." Luster said. "He was playing there, and all of a sudden he started bellering."

"Is you been projecking with his graveyard." Dilsey said.

"I aint touched his graveyard."[61] Luster said.

"Dont lie to me, boy." Dilsey said. We went up the steps and into the kitchen. Dilsey opened th firedoor and drew a chair up in front of it and I sat down. I hushed.

What you want to get her started for, Dilsey said. Whyn't you keep him out of there.

He was just looking at the fire, Caddy said. Mother was telling him his new name. We didn't mean to get her started.[62]

I knows you didn't, Dilsey said. Him at one end of the house and her at the other. You let my things alone, now. Dont you touch noting till I get back.

"Aint you shamed of yourself." Dilsey said. "Teasing him." She set the cake on the table.

"I aint been teasing him." Luster said. "He was playing with that bottle full of dogfennel and all of a sudden je started up bellering. You heard him."

"You aint done nothing to his flowers." Dilsey said.

"I aint touched his graveyard." Luster said. "What I want with his truck. I was just hunting for that quarter."

"You lost it, did you." Dilsey said. She lit the candles on the cake. Some of them were little ones. Some were big ones cut into little pieces.

"I told you to go put it away. Now I reckon you want me to get you another one from Frony."

"I got to go to that show, Benjy or no Benjy." Luster said. "I aint

---

61) 벤지의 "묘지"는 흰꽃독말풀(jimson weed)이 들어 있는 유리병이다.

62) 여기 이탤릭 부분의 문단은 벤지의 이름이 모리에서 벤자민(벤지)으로 바뀌는 시점에서 벌어지고 있는 상황들이 연결되고 있다. 그리고 어머니 캐롤라인의 감정이 매우 불안한 상태로 눈물을 보이는("get her started") 모습이 자주 비춰지고 있는데, 그것은 아마도 벤지가 저능아라는 사실을 알고서 그녀가 받고 있는 슬픔이나 치욕감이 벤지의 이름 변화와 연결되어, 그녀의 그러한 모습을 포착하고 있다.

going to follow him around day and night both."

"You going to do just what he want you to, nigger boy." Dilsey said. "You hear me."

"Aint I always done it." Luster said. "Dont I always does what he wants. Dont I, Benjy."

"Then you keep it up." Dilsey said. "Bringing him in here, bawling and getting her started too. You all go ahead and eat this cake, now, before Jason come. I dont want him jumping on me about a cake I bought with my own money. Me baking a cake here, with him counting every egg that comes into this kitchen. See can you let him alone now, less you dont want to go to that show tonight."

Dilsey went away.

"You cant blow out no candles." Luster said. "Watch me blow them out." He leaned down puffed his face. The candles went away. I began to cry. "Hush." Luser said. "Here. Look at the fire whiles I cuts this cake."

I could hear the clock, and I could hear Caddy standing behind me, and I could hear the roof. It's still raining, Caddy said. I hate rain. I hate everything. And then her head came into my lap and she was crying, holding me, and I began to cry. Then I looked at the fire again and the bright, smooth shapes went again. I could hear the clock and the roof and Caddy.

I ate some cake. Luster's hand came and took another piece. I could hear him eating. I looked at the fire.

A long piece of wire came across my shoulder. It went to the door, and then the fire went away. I began to cry.

"What you howling for now." Luster said. "Look there." The fire was there. I hushed. "Cant you set and look at the fire and be quite like mammy told you." Luster said. "You ought to be ashamed of yourself. Here. Here's you some more cake."

"What you done to him now." Dilsey said. "Cant you never let him alone."

"I was just trying to get him to hush up and not sturb[63)] Miss

Cahline." Luster said. "Something got him started again."

"And I know what that something name." Dilsey said. "I'm going to get Versh to take a stick to you when he comes home. You just trying yourself. You been doing it all day. Did you take him down to the branch."

"Nome."[64] Luster said. "We been right here in this yard all day, like you said."

His hand came for another piece of cake. Dilsey hit his hand. "Reach it again, and I chop it right off with this here butcher knife." Dilsey said.

"I bet he aint had one piece of it."

"Yes he is." Luster said. "He already had twice as much as me. Ask him if he aint."

"Reach hit one more time." Dilsey said. "Just reach it."

That's right, Dilsey said. I reckon it'll be my time to cry next. Reckon Maury going to let me cry on him a while, too.

His name's Benjy now, Caddy said.

How come it is, Dilsey said. He aint wore out the name he was born with yet, is he.

Benjamin came out of the bible,[65] *Caddy said. It's a better name for him than Maury was.*

How come it is, Dilsey said.

Mother says it is, Caddy said.

Huh, Dilsey said. Name aint going to help him. Hurt him, neither. Folks dont have no luck, changing names. My name been Dilsey since

---

63) disturb.

64) No Ma' am.

65) 성경(Genesis 35.17)에서 벤자민은 야곱(Jacob)과 라헬(Rachel)의 막내아들로 태어나지만 라헬은 아이의 출산과 함께 사망한다. 그녀는 죽기 전 아이를 베노니(Benoni: "son of my sorrow")라고 이름 짓지만, 야곱은 그를 벤자민("son of my right hand")으로 개명한다.

fore I could remember and it be Dilsey when they's long forgot me.

How will they know it's Dilsey, when it's long forgot, Dilsey, Caddy said.

It'll be in the Book,[66] *honey, Dilsey said. Writ out.*

Can you read it, Caddy said.

Wont have to, Dilsey said. They'll read it for me. All I got to do is say Ise here.

The long wire came across my shoulder, and the fire went away. I began to cry.

Dilsey and Luster fought.

"I seen you." Dilsey said. "Oho, I seen you." She dragged Luster out of the corner, shaking him. "Wasn't nothing bothering him, was they. You just wait till your pappy come home. I wish I was young like I use to be, I'd tear them years[67] right off your head. I good mind to lock you up in that cellar and not let you go to that show tonight, I sho is."

"Ow, mammy." Luster said. "Ow, mammy."

I put my hand out to where the fire had been.

"Catch him." Dilsey said. "Catch him back."

My hand jerked back and I put it in my mouth and Dilsey caught me. I could still hear the clock between my voice.[68] Dilsey reached back and hit Luster on the head. My voice was going loud every time.

"Get that soda."[69] Dilsey said. She took my hand out of my mouth. My voice went louder then and my hand tried to go back to

---

66) 신의 "생명의 책"으로 그 안에는 구원받은 자들의 이름이 적혀 있다(Revelation 20.12,. 15).

67) ears.

68) 벤지가 계속 울다가 호흡을 들이키기 위해 울음을 잠시 멈추고 있는 사이에 시계 소리를 듣고 있는 모습이다. 벤지가 여기서 자신의 울음소리를 "목소리"라고 표현하는 것은 의미심장하지 않을 수 없다.

69) 탄산음료로 화상 부위에 부으면 고통을 완화하는 효과가 있어 딜시가 가져오라고 말한다.

my mouth, but Dilsey held it. My voice went loud. She sprinkled soda on my hand.

"Look in the pantry and tear a piece off of that rag hanging on the nail." she said. "Hush, now. You dont want to make your maw sick again, does you. Here, look at the fire. Dilsey make your hand stop hurting in just a minute. Look at the fire." She opened the door. I looked at the fire, but my hand didn't stop and I didn't stop. My hand was trying to go to my mouth, but Dilsey held it.

She wrapped the cloth around it. Mother said,

"What is it now. Cant I even be sick in peace. Do I have to get up out of bed to come down to him, with two grown negroes to take care of him."

"He all right now." Dilsey said. "He going to quit. He just burnt his hand a little."

"With two grown negroes, you must bring him into the house, bawling." Mother said. "You got him started on purpose, because you know I'm sick." She came and stood by me. "Hush." she said. "Right this minute. Did you give him this cake."

"I bought it." Dilsey said. "It never come out of Jason's pantry. I fixed him some birthday."

"Do you want to poison him with that cheap store cake." Mother said. "Is that what you are trying to do. Am I never to have one minute's peace."

"You go on back up stairs and lay down." Dilsey said. "It'll quit smarting him in a minute now, and he'll hush. Come on, now."

"And I leave him down here for you all to do something else to." Mother said. "How can I lie there, with him bawling down here. Benjamin. Hush this minute."

"They aint nowhere else to take him." Dilsey said. "We aint got the room we use to have. He cant stay out in the yard, crying where all the neighbors can see him."

"I know, I know." Mother said. "It's all my fault. I'll be gone soon, and you and Jason will both get along better." She began to cry.

"You hush that, now." Dilsey said. "You'll get yourself down again. You come on back up stairs. Luster going to take him to the liberry[70] and play with him till I get his supper done."

Dilsey and Mother went out.

"Hush up." Luster said. "You hush up. You want me to burn your other hand for you. You aint hurt. Hush up."

"Here." Dilsey said. "Stop crying, now." She gave me the slipper, and I hushed. "Take him to the liberry." she said. "And if I hear him again, I going to whip you myself."

We went to the library. Luster turned on the light. The windows went black, and the dark tall place on the wall came and I went and touched it. It was like a door, only it wasn't a door.[71]

The fire came behind me and I went to the fire and sat on the floor, holding the slipper. The fire went higher. It went onto the cushion in Mother's chair.

"Hush up." Luster said. "Cant you never get done for a while. Here I done built you a fire, and you wont even look at it."

Your name is Benjy, Caddy said. Do you hear. Benjy. Benjy.

Dont tell him that, Mother said. Bring him here.

Caddy lifted me under the arms.

Get up, Mau— I mean Benjy, she said.

Dont try to carry him, Mother said. Cant you lead him over here. Is that too much for you to think of.

---

70) library.

71) 이 문단은 해질녘 서재에 들어가 러스터가 불을 켜자 벤지의 눈에는 창문들이 어둡게 명암 처리되고 있다. 그리고 벤지가 다가가서 만지고 있는 벽의 어두운 부분은 원래 거울이 있었던 자리로, 그 거울을 통해 벤지는 집안이나 형제들 간에 일어났던 일들을 보곤 했다. 곧 이어 연상되는, 캐디가 벤지를 위해 만들어준 종이인형들을 가위로 난도질해놓자 벌어지는, 캐디와 제이슨간의 싸움도 이 거울을 통해 그려진다. 또한 여기 빛바랜 벽지 위에 남겨진 거울 흔적을 벤지가 "문"으로 비유하고 있는 점도 매우 상징적이다.

I can carry him, Caddy said. "Let me carry him up, Dilsey."

"Go on, minute." Dilsey said. "You aint big enough to tote a flea. You go on and be quiet, like Mr Jason said."

There was a light at the top of the stairs. Father was there, in his shirt sleeves. The way he looked said Hush. Caddy whispered,

"Is Mother sick."

Versh set me down and we went into Mother's room. There was a fire. It was rising and falling on the walls. There was another fire in the mirror. I could smell the sickness. It was on a cloth folded on Mother's head. Her hair was on the pillow. The fire didn't reach it, but it shone on her hand, where her rings were jumping.

"Come and tell Mother goodnight." Caddy said. We went to the bed. The fire went out of the mirror. Father got up from the bed and lifted me up and Mother put her hand on my head.

"What time is it." Mother said. Her eyes were closed.

"Ten minutes to seven." Father said.

"It's too early for him to go to bed." Mother said. "He'll wake up at daybreak, and I simply cannot bear another day like today."

"There, there." Father said. he touched Mother's face.

"I know I'm nothing but a burden to you." Mother said. "But I'll be gone soon. Then you will be rid of my bothering."

"Hush." Father said. "I'll take him downstairs a while." He took me up. "Come on, old fellow. Let's go down stairs a while. We'll have to be quiet while Quentin is studying, now."

Caddy went and leaned her face over the bed and Mother's hand came into the firelight. Her rings jumped on Caddy's back.

Mother's sick, Father said. Dilsey will put you to bed. Where's Quentin.

Versh getting him, Dilsey said.

Father stood and watched us go fast. We could hear Mother in her room. Caddy said "Hush." Jason was still climbing the stairs. He had his hands in his pockets.

"You all must be good tonight." Father said. "And be quiet, so you wont disturb Mother."

"We'll be quiet." Caddy said. "You must be quiet now, Jason." she said. We tiptoed.

We could hear the roof. I could see the fire in the mirror too. Caddy lifted me again.

"Come on, now." she said. "Then you can come back to the fire. Hush, now."

"Candace." Mother said.

"Hush, Benjy." Caddy said. "Mother wants you a minute. Like a good boy. Then you can come back. Benjy."

Caddy let me down, and I hushed.

"Let him stay here, Mother. When he's through looking at the fire, then you can tell him."

"Candace." Mother said. Caddy stooped and lifted me. We staggered. "Candace." Mother said.

"Hush." Caddy said. "You can still see it. Hush."

"Bring him here." Mother said. "He's too big for you to carry. You must stop trying. You'll injure your back. All of our women have pride themselves on their carriage. Do you want to look like a washerwoman."

"He's not too heavy." Caddy said. "I can carry him."

"Well, I dont want him carried, then." Mother said. "A five year old child. No, no. Not in my lap. Let him stand up."

"If you'll hold him, he'll stop." Caddy said. "Hush." she said. "You can go right back. Here. Here's your cushion. See." [72]

"Dont, Candace." Mother said.

---

72) 캐디는 벤지가 좋아하는 불(벽난로)가로부터 데리고 나와, (벤지를 안으려 하지도 않는) 어머니에게 데려가자 울음을 터뜨리는 그를 향해 난롯가에 다시 곧 데려다 주겠다고 약속한다. 앞서 언급되고 있는 슬리퍼와 함께 여기 쿠션은 캐디가 남기고 간, 벤지에게 그녀를 상기시키는 중요한 페티시(fetish), 즉 그녀의 부재 상태에서 누이에 대한 벤지의 그리움과 욕망을 일시적이나마 대리 충족시켜주는 물건이 되고 있다.

"Let him look at it and he'll be quiet." Caddy said. "Hold up just a minute while I slip it out. There, Benjy. Look."

I looked at it and hushed.

"You humor him too much." Mother said. "You and your father both. You dont realise that I am the one who has to pay for it. Damuddy spoiled Jason that way and it took him two years to outgrow it, and I am not strong enough to go through the same thing with Benjamin."

"You dont need to bother with him." Caddy said. "I like to take care of him. Dont I. Benjy."

"Candace." Mother said. "I told you not to call him that. It was bad enough when your father insisted on calling you by that silly nickname, and I will not have him called by one. Nicknames are vulgar. Only common people use them. Benjamin." she said.

"Look at me." Mother said.

"Benjamin." she said. She took my face in her hands and turned it to hers.

"Benjamin." she said. "Take that cushion away, Candace."

"He'll cry." Caddy said.

"Take that cushion away, like I told you." Mother said. "He must learn to mind."[73]

The cushion went away.

"Hush, Benjy." Caddy said.

"You go over there and sit down." Mother said. "Benjamin." She held my face to hers.

"Stop that." she said. "Stop it."

But I didn't stop and Mother caught me in her arms and I began to cry, and I cried. Then the cushion came back and Caddy held it above Mother's head.[74] She drew Mother back in the chair and

---

73) 어머니는 지체아인 벤지가 스스로를 통제할 수 있도록 엄하게 훈련을 받아야 한다고 생각한다.

Mother lay crying against the red and yellow cushion.

"Hush, Mother." Caddy said. "You go up stairs and lay down, so you can be sick. I'll go get Dilsey." She led me to the fire and I looked at the bright, smooth shapes. I could hear the fire and the roof.

Father took me up. He smelled like rain.

"Well, Benjy." he said. "Have you been a good boy today."

Caddy and Jason were fighting in the mirror.

"You, Caddy." Father said.

They fought. Jason began to cry.

"Caddy." Father said. Jason was crying. He wasn't fighting anymore, but we could see Caddy fighting in the mirror and Father put me down and went into the mirror and fought too. He lifted Caddy up. She fought. Jason lay on the floor, crying. He had scissors in his hand. Father held Caddy.

"He cut up all Benjy's dolls." Caddy said. "I'll slit his gizzle."[75)]

"Candace." Father said.

"I will." Caddy said. "I will." She fought. Father held her. She kicked at Jason. He rolled into the corner, out of the mirror. Father brought Caddy to the fire. They were all out of the mirror. Only the fire was in it. Like the fire was in a door.

"Stop that." Father said. "Do you want to make Mother sick in her room."

Caddy stopped. "He cut up all the dolls Mau—Benjy and I made."

Caddy said. "He did it just for meanness."

"I didn't." Jason said. He was sitting up, crying. "I didn't know

---

74) 어머니가 마지못해 눈물을 보이며 벤지를 무릎에 앉히고 있는데, 사실 캐디는 그 순간 어머니가 보이지 않게 머리 위로 벤지가 좋아하는 (금지된) 쿠션을 들어올려 그의 눈에만 보이게 함으로써, 어머니의 무릎 위에서 벤지가 얌전히 울음 그치고 앉아 있게 만든다.

75) gizzard.

they were his. I just thought they were some old papers."

"You couldn't help but know." Caddy said. "You did it just "

"Hush." Father said. "Jason." he said.

"I'll make you some more tomorrow." Caddy said. "We'll make a lot of them. Here, you can look at the cushion, too."

Jason came in.

I kept telling you to hush, Luster said.

What's the matter now, Jason said.

"He just trying hisself." Luster said. "That the way he been going on all day."

"Why dont you let him alone, then." Jason said. "If you cant keep him quiet, you'll have to take him out to the kitchen. The rest of us cant shut ourselves up in a room like Mother does."

"Mammy say keep him out the kitchen till she get supper." Luster said.

"Then play with him and keep him quiet." Jason said. "Do I have to work all day and then come home to a mad house." He opened the paper and read it.

You can look at the fire and the mirror and the cushion too, Caddy said. You wont have to wait until supper to look at the cushion, now. We could hear the roof. We could hear Jason too, crying loud beyond the wall.

Dilsey said, "You come, Jason. You letting him alone, is you."

"Yessum." Luster said.

"Where Quentin." Dilsey said. "Supper near bout ready."

"I dont know'm." Luster said. "I aint seen her."

Dilsey went away. "Quentin." she said in the hall. "Quentin. Supper ready."

We could hear the roof. Quentin smelled like rain, too.

What did Jason do, he said.

He cut up all Benjy's dolls, Caddy said.

Mother said to not call him Benjy, Quentin said. He sat on the rug by us. I wish it wouldn't rain, he said. You cant do anything.

You've been in a fight, Caddy said. Haven't you.

It wasn't much, Quentin said.

You can tell it, Caddy said. Father'll see it.

I dont care, Quentin said. I wish it wouldn't rain.

Quentin said, "Didn't Dilsey say supper was ready."

"Yessum." Luster said. Jason looked at Quentin. Then he read the paper again. Quentin came in. "She say it bout ready." Luster said. Quentin jumped down in Mother's chair. Luster said.

"Mr Jason."

"What." Jason said.

"Let me have two bits." Luster said.

"What for." Jason said.

"To go to the show tonight." Luster said.

"I thought Dilsey was going to get a quarter from Frony for you."

Jason said.

"She did." Luster said. "I lost it. Me and Benjy hunted all day for that quarter. You can ask him."

"Then borrow one from him." Jason said. "I have to work for mine." He read the paper. Quentin looked at the fire. the fire was in her eyes and on her mouth. Her mouth was red.

"I tried to keep him away from there." Luster said.

"Shut your mouth." Quentin said. Jason looked at her.

"What did I tell you I was going to do if I saw you with that show fellow again." he said. Quentin looked at the fire. "Did you hear me." Jason said.

"I heard you." Quentin said. "Why dont you do it, then."

"Dont you worry." Jason said.

"I'm not." Quentin said. Jason read the paper again.

I could hear the roof. Father leaned forward and looked at Quentin.

Hello, he said. Who won.

"Nobody." Quentin said. "They stopped us. Teachers."[76)]

"Who was it." Father said. "Will you tell."

"It was all right." Quentin said. "He was as big as me."

"That's good." Father said. "Can you tell what it was about."

"It wasn't anything." Quentin said. "He said he would put a frog in her desk[77] and she wouldn't dare to whip him."

"Oh." Father said. "She. And then what."

"Yes, sir." Quentin said. "And then I kind of hit him."

We could hear the roof and the fire, and a snuffling outside the door.

"Where was he going to get a frog in November." Father said.

"I dont know, sir." Quentin said.

We could hear them.

"Jason." Father said. We could hear Jason.

"Jason." Father said. "Come in here and stop that."

We could hear the roof and the fire and Jason.

"Stop that, now." Father said. "Do you want me to whip you again." Father lifted Jason up into the chair by him. Jason snuffled. We could hear the fire and the roof. Jason snuffled a little louder.

"One more time." Father said. We could hear the fire and the roof.

Dilsey said, All right. You all can come on to supper.

Versh smelled like rain. He smelled like a dog, too. We could hear the fire and the roof.

We could hear Caddy walking fast.[78] Father and Mother looked at the door. Caddy passed it, walking fast. She didn't look. She walked fast.

---

76) 퀸턴이 학교에서 캐디 문제로 싸우자 선생님들이 그 싸움을 중단시켰음을 알 수 있다.

77) 퀸턴은 학교에서 싸운 이유의 진실, 즉 캐디의 "명예"를 수호하기 위한 것이었다고 사실대로 말할 수 없어, 아버지께 거짓말을 하고 있다. 뒤에서 "11월에 어디서 개구리를 구했을까"라는 캄슨씨의 의문에서도 드러나듯, 그는 퀸턴이 거짓말하고 있다는 것을 금방 알아차린다.

78) 캐디가 처녀성을 상실하고 돌아온 날 밤, 집안에 들어서면서 기다리고 있는 가족들을 대면하지 않기 위해 빠르게 발걸음을 옮기는 모습이다.

"Candace." Mother said. Caddy stopped walking.

"Yes, Mother." she said.

"Hush, Caroline." Father said.

"Come here." Mother said.

"Hush, Caroline." Father said. "Let her alone."

Caddy came to the door and stood there, looking at Father and Mother. Her eyes flew at me, and away. I began to cry. It went loud and I got up. Caddy came in and stood with her back to the wall, looking at me. I went toward her, crying, and she shrank against the wall and I saw her eyes and I cried louder and pulled at her dress. She put her hands out but I pulled at her dress.[79)] Her eyes ran.

Versh said, Your name Benjamin now. You know how come your name Benjamin now. They making a bluegum[80)] *out of you. Mammy say in old time your granpaw changed nigger's name, and he turn preacher, and when they look at him, he bluegum too. Didn't use to be bluegum, neither. And when family woman look him in the eye in the full of the moon, chile born bluegum. And one evening, when they was about a dozen them bluegum chillen running around the place, he never come home. Possum hunters found him in the woods, et clean. And you know who et him. Them bluegum chillen did.*

We were in the hall. Caddy was still looking at me. Her hand was against her mouth and I saw her eyes and I cried. We went up the stairs. She stopped again, against the wall, looking at me and I cried

---

79) 이 순간 캐디나 벤지가 느끼고 있는 감정(벤지의 분노, 캐디의 치욕감)을 명확히 확인할 수 없지만, 둘 다 이미 울고 있다는 것을 알 수 있으며, 캐디는 동생의 눈을 똑바로 볼 수 없다. 반면 벤지의 행동, 누이의 드레스를 잡아당기는 행위는 다분히 성적으로 생각해 볼 수 있으며, 그가 그 행동을 반복하고 캐디는 그것을 계속 저지하고 있는 것도 알 수 있다.

80) "블루검"의 의미는 분홍색을 띠기보다는 푸른빛이 도는 잇몸을 가진 흑인을 칭하는 말이다. 민담에 의하면, 블루검은 독을 가지고 "살인적으로 물어뜯는 성향"을 가진 흑인 마술사(conjuror)를 말한다.

and she went on and I came on, crying, and she shrank against the wall, looking at me. She opened the door to her room, but I pulled at her dress and we went to the bathroom and she stood against the door, looking at me. Then she put her arm across her face and I pushed at her, crying.

What are you doing to him, Jason said. Why cant you let him alone.

I aint touching him, Luster said. He been doing this way all day long. He needs whipping.

He needs to be sent to Jackson, Quentin said. How can anybody live in a house like this.

If you dont like it, young lady, you'd better get out, Jason said.

I'm going to, Quentin said. Dont you worry.[81)]

Versh said, "You move back some, so I can dry my legs off." He shoved me back a little. "Dont you start bellering, now. You can still see it. That's all you have to do. You aint had to be out in the rain like I is. You's born lucky and dont know it." He lay on his back before the fire.

"You know how come your name Benjamin now." Versh said. "Your mamma too proud for you. What mammy say."

"You be still there and let me dry my legs off." Versh said. "Or you know what I'll do. I'll skin your rinktum."[82)]

We could here the fire and the roof and Versh.

Versh got up quick and jerked his legs back. Father said, "All right, Versh."

"I'll feed him tonight." Caddy said. "Sometimes he cries when Versh feeds him."

"Take this tray up." Dilsey said. "And hurry back and feed Benjy."

"Dont you want Caddy to feed you." Caddy said.

---

81) 미스 퀸턴이 그날 밤 집에서 도망칠 것을 암시하는 부분이다.

82) rectum.

Has he got to keep that old dirty slipper on the table, Quentin said. Why dont you feed him in the kitchen. It's like eating with a pig.

If you dont like the way we eat, you'd better not come to the table, Jason said.

Steam came off of Roskus. He was sitting in front of the stove. The oven door was open and Roskus had his feet in it. Steam came off the bowl. Caddy put the spoon into my mouth easy. There was a black spot on the inside of the bowl.

Now, now, Dilsey said. He aint going to bother you no more.

It got down below the mark.[83)] Then the bowl was empty. It went away. "He's hungry tonight." Caddy said. The bowl came back. I couldn't see the spot. Then I could. "He's starved, tonight." Caddy said. "Look how much he's eaten."

Yes he will, Quentin said. You all send him out to spy on me. I hate this house. I'm going to run away.

Roskus said, "It going to rain all night."

You've been running a long time,[84)] *not to've got any further off than mealtime, Jason said.*

See if I dont, Quentin said.

"Then I dont know what I going to do." Dilsey said. "It caught me in the hip so bad now I cant scarcely move.[85)] Climbing them stairs all evening."

Oh, I wouldn't be surprised, Jason said. I wouldn't be surprised at anything you'd do.

---

83) 캐디가 벤지에게 밥을 먹이는 장면에서 그릇 안에 그려져 있는 (아마도 줄무늬) 표식 아래로 먹고 있는 음식이 줄어들고 있음을 말한다.

84) 앞서 여러 번 미스 퀀틴이 이 집에서 달아나 버릴 것이라고 삼촌에게 위협적으로 말해 왔기에, 그것에 이미 면역이 되어버린 제이슨은 그 말을 믿지 않으면서 조롱하듯 그녀의 말을 되받아치고 있다.

85) 비오는 날씨("it")가 특히 딜시의 엉치 부분을 악화시키고 있는 관절염(류머티즘)의 고통을 말한다.

Quentin threw her napkin on the table.

Hush your mouth, Jason, Dilsey said. She went and put her arm around Quentin. Sit down, honey, Dilsey said. He ought to be shamed of hisself, throwing what aint your fault up to you.[86)]

"She sulling again, is she." Roskus said.

"Hush your mouth." Dilsey said.

Quentin pushed Dilsey away. She looked at Jason. Her mouth was red. She picked up her glass of water and swung her arm back, looking at Jason. Dilsey caught her arm. They fought. The glass broke on the table, and the water ran into the table. Quentin was running.

"Mother's sick again." Caddy said.

"Sho she is." Dilsey said. "Weather like this make anybody sick. When you going to get done eating, boy."

Goddam you, Quentin said. Goddam you. We could hear her running on the stairs. We went to the library.

Caddy gave me the cushion, and I could look at the cushion and the mirror and the fire.

"We must be quiet while Quentin's studying." Father said. "What are you doing, Jason."

"Nothing." Jason said.

"Suppose you come over here to do it, then." Father said.

Jason came out of the corner.

"What are you chewing." Father said.

"Nothing." Jason said.

"He's chewing paper again." Caddy said.

"Come here, Jason." Father said.

Jason threw into the fire. It hissed, uncurled, turning black. Then it was gray. Then it was gone. Caddy and Father and Jason were in

---

86) 딜시는 제이슨이 캐디에 대한 분노를 딸 미스 퀸턴에게 화풀이하고 있다고 믿고 있다. 다음 줄, sulling = sullen or sulking.

Mother's chair. Jason's eyes were puffed shut and his mouth moved, like tasting. Caddy's head was on Father's shoulder. Her hair was like fire, and little points of fire were in her eyes, and I went and Father lifted me into the chair too, and Caddy held me. She smelled like trees.

She smelled like trees. In the corner it was dark, but I could see the window. I squatted there, holding the slipper. I couldn't see it, but my hands saw it, and I could hear it getting night, and my hands saw the slipper but I couldn't see myself, but my hands could see the slipper, and I squatted there, hearing it getting dark.[87)]

Here you is, Luster said. Look what I got. He showed it to me. You know where I got it. Miss Quentin give it to me. I knowed they couldn't keep me out. What you doing, off in here. I thought you done slipped back out doors. Aint you done enough moaning and slobbering today, without hiding off in this here empty room, mumbling and taking on. Come on here to bed, so I can get up there before it starts. I cant fool with you all night tonight. Just let them horns toot the first toot and I done gone.

We didn't go to our room.

"This is where we have the measles." Caddy said. "Why do we have to sleep in here tonight."

"What you care where you sleep." Dilsey said. she shut the door and sat down and began to undress me. Jason began to cry. "Hush." Dilsey said.

---

87) 이 문단은 현시점, 1928년 4월 7일의 하루가 저물면서, 벤지는 서재에 혼자 나와 어두운 방에서 창문 너머로 떨어지는 저녁햇살, 아직 완전히 다 어두워지지 않은 창문가를 보며 앉아 있다. 집안의 이 서재는 앞서 몇 페이지에서 계속되고 있듯이, 어린 시절 캐디와 관련된 가족들의 많은 기억들이 남아 있는 곳이다. 그리고 어둠 속에서 그는 캐디가 남기고 간 슬리퍼 한 짝을 눈으로는 볼 수 없지만 손으로는 볼 수 있다고 말하면서, 벤지는 자신의 거세된 아랫도리("I couldn' t see myself")와 거세된 자신의 성기와 모양이 비슷한 슬리퍼를 연결짓고 있다.

"I want to sleep with Damuddy." Jason said.

"She's sick." Caddy said. "You can sleep with her when she gets well. Cant he, Dilsey."

"Hush, now." Dilsey said. Jason hushed.

"Our nighties are here, and everything." Caddy said. "It's like moving."

"And you better get into them." Dilsey said. "You be unbuttoning Jason."

Caddy unbuttoned Jason. He began to cry.

"You want to get whipped." Dilsey said. Jason hushed.

Quentin, Mother said in the hall.

What, Quentin said beyond the wall. We heard Mother lock the door. She looked in our door and came in and stooped over the bed and kissed me on the forehead.

When you get him to bed, go and ask Dilsey if she objects to my having a hot water bottle, Mother said. Tell her that if she does, I'll try to get along without it. Tell her I just want to know.

Yessum, Luster said. Come on. Get your pants off.

Quentin and Versh came in. Quentin had his face turned away. "What are you crying for." [88] Caddy said.

"Hush." Dilsey said. "You all get undressed, now. You can go on home, Versh."

I got undressed and I looked at myself, and I began to cry.[89] *Hush, Luster said. Looking for them aint going to do no good. They're gone. You keep on like this, and we aint going have you no more birthday. He put my gown on. I hushed, and then Luster stopped, his head toward the window. Then he went to the window and looked out. He came back and took my arm. Here she come, he said. Be*

---

88) 아마도 할머니가 돌아가신 사실을 알았거나 아니면 할머니가 많이 아프시거나, 이유는 분명치 않지만 퀸턴이 울고 있다.

89) 옷을 갈아입으면서 자신의 없어진 아랫부분을 보며 벤지는 울고 있다.

quiet, now. We went to the window and looked out. It came out of Quentin's window and climbed across into the tree. We watched the tree shaking. The shaking went down the tree, then it came out and we watched it go away across the grass. Then we couldn't see it.[90)]*Come on, Luster said. There now. Hear them horns. You get in that bed while my foots behaves.*

There were two beds.[91)] Quentin got in the other one. He turned his face to the wall. Dilsey put Jason in with him. Caddy took her dress off.

"Just look at your drawers." Dilsey said. "You better be glad your maw aint seen you."

"I already told on her." Jason said.

"I bound you would." Dilsey said.

"And see what you got by it." Caddy said. "tattletale."

"What did I get by it." Jason said.

"Whyn't you get your nightie on." Dilsey said. She went and helped Caddy take off her bodice and drawers. "Just look at you." Dilsey said. She wadded the drawers and scrubbed Caddy behind with them. "It done soaked clean through onto you." she said. "But you wont get no bath this night. Here." She put Caddy's nightie on her and Caddy climbed into the bed and Dilsey went to the door and stood with her hand on the light. "You all be quiet now, you hear." She said.

"All right." Caddy said. "Mother's not coming in tonight." She

---

90) 이 문단에서 벤지에게 옷을 다 입힌 후 이어지는 장면은, 벤지와 러스터가 그날 밤 미스 퀸턴이 이층 그녀의 방에서 창문을 통해 나와 나무를 타고 내려와서는 기다리던 차를 타고 도망치는 것을 목격하는 부분이다. 어둠 속에서 그녀를 알아볼 수 없는 벤지의 눈은 그녀를 "it"으로 묘사한다.

91) 벤지 장의 마지막을 장식하는 기억은 어린 시절 캐디와 함께 같은 침대에서 자던 시점으로 돌아가고 있다. 물론 제이슨은 할머니 곁에서 자곤 했지만, 다른 침대는 퀸턴과 제이슨이 사용하였다.

said. "So we still have to mind me."

"Yes." Dilsey said. "Go to sleep, now."

"Mother's sick." Caddy said. "She and Damuddy are both sick."

"Hush." Dilsey said. "You go to sleep."

The room went black, except the door. Then the door went black.[92] Caddy said, "Hush, Maury" putting her hand on me. So I stayed hushed. We could hear us. We could hear the dark.[93]

It went away, and Father looked at us. He looked at Quentin and Jason, then he came and kissed Caddy and put his hand on my head.

"Is Mother very sick." Caddy said.

"No." Father said. "Are you going to take good care of Maury."

"Yes." Caddy said.

Father went to the door and looked at us again. Then the dark came back, and he stood black in the door, and then the door turned black again. Caddy held me and I could hear us all, and the darkness, and something I could smell. And then I could see the windows, where the trees were buzzing. Then the dark began to go in smooth, bright shapes, like it always does, even when Caddy says that I have been asleep.

92) 딜시가 방안의 불을 끄자 복도의 불 때문에 방문 쪽은 불빛이 들어오고 있는 상태이며, 딜시가 방을 나가 복도의 불을 끄자 방문도 깜깜해지고 있다.

93) 아마 어둠 속에서 형제들의 숨결소리를 벤지는 이렇게 표현하고 있는지 모른다.

June Second, 1910

When the shadow of the sash appeared on the curtains it was between seven and eight oclock and then I was in time again, hearing the watch. It was Grandfather's and when Father gave it to me he said I give you the mausoleum of all hope and desire; it's rather excruciating-ly[1] apt that you will use it to gain the reducto absurdum[2] of all human experience which can fit your individual needs no better than it fitted his or his father's. I give it to you not that you may remember time, but that you might forget it now and then for a moment and not spend all your breath trying to conquer it. Because no battle is ever won he said. They are not even fought. The field only reveals to man his own folly and despair, and victory is an illusion of philosophers and fools.[3]

It was propped against the collar box and I lay listening to it. Hearing it, that is. I dont suppose anybody ever deliberately listens to a watch or a clock. You dont have to. You can be oblivious to the sound for a long while, then in a second of ticking it can create in the mind unbroken the long diminishing parade of time you didn't hear. Like Father said down the long and lonely light-rays you might see Jesus walking, like. And the good Saint Francis that said Little Sister

---

1) 여기 작가의 특이한 하이픈 사용은 특별히 "ly"의 발음을 강조하기 위해서이다.

2) 정확한 라틴어 표현은 "reductio ad absurdum"(reduced to absurdity)이다.

3) 이 첫 문단은 그의 장에서 퀸턴이 가장 집착하고 있는 이슈 중 하나인, 시간/과거에 대한 철학적이면서도 통렬한 성찰이 아버지와 오갔던 대화를 통해 기억되고 있다.

Death, that never had a sister.[4)]

Through the wall I heard Shreve's[5)] bed-springs and then his slippers on the floor hishing. I got up and went to the dresser and slid my hand along it and touched the watch and turned it face-down and went back to bed. But the shadow of the sash was still there and I had learned to tell almost to the minute, so I'd have to turn my back to it, feeling the eyes animals used to have in the back of their heads when it was on top, itching. It's always the idle habits you acquire which you will regret. Father said that. That Christ was not crucified: he was worn away by a minute clicking of little wheels. That had no sister.[6)]

And so as soon as I knew I couldn't see it, I began to wonder what time it was. Father said that constant speculation regarding the position of mechanical hands on an arbitrary dial which is a symptom of mind-function. Excrement Father said like sweating.[7)]

---

4) 퀸턴 장의 2번째 문단은 퀸턴이 집착하고 있는, 그의 실존의 또 다른 비극적 딜레마인 "누이"라는 말이 등장한다. "Little Sister Death"는 성서(Armstrong 239)에서 유래한 말로, 속세의 고통을 누이("sisters")에 비유하였던 성 프란시스(of Assisi)가 자신의 죽음을 맞으면서 그 죽음을 기꺼이 받아들이는 제스처로 "Then be welcome Sister Death!"라고 말한 데서 기인한다. 하지만 작품에서 이 말은 여성(캐디)의 성과 남성(퀸턴)의 죽음과의 연관성을 암시하고 있다.

5) 쉬리브는 퀸턴의 캐나다 출신 룸메이트이다.

6) 퀸턴 장에서 퀸턴이 아버지 캄슨씨의 말을 인용할 때마다, 그가 아버지의 염세주의적 인생철학에 동조하면서 말하고 있는 것인지, 아니면 단순히 아버지의 말을 반복하고 있는 것인지는 확실하지 않다. 여기 아버지는 그리스도의 죽음조차도 시간의 흐름 속에서 보통 사람의 죽음과 다를 바 없다고 말한다. 마지막 문장은 앞서 성 프란시스와 관련하여 그가 여동생이 없다는 얘기를 반복하는 말일 수도 있고, 아니면 그리스도도 여동생이 없다는 말일 수도 있으며, 그리고 아버지 역시 (포크너처럼) 여동생이 없다는 의미로 읽어낼 수 있다. 무엇보다 이 말은 (캐디처럼 '치명적인') 누이를 가져보지 않은 자는 퀸턴 자신이 지금 당하고 있는 (결국 그를 죽음에 이르게 하는) 고통의 깊이를 결코 이해할 수 없음을 암시한다.

And I saying All right. Wonder. Go on and wonder.

If it had been cloudy I could have looked at the window, thinking what he said about idle habits. Thinking it would be nice for them down at New London[8)] if the weather held up like this. Why shouldn't it? The month of brides, the voice that breathed[9)] *She ran right out of the mirror, out of the banked scent.*[10)] *Roses. Roses. Mr and Mrs Jason Richmond Compson announce the marriage of. Roses.* Not virgins like dogwood, milkweed.[11)] I said I have committed incest, Father I said.[12)] Roses. Cunning and serene. If you attend Harvard one year, but dont see the boat-race, there should be a refund. Let Jason have it. Give Jason a year at Harvard.

Shreve stood in the door, putting his collar on, his glasses glinting rosily, as though he had washed them with his face. "You taking a cut this morning?"

---

7) 아버지는 인간의 감정이라는 것은 배설물이나 땀 같은 몸의 기능과도 같은 것이라 말하며, 과거와 캐디를 두고 고통하는 퀀턴을 향해 시간이 지나면 모든 것이 해결될 것이라는 말을 계속하고 있다.

8) 미국 코네티컷주에 소재한 도시로, 하버드 대학과 예일 대학 간에 보트경주가 열리던 장소이다.

9) "그 목소리"는 벤지가 내는 소리를 말한다.

10) 1910년 4월 25일 캐디의 결혼식 날, 거울 속에서 보이던 그녀의 모습이 사라지면서, 그녀는 웨딩드레스를 입은 채 벤지를 위로하기 위해 식장 밖으로 뛰어나가고 있다.

11) 전통적으로 장미는 열정적이고 성적인 사랑을 의미하거나 혹자는 여성의 성기를 상징하는 꽃으로 알려져 있으며, 반면 dogwood(산딸나무류)나 milkweed(흰 유액을 분비하는 풀)의 하얀 색은 순결/처녀성을 상징한다.

12) 1909년 여름, 퀀턴이 아버지와 나누는 대화에서 계속 반복하는 문장이다. 하지만 작품에서 퀀턴이 캐디와 근친상간을 범했다고 아버지께 실제로 고백하고 있는지, 아니면 그 고백을 상상하고만 있는지는 분명치 않다. 작가는 둘 간의 근친상간은 결코 일어나지 않았으며, 퀀턴이 아버지께 그 말을 할 수 있기를 단지 바랄 뿐이라고 쓰고 있다(*Faulkner in the University*. Eds. F. Gwynn and J. Blotner. Charlottesville: UP of Virginia, 1959. p.262).

"Is it that late?"

He looked at his watch. "Bell in two minutes."

"I didn't know it was that late." He was still looking at the watch, his mouth shaping. "I'll have to hustle. I cant stand another cut. The dean told me last week—" He put the watch back into his pocket. Then I quit talking.

"You'd better slip on your pants and run," he said. He went out.

I got up and moved about, listening to him through the wall. He entered the sitting-room, toward the door.

"Aren't you ready yet?"

"Not yet. Run along. I'll make it."

He went out. The door closed. His feet went down the corridor. Then I could hear the watch again. I quit moving around and went to the window and drew the curtains aside and watched them running for chapel, the same ones fighting the same heaving coat-sleeves, the same books and flapping collars flushing past like debris on a flood, and Spoade. Calling Shreve my husband.[13] Ah let him alone, Shreve said, if he's got better sense than to chase after the little dirty sluts, whose business. In the South you are ashamed of being a virgin. Boys. Men. They lie about it. Because it means less to women, Father said. He said it was men invented virginity not women. Father said it's like death: only a state in which the others are left and I said, But to believe it doesn't matter and he said, That's what's so sad about anything: not only virginity and I said, Why couldn't it have been me and not her who is unvirgin and he said, That's why that's sad too; nothing is even worth the changing of it,[14] and Shreve said

---

13) 하버드 대학 친구인 스포드가 퀸턴이 여자들에겐 관심이 없는 면과 룸메이트인 쉬리브와의 가까운 사이를 꼬집어서 하는 말이다.

14) "Because"로 시작하는 부분에서 여기까지는, 여성의 성 도덕에 대한 캄슨씨의 냉소주의를 반영한다. 물론 퀸턴은 아버지의 이러한 말을 납득할 수 없으며, 그에게 (캐디의/여성의) 처녀성이 중요함은 말할 여지도 없다. 하지만 아버지는 퀸턴이 처

if he's got better sense than to chase after the little dirty sluts and I said Did you ever have a sister? Did you? Did you?

Spoade was in the middle of them like a terrapin in a street full of scuttering dead leaves, his collar about his ears, moving at his customary unhurried walk. He was from South Carolina, a senior. It was his club's boast that he never ran for chapel and had never got there on time and had never been absent in four years and had never made either chapel or first lecture with a shirt on his back and socks on his feet. About ten oclock he'd come in Thompson's,[15] get two cups of coffee, sit down and take his socks out of his pocket and remove his shoes and put them on while the coffee cooled. About noon you'd see him with a shirt and collar on, like anybody else. The others passed him running, but he never increased his pace at all. After a while the quad was empty.

A sparrow slanted across the sunlight, onto the window ledge, and cocked his head at me. His eye was round and bright. First he'd watch me with one eye, then flick! and it would be the other one, his throat pumping faster than any pulse. The hour began to strike. The sparrow quit swapping eyes and watched me steadily with the same one until the chimes ceased, as if he were listening too. Them he flicked off the ledge and was gone.

It was a while before the last stroke ceased vibrating. It stayed in the air, more felt than heard, for a long time. Like all the bells that ever rang still ringing in the long dying light-rays and Jesus and Saint Francis talking about his sister. Because if it were just to hell; if

---

녀성을 (죽음처럼) 단순히 하나의 상황 내지는 상태("state")로 인지하기를 원하며, 여성의 처녀성을 죽음에 비유하는 아버지의 발언은 퀸턴에게 더 큰 절망감만 안겨 줄 뿐이다.

15) "탐슨즈"는 보스톤의 워싱턴가에 있는 유명한 레스토랑이다. 주목할 점은 퀸턴이 시간으로부터 도망치려는 갖은 노력에도 불구하고, 오히려 그가 얼마나 시간에 집착하고 있는지를 여러 각도에서 보여주는 부분이다.

that were all of it. Finished. If things just finished themselves. Nobody else there but her and me. If we could just have done something so dreadful that they would have fled hell except us. *I have committed incest I said Father it was I it was not Dalton Ames*

And when he put Dalton Ames. Dalton Ames. Dalton Ames. When he put the pistol in my hand I didn't. That's why I didn't.[16] He would be there and she would and I would. Dalton Ames. Dalton Ames. Dalton Ames. If we could have just done something so dreadful and Father said That's sad too people cannot do anything that dreadful they cannot do anything very dreadful at all they cannot even remember tomorrow what seemed dreadful today and I said, You can shirk all things and he said, Ah can you. And I will look down and see my murmuring bones and the deep water like wind, like a roof of wind, and after a long time they cannot distinguish even bones upon the lonely and inviolate sand. Until on the Day when He says Rise only the flat-iron would come floating up.[17] It's not when you realise that nothing can help you—religion, pride, anything—it's when you realise that you dont need any aid. Dalton Ames. Dalton Amnes. Dalton Ames. If I could have been his mother lying with open body lifted laughing, holding his father with my hand refraining, seeing, watching him die before he lived.[18] *One*

---

16) 달턴 에임스가 처음 소개되며, 그를 두고 기억들이 교차하고 있다. 그는 1909년 여름 캐디가 사귀던 남자로 미스 퀸턴의 아버지일 확률이 가장 높다. 이 장면은 뒤에서 자세히 묘사되는데, 미리 설명하자면, 퀸턴이 달턴과의 대면에서 후자가 건넨 총으로 그를 죽일 수 없는 이유를 말하고 있다. 만약 그 순간 퀸턴이 달턴을 죽였다면 후자 또한 그들과 함께 지옥으로 떨어질 것이기에, 지옥일지라도 캐디와 둘만 있고 싶은 퀸턴의 욕망 때문에 그는 달턴을 죽이지 않았다고 말한다.

17) 퀸턴이 오늘 물에 빠져 죽을 것을 처음으로 시사하는 부분이다.

18) 이 부분은 노골적으로 성적인 이미지가 암시되고 있다. 여기 퀸턴의 환상은 자신을 여성(달턴의 어머니)으로 상상하며, 달턴이 아예 태어나지도 말았으면 하는 소망을 내포하고 있다.

minute she was standing in the door

I went to the dresser and took up the watch, with the face still down. I tapped the crystal on the corner of the dresser and caught the fragments of glass in my hand and put them into the ashtray and twisted the hands off and put them in the tray. The watch ticked on. I turned the face up, the blank dial with little wheels clicking and clicking behind it, not knowing any better. Jesus walking on Galilee and Washington not telling lies.[19] Father brought back a watch-charm from the Saint Louis Fair to Jason: a tiny opera glass into which you squinted with one eye and saw a skyscraper, a ferris wheel all spidery, Niagara Falls on a pinhead. There was a red smear on the dial. When I saw it my thumb began to smart. I put the watch down and went into Shreve's room and got the iodine and painted the cut. I cleaned the rest of the glass out of the rim with a towel.

I laid out two suits of underwear, with socks, shirts, collars and ties, and packed my trunk. I put in everything except my new suit and an old one[20] and two pairs of shoes and two hats, and my books. I carried the books into the sitting-room and stacked them on the table, the ones I had brought from home and the ones *Father said it used to be a gentlemen was known by his books; nowadays he is known by the ones he has not returned* and locked the trunk and addressed it. The quarter hour sounded. I stopped and listened to it until the chimes ceased.

I bathed and shaved. The water made my finger smart a little, so I painted it again. I put on my new suit and put my watch on and packed the other suit and the accessories and my razor and brushes in

---

19) 이제 시계의 앞면도 박살난 상황에서 퀀턴에게 현재와 과거의 모든 사건들은 시간과 관련하여 같은 차원 내에서 존재한다. 그것이 그리스도가 수면 위를 걸어 다니던 고대의 기적이든, 아니면 조지 워싱턴의 진실성에 대한 미국의 전설적 일화이든 간에.

20) 양복 두벌만 빼고 짐을 싸고 있는 퀀턴은 곧 새 양복을 입고 길을 나서지만, 나중에 그는 기숙사로 다시 돌아와 헌 양복으로 갈아입은 후 죽음을 향해 길을 나서게 될 것이다.

my hand bag, and folded the trunk key into a sheet of paper and put it in an envelope and addressed it to Father, and wrote the two notes and sealed them.[21)]

The shadow hadn't quite cleared the stoop. I stopped inside the door, watching the shadow move. It moved almost perceptibly, creeping back inside the door, driving the shadow back into the door. *Only she was running already when I heard it. In the mirror she was running before I knew what it was. That quick her train caught up over her arm she ran out of the mirror like a cloud, her veil swirling in long glints her heels brittle and fast clutching her dress onto her shoulder with the other hand, running out of the mirror the smells roses roses the voice that breathed o'er Eden. Then she was across the porch I couldn't hear her heels then in the moonlight like a cloud, the floating shadow of the veil running across the grass, into the bellowing. She ran out of her dress, clutching her bridal, running into the bellowing where T. P. in the dew Whooey Sassprilluh Benjy under the box bellowing. Father had a V-shaped silver cuirass on his running chest*

Shreve said, "Well, you didn't . . . . Is it a wedding or a wake?"

"I couldn't make it," I said.

"Not with all that primping. What's the matter? You think this was Sunday?"

"I reckon the police wont get me for wearing my new suit one time," I said.

"I was thinking about the Square students. They'll think you go to Harvard. Have you got too proud to attend classes too?"

---

21) 퀸턴은 집에 보낼 가방을 싸면서 아버지께 보낼 편지 속에 그 열쇠를 싸는데, 그것이 아버지께 보내는 자살노트인지는 여기서 확실치 않다. 반면 그는 쉬리브에게 2개의 노트(편지)를 남기고 있는데, 하나는 뒤에서 드러나듯 디콘에게 주길 원하는 자신의 옷가지들에 대한 지시사항을 적은 노트이며, 다른 하나는 아마도 쉬리브에게 남기는 퀸턴의 자살노트로 추정할 수 있다.

"I'm going to eat first." The shadow on the stoop was gone. I stepped into sunlight, finding my shadow again. I walked down the steps just ahead of it. The half hour went. Then the chimes ceased and died away.

Deacon wasn't at the postoffice either. I stamped the two envelopes and mailed the one to Father and put Shreve's in my inside pocket, and then I remembered where I had last seen the Deacon. It was on Decoration Day, in a G.A.R. uniform,[22)] in the middle of the parade. If you waited long enough on any corner you would see him in whatever parade came along. The one before was on Columbus' or Garibalde's[23)] or somebody's birthday. He was in the Street Sweepers' section,[24)] in a stovepipe hat, carrying a two inch Italian flag, smoking a cigar among the brooms and scoops. But the last time was the G.A.R. one, because Shreve said:

"There now. Just look at what your grandpa did to that poor old nigger."

"Yes," I said. "Now he can spend day after day marching in parades. If it hadn't been for my grandfather, he'd have to work like whitefolks."

I didn't see him anywhere. But I never knew even a working nigger that you could find when you wanted him, let alone one that lived off the fat of the land. A car came along. I went over to town and went to Parker's and had a good breakfast.[25)] While I was eating I heard a clock strike the hour. But then I suppose it takes at least one hour to

---

22) "D. Day"는 남북전쟁에서 죽은 병사들을 기리는 날로, 1868년 5월 30일 Memorial Day(전몰장병 추도 기념일)로 개명되었다. G. A. R.(the Grand Army of the Republic)는 남북전쟁 시 북군을 의미한다.

23) Giuseppe Garibaldi(1807-1882), 이탈리아 자유에 기여한 국가적 영웅.

24) 거리 청소부들은 기념일 행렬에서 말들의 뒤를 따르며 거리를 치운다.

25) 퀸턴은 (시내 전)차를 타고 보스톤으로 들어가, 디킨스, 호손, 에머슨 등이 머문 곳으로도 유명한 파커 호텔(Parker House)에서 아침식사를 한다.

lose time in, who has been longer than history getting into the mechanical progression of it.

When I finished breakfast I bought a cigar. The girl said a fifty cent one was the best, so I took one and lit it and went out to the street. I stood there and took a couple of puffs, then I held it in my hand and went to toward the corner. I passed a jeweller's window, but I looked away in time. At the corner two bootblacks caught me, one on either side, shrill and raucous, like blackbirds. I gave the cigar to one of them, and the other one a nickel. Then they let me alone. The one with the cigar was trying to sell it to the other for the nickel.

There was a clock, high up in the sun, and I thought about how, when you dont want to do a thing, your body will try to trick you into doing it, sort of unawares. I could feel the muscles in the back of my neck, and then I could hear my watch ticking away in my pocket and after a while I had all the other sounds shut away, leaving only the watch in my pocket. I turned back up the street, to the window. He was working at the table behind the window. He was going bald. There was a glass in his eye—a metal tube screwed into his face. I went in.

The place was full of ticking, like crickets in September grass, and I could hear a big clock on the wall above his head. He looked up, his eye big and blurred and rushing beyond the glass. I took mine out and handed it to him.

"I broke my watch."

He flipped it over in his hand. "I should say you have. You must have stepped on it."

"Yes, sir. I knocked it off the dresser and stepped on it in the dark. It's still running though."

He pried the back open and squinted into it. "Seems to be all right. I cant tell until I go over it, though. I'll go into it this afternoon."

"I'll bring it back later," I said. "Would you mind telling me if any of those watches in the window are right?"

He held my watch on his palm and looked up at me with his

blurred rushing eye.

"I made a bet with a fellow," I said. "And I forgot my glasses this morning."

"Why, all right," he said. He laid the watch down and half rose on his stool and looked over the barrier. Then he glanced up at the wall. "It's twen——."

"Dont tell me," I said, "please sir. Just tell me if any of them are right."

He looked at me again. He sat back on the stool and pushed the glass up onto his forehead. It left a red circle around his eye and when it was gone his whole face looked naked. "What're you celebrating today?" he said. "That boat race aint until next week, is it?"

"No, sir. This is just a private celebration. Birthday. Are any of them right?"

"No. But they haven't been regulated and set yet. If you're thinking of buying one of them——"

"No, sir. I dont need a watch. We have a clock in our sitting room. I'll have this one fixed when I do." I reached my hand.

"Better leave it now."

"I'll bring it back later." He gave me the watch. I put it in my pocket. I couldn't hear it now, above all the others. "I'm much obliged to you. I hope I haven't taken up your time."

"That's all right. Bring it in when you are ready. And you better put off this celebration until after we win that boat race."

"Yes, sir. I reckon I had."

I went out, shutting the door upon the ticking. I looked back into the window. He was watching me across the barrier. There were about a dozen watches in the window, a dozen different hours and each with the same assertive and contradictory assurance that mine had, without any hands at all. Contradicting one another. I could hear mine, ticking away inside my pocket, even though nobody could see it, even though it could tell nothing if anyone could.

And so I told myself to take that one. Because Father said clocks slay time. He said time is dead as long as it is being clicked off by little wheels; only when the clock stops does time come to life.[26)] The hands were extended, slightly off the horizontal at a faint angle, like a gull tilting into the wind. Holding all I used to be sorry about like the new moon holding water, niggers say. The jeweller was working again, bent over his bench, the tube tunnelled into his face. His hair was parted in the center. The part ran up into the bald spot, like a drained marsh in December.

I saw the hardware store from across the street. I didn't know you bought flat-irons by the pound.

"Maybe you want a tailor's goose,"[27)] the clerk said. "They weigh ten pounds." Only they were bigger than I thought. So I got two six-pound little ones, because they would look like a pair of shoes wrapped up. They felt heavy enough together, but I thought again how Father had said about the reducto absurdum of human experience, thinking how the only opportunity I seemed to have for the application of Harvard.[28)] Maybe by next year; thinking maybe it takes two years in school to learn to do that properly.

But they felt heavy enough in the air. A car came. I got on. I didn't see the placard on the front. It was full, mostly prosperous looking

---

26) 시간에 대한 아버지의 철학을 엿볼 수 있으며, 작가(퀸턴)의 시간 개념과도 밀접한 관계가 있다. 기계적인 시간의 흐름은 아무런 의미가 없으며, 인간의 감정이나 심상이 느낄 수 있는 시간만이 진정한 의미를 가지며 그러한 시간의 의미는 결코 기계적으로 가늠할 수 없는 것이다. 이어지는 문장의 시공간 속에서 정지된 이미지는 시간과 움직임으로부터 (삶 자체로부터) 도망하려는, 즉 어느 것도 변하지 않을 순수와 정적의 안전한 공간으로 도망하려는 퀸턴의 욕망을 반영한다.

27) 주로 재봉사들이 사용하는 거위 목 모양의 손잡이가 달린 납작한 다리미.

28) 자신이 익사하기 위해 필요한 무게가 얼마인가를 아는 것이 그가 하버드 대학에서 받은 교육으로부터 실질적인 목적을 위해 적용한 유일한 지식임을 냉소적으로 말하고 있다.

people reading newspapers. The only vacant seat was beside a nigger. He wore a derby and shined shoes and he was holding a dead cigar stub. I used to think that a Southerner had to be always conscious of niggers. I thought that Northerners would expect him to. When I first came East I kept thinking You've got to remember to think of them as colored people not niggers, and if it hadn't happened that I wasn't thrown with many of them, I'd have wasted a lot of time and trouble before I learned that the best way to take all people, black or white, is to take them for what they think they are, then leave them alone. That was when I realised that a nigger is not a person so much as a form of behavior; a sort of obverse reflection of the white people he lives among.[29)] But I thought at first that I ought to miss having a lot of them around me because I thought that Northerners thought I did, but I didn't know that I really had missed Roskus and Dilsey and them until that morning in Virginia. The train was stopped when I waked and I raised the shade and looked out. The car was blocking a road crossing, where two white fences came down a hill and then sprayed outward and downward like part of the skeleton of a horn, and there was a nigger on a mule in the middle of the stiff ruts, waiting for the train to move. How long he had been there I didn't know, but he sat straddle of the mule, his head wrapped in a piece of blanket, as if they had been built there with the fence and the road, of with the hill, carved out of the hill itself, like a sign put there saying You are home again. He didn't have a saddle and his feet dangled almost to the ground. The mule looked like a rabbit. I raised the window.

"Hey, Uncle," I said. "Is this the way?"

---

29) 퀸턴은 여기서 "검둥이", 즉 흑인의 정체성은 인간으로보다는 "하나의 행동양상"으로 정의하면서 그들의 인간성은 백인들과의 관계 속에서만 그리고 백인들의 시선(표면에 반영된 이미지)을 통해서 규명됨을 말한다. 물론 퀸턴의 이러한 정의는 남부 백인들의 인종관을 반영한다.

"Suh?" He looked at me, then he loosened the blanket and lifted it away from his ear.

"Christmas gift!" I said.[30)]

"Sho comin, boss. You done caught me, aint you."

"I'll let you off this time." I dragged my pants out of the little hammock and got a quarter out. "But look out next time. I'll be coming back through here two days after New Year, and look out then" I threw the quarter out the window. "Buy yourself some Santy Claus."

"Yes, suh," he said. He got down and picked up the quarter and rubbed it on his leg." Thanky, young marster. Thanky." Then the train began to move. I leaned out the window, into the cold air, looking back. He stood there beside the gaunt rabbit of a mule, the two of them shabby and motionless and unimpatient. The train swung around the curve, the engine puffing with short, heavy blasts, and they passed smoothly from sight that way, with that quality about them of shabby and timeless patience, of static serenity: that blending of childlike and ready incompetence and paradoxical reliability that tends and protects them it loves out of all reason and robs them steadily and evades responsibility and obligations by means too barefaced to be called subterfuge even and is taken in theft or evasion with only that frank and spontaneous admiration for the victor which a gentleman feels for anyone who beats him in a fair contest, and withal a fond and unflagging tolerance for whitefolks' vagaries like that of a grandparent for unpredictable and troublesome children, which I had forgotten. And all that day, while the train wound through rushing gaps and along ledges where movement was

30) 여기 둘 간의 대화에서, "Uncle"은 특히 남부에서 백인들이 나이든 흑인남자들을 두고, 실제 혈연관계를 말하기보다는, 인종적으로 '생색내는' 차원에서 부르는 호칭이다. "Christmas gift"은 남부에서 주로 흑백 간에 오가는 관습으로, 먼저 "크리스마스 선물"이라고 말한 사람이 선물을 얻게 되는 게임이다.

only a laboring sound of the exhaust and groaning wheels and the eternal mountains stood fading into the thick sky, I thought of home, of the bleak station and the mud and the niggers and country folks thronging slowly about the square, with toy monkeys and wagons and candy in sacks and roman candles[31)] sticking out, and my insides would move like they used to do in school when the bell rang.

I wouldn't begin counting until the clock struck three. Then I would begin, counting to sixty and folding down one finger and thinking of the other fourteen fingers waiting to be folded down, or thirteen or twelve or eight or seven, until all of a sudden I'd realise silence and the unwinking minds, and I'd say "Ma'am?" "Your name is Quentin, isn't it?" Miss Laura[32)] would say. Then more silence and the cruel unwinking minds and hands jerking into the silence. "Tell Quentin who discovered the Mississippi River, Henry." "DeSoto."[33)] Then the minds would go away, and after a while I'd be afraid I had gotten behind and I'd count fast and fold down another finger, then I'd be afraid I was going too fast and I'd slow up, then I'd get afraid and count fast again. So I never could come out even with the bell, and the released surging of feet moving already, feeling earth in the scuffed floor, and the day like a pane of glass struck a light, sharp blow, and my insides would move, sitting still. *Moving sitting still. My bowels moved for thee. One minute she was standing in the door. Benjy. Bellowing. Benjamin the child of mine old age bellowing. Caddy! Caddy!*

---

31) 폭죽. 남북전쟁 이후 (패배한) 남부인들은 수년 동안 미국의 가장 큰 경축일인 독립기념일(July 4th)에 폭죽을 터뜨리지 않았다. 하지만 공휴일은 여전히 폭죽놀이와 함께 즐기길 원했기에 크리스마스 축하놀이 중 그들은 폭죽 터뜨리는 놀이를 하곤 했다.

32) 초등학교 여선생님. 남부에서는 호칭 사용 시 미스 다음에 성이 아닌 이름을 쓰는 습관이 있다.

33) Hernando de Soto (1500?-1542?), 1541년 미시시피 강을 발견한 스페인 탐험가이다.

I'm going to run away. He began to cry she went and touched him. Hush. I'm not going to. Hush. He hushed. Dilsey.

He smell what you tell him when he want to. Dont have to listen nor talk.

Can he smell that new name they give him? Can he smell bad luck?

What he want to worry about luck for? Luck cant do him no hurt.

What they change his name for then if aint trying to help his luck?

The car stopped, started, stopped again. Below the window I watched the crowns of people's heads passing beneath new straw hats not yet unbleached. There were women in the car now, with market baskets, and men in work-clothes were beginning to outnumber the shined shoes and collars.

The nigger touched my knee. "Pardon me," he said. I swung my legs out and let him pass. We were going beside a blank wall, the sound clattering back into the car, at the women with market baskets on their knees and a man in a stained hat with a pipe stuck in the band. I could smell water, and in a break in the wall I saw a glint of water and two masts, and a gull motionless in midair, like on an invisible wire between the masts, and I raised my hand and through my coat touched the letters I had written. When the car stopped I got off.

The bridge was open to let a schooner through. She was in tow, the tug nudging along under her quarter, trailing smoke, but the ship herself was like she was moving without visible means. A man naked to the waist was coiling down a line on the fo'c's'le head.[34) His body was burned the color of leaf tobacco. Another man in a straw hat without any crown was at the wheel. The ship went through the bridge, moving under bare poles like a ghost in broad day, with three gulls hovering above the stern like toys on invisible wires.

When it closed I crossed to the other side and leaned on the rail

---

34) 선수루(forecastle), 배 갑판의 앞부분.

above the boathouses. The float was empty and the doors were closed. Crew just pulled in the late afternoon now, resting up before. The shadow of the bridge, the tiers of railing, my shadow leaning flat upon the water, so easily had I tricked it that would not quit me. At least fifty feet it was, and if I only had something to blot it in to the water, holding it until it was drowned, the shadow of the package like two shoes wrapped up lying on the water.[35)] Niggers say a drowned man's shadow was watching for him in the water all the time. It[36)] twinkled and glinted, like breathing, the float slow like breathing too, and debris half submerged, healing out to the sea and the caverns and the grottoes of the sea. The displacement of water is equal to the something of something.[37)] Reducto absurdum of all human experience, and two six-pound flat-irons weigh more than one tailor's goose. What a sinful waste Dilsey would say. Benjy knew it when Damuddy died. He cried. *He smell hit. He smell hit.*

The tug came back downstream, the water shearing in long rolling cylinders, rocking the float at last with the echo of passage, the float lurching onto the rolling cylinder with a plopping sound and a long jarring noise as the door rolled back and two men emerged, carrying a shell. They set it in the water and a moment later Bland came out, with the sculls. He wore flannels, a gray jacket and a stiff straw hat. Either he or his mother had read somewhere that Oxford students pulled in flannels and stiff hats, so early one March they bought Gerald a one pair shell[38)] and in his flannels and stiff hat he went on

---

35) 자신의 그림자로부터 도망하려는 퀸턴은 여기서 그 그림자가 익사하는 장면을 상상하고 있다("blot[ting] it into the water"). 그리고 두개의 신을 싼 것 같은 뭉치는 철물점에서 산 다리미 두개를 포함하고 있으며, 이 장면은 자신의 수사(drowning himself)를 명료히 드러내는 부분이기도 하다.

36) 수면 위의 퀸턴의 그림자.

37) 아르키메데스(Archimedes)의 원리.

38) 한 세트의 노를 가진 경주용 보트.

the river. The folks at the boathouse threatened to call a policeman,[39] but he went anyway. His mother came down in a hired auto, in a fur suit like an arctic explorer's, and saw him off in a twenty-five mile wind and a steady drove of ice floes like dirty sheep. Ever since then I have believed that God is not only a gentleman and a sport; he is a Kentuckian too. When he sailed away she made a detour and came down to the river again and drove along parallel with him, the car in low gear. They said you couldn't have told they'd ever seen one another before, like a King and Queen, not even looking at one another, just moving side by side across Massachusetts on parallel courses like a couple of planets.

He got in and pulled away. He pulled pretty well now. He ought to. They said his mother tried to make him give rowing up and do something else the rest of his class couldn't or wouldn't do, but for once he was stubborn. If you could call it stubbornness, sitting in his attitudes of princely boredom, with his curly yellow hair and his violet eyes and his eyelashes and his Now York clothes, while his mamma was telling us about Gerald's horses and Gerald's niggers and Gerald's women. Husbands and fathers in Kentucky must have been awful glad when she carried Gerald off to Cambridge. She had an apartment over in town, and Gerald had one there too, besides his rooms in college. She approved of Gerald associating with me because I at least revealed a blundering sense of noblesse oblige by getting myself born below Mason and Dixon,[40] and a few others whose Geography met the requirements (minimum). Forgave, at least. Or condoned. But since she met Spoade coming out of chapel

---

39) 아마도 3월에 보트 경주를 하는 것은 너무 위험하다고 생각되기에.

40) 메이슨-딕슨 경계선(Mason-Dixon line)은 메릴랜드 주와 펜실베이니아 주 경계를 가르는 선으로, 노예제도가 성행하던 남부와 그렇지 않은 북부를 분리시킨 경계이다. 1763-1767년, 경계 분쟁을 해결하기 위해 그 선을 조사했던 영국의 두 천문학자, 메이슨(Charles Mason)과 딕슨(Jeremiah Dixon)의 이름에서 유래하고 있다.

one[41] He said she couldn't be a lady no lady would be out at that hour of the night she never had been able to forgive him for having five names, including that of a present English ducal house. I'm sure she solaced herself by being convinced that some misfit Maingault or Mortemar had got mixed up with the lodge-keeper's daughter. Which was quite probable, whether she invented it or not. Spoade was the world's champion sitter-around, no holds barred and gouging discretionary.

The shell was a speck now, the oars catching the sun in spaced glints, as if the hull were winking itself along him along. *Did you ever have a sister? No but they're all bitches. Did you ever have a sister? One minute she was, Bitches. Not bitch one minute she stood in the door* Dalton Ames. Dalton Ames. Dalton Shirts. I thought all the time they were khaki, army issue khaki, until I saw they were of heavy Chinese silk or finest flannel because they made his face so brown his eyes so blue. Dalton Ames. It just missed gentility. Theatrical fixture. Just papier-mache, then touch. Oh. Asbestos. Not quite bronze. *But wont see him at the house.*

Caddy's a woman too remember. She must do things for women's reasons too.

Why wont you bring him to the house, Caddy? Why must you do like nigger women do in the pasture the ditches the dark woods hot hidden furious in the dark woods.

And after a while I had been hearing my watch for some time and I

---

41) 여기 스포드가 "제1 예배당"에서 한 짓은 묘사되지 않고 있지만, 연결되는 블랜드 부인의 반응, 즉 스포드가 유럽의 명문가("Maingault or Mortemar")에 속하는 이름("five names")을 가졌음에도 불구하고, 그날 밤("one night") 그곳에 모습을 드러낸 사실만으로, 아들인 제랄드의 친구로 스포드를 인정할 수 없다는 그녀의 반응에서, 그곳에서 스포드는 아마 성적으로(동성애적으로) 연루된 어떤 짓을 하였음을 추측할 수 있다. 당시 대학 "예배당들"은, 전해오던 대학가의 전설에 의하면 그리고 실제로도, 학생들의 성적 유희장으로 악명 높은 장소이기도 했다.

could feel the letter crackle through my coat, against the railing, and I leaned on the railing, watching my shadow, how I had tricked it. I moved along the rail, but my suit was dark too and I could wipe my hands, watching my shadow, how I had tricked it. I walked it into the shadow of the quai. Then I went east.

Harvard my Harvard boy Harvard harvard That pimple-faced infant she met at the field-meet with colored ribbons. Skulking along the fence trying to whistle her out like a puppy. Because they couldn't cajole him into the diningroom Mother believed he had some sort of spell he was going to cast on her when he got her alone. Yet any blackguard *He was lying beside the box under the window bellowing* that could drive up in a limousine with a flower in his buttonhole. *Harvard. Quentin this is Herbert. My Harvard boy. Herbert will be a big brother has already promised Jason*

Hearty, celluloid like a drummer.[42)]Face full of teeth white but not smiling. *I've heard of him up there.* All teeth but not smiling. *You going to drive?*

Get in Quentin

You going to drive.

It's her car aren't you proud of your little sister owns first auto in town Herbert his present.[43)] *Louis has been giving her lessons every morning didn't you get my letter* Mr and Mrs Jason Richmond Compson announce the marriage of their daughter Candace to Mr Sydney Herbert Head on the twenty-fifth of April one thousand nine

---

42) 허버트에 대한 퀜턴의 생각이 명료히 드러나는 부분으로, "셀룰로이드" 칼라를 입고 있는 전형적인 떠돌이 영업사원("drummer") 같은 허버트의 이미지는 그의 진솔하지 못하면서도 가공적인 모습이 강조된다.

43) 이 대화는 캐디, 캄슨 부인, 그리고 허버트가 하버드에서 캐디의 결혼식에 참석하기 위해 돌아온 퀜턴을 기차역에서 맞고 있는 부분이다. 여기 캐디는 허버트가 선물한 차를 운전하고 있으며, 더욱 낯설어진 여동생의 모습에 두 번이나 "네가 운전할거냐?"라고 묻는데서 퀜턴의 충격을 엿볼 수 있다.

hundred and ten at Jefferson Mississippi. At home after the first of August number Something Something Avenue South Bend Indiana. Shereve said Aren't you even going to open it? *Three days. Times. Mr and Mrs Jason Richmond Compson* Young Lochinvar[44] rode out of the west a little too soon, didn't he?

I'm from the south. You're funny, aren't you.

O yes I knew it was somewhere in the county.

You're funny, aren't you. You ought to join the circus.

I did. That's how I ruined my eyes watering the elephant's fleas. *Three times* These country girls. You cant ever tell about them, can you. Well, any way Byron never had his wish,[45] thank God. *But not hit a man in glasses* Aren't you even going to open it? *It lay on the table a candle burning at each corner upon the envelope tied in a soiled pink garter two artificial flowers. Not hit a man in glasses.*

Country people poor thing they never saw an auto before lots of them honk the horn Candace so *She wouldn't look at me* they'll get out of the way *wouldn't look at me.* your father wouldn't like it if you were to injure one of them I'll declare your father will simply have to get an auto now I'm almost sorry you brought it down Herbert I've enjoyed it so much of course there's the carriage but so often when I'd like to ho out Mr Compson has the darkies doing something it would be worth my head to interrupt he insists that Roskus is at my call all the time but I know what that means I know how often people make promises just to satisfy their consciences are

---

44) 월터 스캇의 시("Marmion")에 등장하는 인물로, 결혼식장에서 신랑과 하객들을 남겨둔 채 자신이 사랑하는 여자를 구해 도망하는 용감한 젊은이이다. 캐디의 "명예"에 집착하지만 용기 없는 퀜턴을 조롱하는 비유라 하겠다.

45) 혹자는 이 말을 하는 이가 퀜턴이라고 단정하지만, 그가 쉬리브인지 허버트인지, 아니면 퀜턴 자신인지는 확실치 않다. 바이런(Lord Byron)이 의붓동생(Augusta Leigh)에게 근친상간의 욕망을 결코 이루지 못했다고 여기서 말하고 있지만, 바이런의 근친상간은 이루어졌다.

you going to treat my little baby girl that way Herbert but I know you wont Herbert has spoiled us all to death Quentin did I write you that he is going to take Jason into his bank when Jason finishes high school Jason will make a splendid banker he is the only one of my children with any practical sense you can thank me for that he take after my people the others are all Compson *Jason furnished the flour. They made kites on the back porch and sold them for a nickel a piece, he and the Patterson boy. Jason was treasurer.*

There was no nigger in this car, and the hats unbleached as yet flowing past under the window. Going to Harvard. We have sold Benjy's *He lay on the ground under the window, bellowing. We have sold Benjy's pasture so that Quentin may go to Harvard* a brother to you. Your little brother.

You should have a car it's done you no end of good dont you think so Quentin I call him Quentin at once you see I have heard so much about him from Candace.

Why shouldn't you I want my boys to be more than friends yes Candace and Quentin more than friends *Father I have committed*

What a pity you had no brother or sister *No sister no sister had no sister*

Dont ask Quentin he and Mr Compson both feel a little insulted when I am strong enough to come down to the table I am going on nerve now I'll pay for it after it's all over and you have taken my little daughter away from me *My little sister had no.*[46)] *If I could say Mother. Mother*

Unless I do what I am tempted to and take you instead I dont think Mr Compson could overtake the car.

Ah Herbert Candace do you hear that *She wouldn't look at me soft stubborn jaw-angle not back-looking* You needn't be jealous

46) 성경(Song of Solomon 8.8): "We have a little sister, and she hath no breasts: what shall we do for our sister in the day when she shall be spoken for?"

though it's just an old woman he's flattering a grown married daughter I cant believe it.

Nonsense you look like a girl you are lots younger than Candace color in your cheeks like a girl.[47] *A face reproachful tearful an odor of camphor and of tears a voice weeping steadily and softly beyond the twilit door the twilight-colored smell of honeysuckle. Bringing empty trunks down the attic stairs they sounded like coffins French Lick*[48] *Found not death at the salt lick*

Hats not unbleached and not hats. In three years I can not wear a hat.[49] I could not. Was. Will there be hats then since I was not and not Harvard then. Where the best of thought Father said clings like dead ivy vines upon old dead brick. Not Harvard then. Not to me, anyway. Again. Sadder than was. Again. Saddest of all. Again.

Spoade had a shirt on; then It must be. When I can see my shadow again If not careful that I tricked into the water shall tread again upon my impervious shadow.[50] But no sister. *I wouldn't have done it. I wont have my daughter spied on* I wouldn't have.

How can I control any of them when you have always taught them to have no respect for me and my wishes I know you look down on my people but is that any reason for teaching my children my own children I suffered for to have no respect Trampling my shadow's bones into the concrete with hard heels and then I was hearing the

---

47) 허버트가 캄슨 부인이 소녀 같다고 아부하는 찬사.

48) 20세기 초 남부의 졸부들이 즐겨가던 인디애나 주 남쪽에 있는 휴양지. 캄슨 부인은 임신한 캐디에게 남편감을 찾아주기 위해 이곳을 선택하며, 거기서 캐디는 허버트를 만나게 된다. 원래 사냥꾼들이 사슴(이나 동물들) 사냥을 할 때 커다란 소금덩이를 숲에 내놓아 사슴들이 소금을 빨아먹을 때 정지된 그 먹이감을 향해 더욱 손쉽게 사냥을 할 수 있는 "salt lick"이라는 말이 있다. 때문에 여기 "French Lick"은 남자(남편감)들이 겨냥하고 있는 일종의 정지된 목표물, 즉 여자들을 상징한다고 할 수 있다.

49) 당시 하버드 대학에서는 4학년생만 모자를 쓰지 않았기에, 1년생인 퀸턴이 하는 말이다.

50) 자신의 그림자를 밟으면 죽게 된다는 미신이 있다.

watch, and I touched the letters through my coat.

I will not have my daughter spied on by you or Quentin or anybody no matter what you think she has done

At least you agree there is reason for having her watched

I wouldn't have I wouldn't have. *I know you wouldn't I didn't mean to speak so sharply but women have no respect for each other for themselves*

But why did she The chimes began as I stepped on my shadow, but it was the quarter hour. The Deacon wasn't in sight anywhere. *think I would have could have*

She didn't mean that that's the way women do things it's because she loves Caddy

The street lamps would go down the hill then rise toward town I walked upon the belly of my shadow. I could extend my hand beyond it. *feeling Father behind me beyond the rasping darkness of summer and August the street lamps* Father and I protect women from one another from themselves our women *Women are like that they dont acquire knowledge of people we are for that they are just born with a practical fertility of suspicion that makes a crop every so often and usually right they have an affinity for evil for supplying whatever the evil lacks in itself for drawing it about them instinctively as you do bed-clothing in slumber fertilising the mind for it until the evil has served its purpose whether it ever existed or no* He was coming along between a couple of freshmen. He hadn't quite recovered from the parade, for he gave me a salute, a very superior-officerish kind.

"I want to see you a minute," I said, stopping.

"See me? All right. See you again, fellows," he said, stopping and turning back; "glad to have chatted with you." That was the Deacon, all over. Talk about your natural psychologists. They said he hadn't missed a train at the beginning of school in the forty years, and that he could pick out a southerner with one glance. He never missed, and once he had heard you speak, he could name your state. He had a regular uniform he met trains in, a sort of Uncle Tom's cabin outfit[51], patches and all.

"Yes, suh. Right dis way, young master, hyer we is," taking your bags. "Hyer, boy, come hyer and git dese grips." Whereupon a moving mountain of luggage would edge up, revealing a white boy of about fifteen, and the Deacon would hang another bag on him somehow and drive him off. "Now, den, dont you drap hit. Yes, suh, young master, jes give de old nigger yo room number, and hit'll be done got cold dar when you arrives."

From then on until he had you completely subjugated he was always in or out of your room, ubiquitous and garrulous, though his manner gradually moved northward as his raiment improved, until at last when he had bled you until you began to learn better he was calling you Quentin or whatever,[52] and when you saw him next he'd be wearing a cast-off Brooks suit and a hat with a Princeton club I forget which band that someone had given him and which he was pleasantly and unshakably convinced was a part of Abe Lincoln's military sash. Someone spread the story years ago, when he first appeared around college from wherever he came from, that he was graduate of the divinity school. And when he came to understand what it meant he was so taken with it that he began to retail the story himself, until at least he must have come to believe he really had. Anyway he related long pointless anecdotes of his undergraduate days, speaking familiarly of dead and departed professors by their first names, usually incorrect ones. But he had been guide mentor and friend to unnumbered crops of innocent and lonely freshmen,

---

51) 스토우 부인(Harriet Beecher Stowe)의 1852년 작품(*Uncle Tom's Cabin*)에 등장하는 엉클 톰은 백인가족에 헌신적인 흑인노예를 상징하는 인물이다.

52) 1910년대 미국남부의 흑인들은 젊은 백인들을 첫 이름으로 부르지 않고 "Mr. 퀀턴"으로 부르는 게 상례였다. 하지만 여기 디콘의 태도는 더 이상 남부의 관례를 따르지 않는다.

and I suppose that with all his petty chicanery end hypocrisy he stank no higher in heaven's nostrils than any other.

"Haven't seen you in three-four days," he said, staring at me from his still military aura. "You been sick?"

"No, I've been all right. Working, I reckon. I've seen you though."

"Yes?"

"In the parade the other day."

"Oh, that. Yes, I was there. I dont care nothing about that sort of thing, you understand, but the boys likes to have me with them, the vet'runs does. Ladies wants all the old vet'runs to turn out, you know. So I has to oblige them."

"And on that Wop holiday[53)] too," I said. "You were obliging the W. C. T. U.[54)] then, I reckon."

"That? I was dong that for my son-in-law. He aims to get a job on the city forces. Street cleaner. I tells him all he wants is a broom to sleep on. You saw me, did you?"

"Both times. Yes."

"I mean, in uniform. How'd I look?"

"You looked fine. You looked better than any of them. They ought to make you a general, Deacon."

He touched my arm, lightly, his hand that worn, gentle quality of niggers' hands. "Listen. This aint for outside talking. I dont mind telling you because you and me's the same folks, come long and short." He leaned a little to me, speaking rapidly, his eyes not looking at me. "I've got strings out, right now. Wait till next year. Just wait.

---

53) 콜럼버스 기념일(Columbus Day, 10월 12일) 아니면 가리발디 기념일(Garibaldi's Birthday, 7월 4일)을 지칭.

54) 여성기독교 금연동맹(Women's Christian Temperance Union), 1874년에 창설되었으며, 술 판매와 소비를 금하거나 절제하는데 헌신한 여성 조직이다. 여기 퀸턴은 이탈리아 남자들의 악명 높은 술 소비행태를 두고 농담하고 있으며, 그것은 당시 미국인들의 사회적 편견을 퀸턴 역시 아무런 여과 없이 그대로 받아들이고 있음을 보여준다.

Then see where I'm marching. I wont need to tell you how I'm fixing it; I say, just wait and see, my boy." He looked at me now and clapped me lightly on the shoulder and rocked back on his heels, nodding at me. "Yes, sir. I didn't turn Democrat three years ago for nothing. My son-in-low on the city; me—Yes, sir. If just turning Democrat'll make that son of a bitch go to work . . . . And me; just you stand on that corner yonder a year from two days ago, and see."

"I hope so. You deserve it, Deacon. And while I think about it—" I took the letter from my pocket. "Take this around to my room tomorrow and give it to Shreve. He'll have something for you. But not till tomorrow, mind."

He took the letter and examined it. "It's sealed up."

"Yes. And it's written inside, Not good until tomorrow."

"H'm," "he said. He looked at the envelope, his mouth pursed. "Something for me, you say?"

"Yes. A present I'm making you."

He was looking at me now, the envelope white in his black hand, in the sun. His eyes were soft and irisless and brown, and suddenly I saw Roskus watching me from behind all his whitefolks' claptrap of uniforms and politics and Harvard manner, diffident, secret, inarticulate and sad. "You aint playing a joke on the old nigger, is you?"

"You know I'm not. Did any Southerner ever play a joke on you?"

"You're right. They're fine folks. But you cant live with them."

"Did you ever try?" I said. But Roskus was gone. Once more he was that self he had long since taught himself to wear in the world's eye, pompous, spurious, not quite gross.

"I'll confer to your wishes, my boy." [55)]

---

55) 여기 디콘은 "confer"를 "defer"로 혼동하여 쓰고 있다. 그리고 그는 퀀틴을 "my boy"로 부르고 있는데, 남부에서는 실제 젊은 백인들이 흑인(성인)남자들을 부를 때 "boys"라는 호칭을 쓰고 있는 점에서, 디콘은 여기서도 남부의 인종적 언어습관을 전복하고 있다.

"Not until tomorrow, remember."

"Sure," he said; "understood, my boy. Well—"

"I hope—" I said. He looked down at me, benignant, profound. Suddenly I held out my hand and we shook, he gravely, from the pompous height of his municipal and military dream. "You're a good fellow, Deacon. I hope . . . . You've helped a lot of young fellows, here and there."

"I've tried to treat all folks right," he said. "I draw no petty social lines. A man to me is a man, wherever I find him."

"I hope you'll always find as many friends as you've made."

"Young fellows. I get along with them. They dont forget me, neither," he said, waving the envelope. He put in into his pocket and buttoned his coat. "Yes, sir," he said. "I've had good friends."

The chimes began again, the half hour. I stood in the belly of my shadow and listened to the strokes spaced and tranquil along the sunlight, among the thin, still little leaves. Spaced and peaceful and serene, with that quality of autumn always in bells even in the month if brides.[56] *Lying on the ground under the window bellowing* He took one look at her and knew. Out of the mouths of babes.[57] *The street lamps* The chimes ceased. I went back to the postoffice, treading my shadow into pavement. *go down the hill then they rise toward town like lanterns hung one above another on a wall.* Father said because she loves Caddy she loves people through their shortcomings. Uncle Maury straddling his legs before the fire must remove one hand long enough to drink Christmas. Jason ran on, his hands in his pockets fell down and lay there like a trussed fowl until Versh set him up. *Whyn't you keep them hands outen your pockets*

---

56) 퀸턴에게 종소리는 시간을 상징하면서 동시에 6월에조차도 가을의 느낌을 안겨주는, 즉 어떤 것의 종결점을 향하는 심상을 느끼게 한다고 말한다.

57) 성경(Matthews 21.16): "Out of the mouths of babes and sucklings thou hast perfected praise."

when you running you could stand up then Rolling his head in the cradle rolling it flat across the back. Caddy told Jason and Versh that the reason Uncle Maury didn't work was that he used to roll his head in the cradle when he was little.

Shreve was coming up the walk, shambling, fatly earnest, his glasses glinting beneath the running leaves like little pools.

"I gave Deacon a note for some things. I may not be in this afternoon, so dont you let him have anything until tomorrow, will you?

"All right." He looked at me. "Say, what're you doing today, anyhow? All dressed up and mooning around like the prologue to a suttee.[58)] Did you go to Psychology this morning?"

"I'm not doing anything. Not until tomorrow, now."

"What's that you got there?"

"Nothing. Pair of shoes I had half-soled. Not until tomorrow, you hear?"

"Sure. All right. Oh, by the way, did you get a letter off the table this morning?"

"No."

"It's there. From Semiramis.[59)] Chauffeur brought it before ten oclock."

"All right. I'll get it. Wonder what she wants now."

"Another band recital, I guess. Tumpty ta ta Gerald blah. 'A little louder on the drum, Quentin'. God, I'm glad I'm not a gentleman." He went on, nursing a book, a little shapeless, fatly intent.[60)] *The*

---

58) 인도에서는 남편이 죽으면 아내가 자신을 희생하여 죽은 남편과 함께 산 채로 매장되는 풍습이 있다.

59) 퀸턴과 쉬리브가 블랜드 부인을 두고 조롱투로 부르는 별명으로, Semiramis는 지혜와 미모를 겸비한 고대 아시리아의 전설적인 여왕이며, 그녀는 남편(Ninus)보다 오래 살아남아 바빌론(the city of Babylon)을 건설하였다.

60) 쉬리브가 걸으면서 책을 읽거나 아니면 책을 마치 아이에게 젖을 먹이듯 가슴에 안고 있는 이미지로, 대상을 성적으로 그리고 여성적 시선으로 바라보는 퀸턴을 볼 수 있다.

street lamps do you think so because one of our forefathers was a governor and three were generals and Mother's werent

any live man is better than any dead man but no live or dead man is very much better than any other live or dead man *Done in mother's mind though. Finished. Finished. Then we were all poisoned* You are confusing sin and morality women dont do that your mother is thinking of morality whether it be sin or not has not occurred to her

Jason I must go away you keep the others I'll take Jason and go where nobody knows us so he'll have a chance to grow up and forget all this the others dont love me they have never loved anything with that streak of Compson selfishness and false pride Jason was the only one my heart went out to without dread

nonsense Jason is all right I was thinking that as soon as you feel better you and Caddy might go up to French Lick

and leave Jason here with nobody but you and the darkies[61)]

she will forget him then all the talk will die away *found not death at the salt licks*

maybe I could find a husband for her *not death at the salt licks*

The car came up and stopped. The bells were still ringing the half hour. I got on and it went on again, blotting the half hour. No: the three quarters. Then it would be ten minutes anyway. To leave Harvard *your mother's dream for sold Benjy's pasture for*

what have I done to have been given children like these Benjamin was punishment enough and now for her to have no more regard for me her own mother I've suffered for her dreamed and planned and sacrificed I went down into the valley[62)] yet never since she opened

---

61) "darkies"는 남부에서 흑인들을 총칭하는 말이다. 혹자는 이 말이 경멸적인 뜻을 함의하기보다는 "관대하고 애정 어린" 차원에서 사용되는 용어로 보지만, 그것은 다분히 인종과 계층 차별적인 말이다.

62) 성경(Psalms 23.4): "the valley of the shadow of death." 캄슨 부인은 자기 연민에 빠

her eyes has she given me one unselfish thought at times I look at her I wonder if she can be my child except Jason he has never given me one moment's sorrow since I first held him in my arms I knew then that he was to be my joy and my salvation I thought that Benjamin was punishment enough for any sins I have committed I thought he was my punishment for putting aside my pride and marrying a man who held himself above me I dont complain I loved him above all of them because of it because my duty though Jason pulling at my heart all the while but I see now that I have not suffered enough I see now that I must pay for your sins as well as mine what have you done what sins have your high and mighty people visited upon me but you'll take up for them you always have found excuses for your own blood only Jason can do wrong because he is more Bascomb than Compson while your own daughter my little daughter my baby girl she is she is no better than that when I was a girl I was unfortunate I was only a Bascomb I was taught that there is no halfway ground that a woman is either a lady or not but I never dreamed when I held her in my arms that any daughter of mine could let herself dont you know I can look at her eyes and tell you may think she'd tell you but she doesn't tell things she is secretive you dont know her I know things she's done that I'd die before I'd have you know that's it go on criticise Jason accuse me of setting him to watch her as if it were a crime while your own daughter can I know you dont love him that you wish to believe faults against him you never have yes ridicule him as you always have Maury[63] you cannot hurt me any more than your children already have and then I'll be gone and Jason with no

---

져 자신의 고통과 불만을 토로하기 위해 성경 속의 상투적인 표현들을 자주 쓰곤 한다. 곧이어 그녀는 제이슨을 "my joy and my salvation"(Psalms 51.2)라고 부르기도 한다.

63) 이 문장의 모리는 모리 삼촌(Maury Bascomb)을 말하며, 캄슨 부인은 남편이 동생을 조롱하는데 불만을 토로하고 있다.

one to love him shield him from this I look at him every dat dreading to see this Compson blood beginning to show in him at last with his sister slipping out to see what do you call it then have you ever laid eyes on him will you even let me try to find out who he is it's not for myself I couldn't bear to see him it's for your sake to protect you but who can fight against bad blood you wont let me try we are to sit back with our hands folded while she not only drags your name in the dirt but corrupts the very air your children breathe Jason you must let me go away I cannot stand it let me have Jason[64] and you keep the others they're not my flesh and blood like he is strangers nothing of mine and I am afraid if them I can take Jason and go where we are not known I'll go down on my knees and pray for the absolution of my sins that he may escape this curse try to forget that the others ever were

If that was the three quarters, not over ten minutes now. One car had just left, and people were already waiting for the next one. I asked, but he didn't know whether another one would leave before noon or not because you'd think that interurbans. So the first one was another trolley. I got on. You can feel noon. I wonder if even miners in the bowels of the earth. That's why whistles: because people that sweat, and if just far enough from sweat you wont hear whistles and in eight minutes you should be that far from sweat in Boston. Father said a man is the sum of his misfortunes. One day you'd think misfortune would get tired, but then time is your misfortune Father said. A gull on an invisible wire attached through space dragged. You carry the symbol of your frustration into eternity. Then the wings are bigger Father said only who can play a harp.

I could hear my watch whenever the car stopped, but not often they were already eating *Who would play a* Eating the business of eating inside of you space too space and time confused Stomach

---

64) 전자는 남편 캄슨씨이며, 후자는 아들 제이슨이다.

saying noon brain saying eat oclock[65] All right I wonder what time it is what of it. People were getting out. The trolley didn't stop so often now, emptied by eating.

Then it was past.[66] I got off and stood in my shadow and after a while a car came along and I got on and went back to the interurban station. There was a car ready to leave, and I found a seat next the window and it started and I watched it[67] sort of frazzle out into slack tide flats, and then trees. Now and then I saw the river and I thought how nice it would be for them down at New London if the weather and Gerald's shell going solemnly up the glinting forenoon and I wondered what the old woman would be wanting now, sending me a note before ten oclock in the morning. What picture of Gerald I to be one of the *Dalton Ames oh asbestos Quentin has shot* background. Something with girls in it. Women do have *always his voice above the gabble voice that breathed* an affinity for evil, for believing that no woman is to be trusted, but that some men are too innocent to protect themselves. Plain girls. Remote cousins and family friends[68] whom mere acquaintanceship invested with a sort of blood obligation noblesse oblige. And she sitting there telling us before

65) 비록 시간을 의식적으로 피하고 있을지라도, 퀸턴은 인간의 육체가 시간 속에서 그 자리를 어떻게 찾아내고 있는지에 대해 계속 명상하고 있다. 마치 정오가 되면 위가 먹을 때라는 것을 두뇌로 신호를 보내 알려주듯.

66) 정오가 지나갔음을 말한다. 퀸턴은 (시간을 알리는 거리의 종소리가 들리지 않는) 차를 타고 정오라는 시간으로부터 도망하고자 하는 욕망을 드러낸다. 물론 배고픔을 알리는 자신의 뱃속 시계와 함께, 차 내에서조차도 퀸턴은 끊임없이 시간을 의식하고 있지만.

67) "it"은 창문을 통해 보이는, 도시에서 시골로 들어서면서 펼쳐지는 주변 경관을 말한다.

68) 아버지와의 대화에서 언급된 여성관("악과 친화력을 가진", "믿을 수 없는")을 생각하다, 퀸턴은 제랄드와 친구들의 외출에 동원된 여자들을 생각한다. 블랜드 부인에게 그들은 외모가 수수하고 집안의 먼 친척뻘이나 친분이 있는 집안의 딸들이라 아들 제랄드에게 위협적이기보다는 "믿을 수 있는" 상대라고 생각한다.

their faces what a shame it was that Gerald should have all the family looks because a man didn't need it, was better off without it but without it a girl was simply lost. Telling us about Gerald's women in a *Quentin has shot Herbert he shot his voice through the floor of Caddy's room* tone of smug approbation.[69] "When he was seventeen I said to him one day 'What a shame that you should have a mouth like that it should be on a girl's face' and can you imagine. *the curtains leaning in on the twilight upon the odor of the apple tree her head against the twilight her arms behind her head kimono-winged the voice that breathed o'er eden clothes upon the bed by the nose seen above the apple* what he said? just seventeen, mind. 'Mother' he said 'it often is'." And him sitting there in attitudes regal watching two or three of them through his eyelashes. They gushed like swallows swooping his eyelashes. Shreve said he always had *Are you going to look after Benjy and Father*

The less you say about Benjy and Father the better when have you ever consider them Caddy

Promise

You needn't worry about them you're getting out in good shape

Promise I'm sick you'll have to promise wondered who invented that joke[70] but then he always had considered Mrs Bland a remarkably preserved woman he said she was grooming Gerald to seduce a duchess sometime. She called Shreve that fat Canadian youth twice she arranged a new room-mate for me without consulting me at all, once for me to move out, once for

---

69) 블랜드 부인이 아들의 여성편력을 두고 자랑하자, 퀸턴은 제랄드와 같은 부류의 허버트를 생각하면서, 그의 기억은 캐디의 결혼 전날 밤 캐디 방에서 자신과 캐디가 나누는 대화 장면으로 돌아가, 아래층에서 들려오는 허버트의 목소리를 들으며 총으로 층을 뚫어 허버트와 그의 목소리를 쏴버리는 환상을 드러내고 있다.

70) 여기 "농담"은 앞서 언급된 제랄드가 자신의 입(술)이 자주 여자들의 얼굴 위에서 발견된다는 익살맞은 얘기를 말한다.

He opened the door in the twilight.[71] His face looked like a pumpkin pie.

"Well, I'll say a fond farewell. Cruel fate may part us, but I will never love another. Never."

"What are you talking about?"

"I talking about cruel fate in eight yards of apricot silk and more metal pound for pound than a galley slave and the sole owner and proprietor of the unchallenged peripatetic john of the late Confederacy."[72] Then he told me how she had gone to the proctor to have him moved out and how the proctor had revealed enough low stubbornness to insist on consulting Shreve first. Then she suggested that he send for Shreve right off and do it, and he wouldn't do that, so after that she was hardly civil to Shreve. "I make it a point never to speak harshly of females," Shreve said, "but that woman has got more ways like a bitch than any lady in these sovereign states and dominions." and now Letter on the table by hand, command orchid scented colored If she knew I had passed almost beneath the window knowing it there without   My dear Madam I have not yet had an opportunity of receiving your communication but I beg in advance to be excused today or yesterday and tomorrow or when As I remember that the next one is to be how Gerald throws his nigger downstairs and how the nigger plead to be allowed to matriculate in the divinity school to be near marster marse gerald[73] and How he ran all the way

---

71) 퀜틴의 기억은 블랜드 부인이 쉬리브가 자신의 룸메이트로 적절치 않다고 생각하며—아마 그가 외국인/캐나다인이고 남부의 상류층 출신이 아니어서—자신에게 새 룸메이트를 구해주려던 시점으로 옮아가고 있다.

72) 생애 마지막 날을 배회하고 있는 듯한("unchallenged peripatetic") 퀜틴의 모습을 상징적으로 드러내면서, 남부인인("john of the late Confederacy") 퀜틴을 마치 "소유"하기라도 하듯 행동하는 블랜드 부인의 태도를 쉬리브가 조롱투로 언급하고 있다.

73) 남부에서 백인노예주를 두고, 자신들의 삶보다 더 소중한 백인들을 위해 스스로를 희생하던 충실한 흑인노예들이 구어적으로 노예주(master)를 흔히 "marster"나

to the station beside the carriage with tears in his eyes when marse gerald rid away I will wait until the day for the one about the sawmill husband[74] came to the kitchen door with a shotgun Gerald went down and bit the gun in two and handed it back and wiped his hands on a silk handkerchief threw the handkerchief in the stove I've only heard that one twice

shot him through the I saw you come in here so I watched my chance and came along thought we might get acquainted have a cigar

Thanks I dont smoke

No things must have changed up there since my day mind if I light up

Help yourself

Thanks I've heard a lot guess your mother wont mind if I put the match behind the screen will she a lot about you Candace talked about you all the time up there at the Licks I got pretty jealous I says to myself who is this Quentin anyway I must see what this animal looks like because I was hit pretty hard see soon as I saw the little girl I dont mind telling you it never occurred to me it was her brother she kept talking about she couldn't have talked about you any more if you'd been the only man in the world husband wouldn't have been in it you wont change your mind and have a smoke

I dont smoke

In that case I wont insist even though it is a pretty fair weed cost me twenty-five bucks a hundred wholesale friend of in Havana yes I guess there are lots of changes up there I keep promising myself a visit but I never get around to it been hitting the ball now for ten

---

"marse"라고 부르곤 하였다.

74) 블랜드 부인이 아들 제랄드를 두고 하는 이야기이지만, 그것은 미국 "남서부 휴머 전통"에 등장하는 이야기 중 하나이다. 물론 그 효과는 퀸턴이 블랜드 부인을 풍자적으로 비판하는 면도 있지만, 동시에 이야기의 틀은 퀸턴 자신과 캐디(의 명예) 그리고 달턴과의 관계 또한 상징적으로 엿볼 수 있다.

years I cant get away from the bank during school fellow's habits change things that seem important to an undergraduate you know tell me about things up there

I'm not going to tell Father and Mother if that's what you are getting at Not going to tell not going to oh that that's what you are talking about is it you understand that I dont give a damn whether you tell or not understand that a thing like that unfortunate but no police crime I wasn't the first or the last I was just unlucky you might have been luckier[75)]

You lie

Keep your shirt on I'm not trying to make you tell anything you dont want to meant no offense of course a young fellow like you would consider a thing of that sort a lot more serious than you will in five years

I dont know but one way to consider cheating I dont think I'm likely to learn different at Harvard

We're better than a play you must have made the Dramat[76)] well you' re right no need to tell them we'll let bygones be bygones eh no reason why you and I should let a little thing like that come between us I like you Quentin I like your appearance you dont look like these other hicks I'm glad we're going to hit it off like this I've promised your mother to do something for Jason but I would like to give you a

---

75) 퀸턴이 허버트와 나누는 대화는 하바드 대학에서 허버트가 연루된 (카드게임과 중간고사에서의) 속임수 스캔들뿐만 아니라 허버트와 캐디와의 성관계를 암시하기도 한다. 따라서 앞 문장이 허버트의 스캔들과 캐디와의 성관계를 부모님께 퀸턴이 말하지나 않을까 하는 맥락을 전하고 있다면, 반면 두 번째 문장은 허버트가 하버드에서 그런 불미스러운 짓을 한 사람이 오직 자신만이 아니며 그냥 재수가 없었을 뿐이었다는 변명과 함께, 캐디의 임신이 자신과의 성관계에서 발생한 것으로 생각하며 때문에 결혼을 강행할 수밖에 없는 자신이 재수 없다는 의미로도 유추할 수 있을 것이다.

76) 하버드대학 내, 드라마 클럽.

hand too Jason would be just as well off here but there's no future in a hole like this for a young fellow like you

Thanks you'd better stick to Jason he'd suit you better than I would

I'm sorry about that business but a kid like I was then I never had a mother like yours to teach me the finger points it would just hurt her unnecessarily to know it yes you're right no need to that includes Candace of course

I said Mother and Father

Look here take a look at me how long do you think you'd last with me

I wont have to last long if you learned to fight up at school too try and see how long I would

You damned little what do you think you're getting at

Try and see

My God the cigar what would your mother say if she found a blister on her mantel just in time too look here Quetin we're about to do something we'll both regret I like you liked you as soon as I saw you I says he must be a damned good fellow whoever he is or Candace wouldn't be so keen on him listen I've been out in the world now for ten years things dont matter so much then you'll find that out let's you and I get together on this thing sons of old Harvard and all I guess I wouldn't know the place now best place for a young fellow in the world I'm going to send my sons there give them a better chance than I had wait dont go yet let's discuss this thing a young man gets these ideas and I'm all for them does him good while he's in school forms his character good for tradition the school but when he gets out into the world he'll have to get his the best way he can because he'll find that everybody else is doing the same thing and be damned to here let's shake hands and let bygones be bygones for your mother's sake remember her health come on give me your hand here look at it it's just out of convent[77] look not a blemish not even been creased yet see here

To hell with your money

No no come on I belong to the family now see I know how it is with a young fellow he has lots of private affairs it's always pretty hard to get the old man to stump up for I know haven't I been there and not so long ago either but now I'm getting married and all specially up there come on dont be a fool listen when we get a chance for a real talk I want to tell you about a little widow over in town[78)]
I've heard that too keep your damned money
Call it a loan then just shut your eyes a minute and you'll be fifty
Keep your hands off of me you'd better get that cigar off the mantel
Tell and be damned then see what it gets you if you were not a damned fool you'd have seen that I've got them too tight for any half-baked Galahad[79)] of a brother your mother's told me about your sort with your head swelled up come in oh come in dear Quentin and I were just getting acquainted talking about Harvard did you want me cant stay away from the old man can she
Go out a minute Herbert I want to talk to Quentin
Come in come in let's all have a gabfest and get acquainted I was just telling Quentin
Go on Herbert go out a while
Well all right then I suppose you and bubber[80)] do want to see one another once more eh
You'd better take that cigar off the mantel
Right as usual my boy then I'll toddle along let them order you around while they can Quentin after day after tomorrow it'll be pretty

---

77) 허버트가 퀸턴에게 (다분히 뇌물성의) 새 돈을 건네주며 하는 이 말에도, 퀸턴의 언어가 얼마나 성적으로 집착하고 있음을 알 수 있다. 그 돈이 "막 수녀원에서 나온" (just out of convent), 순결한 처녀와도 같다고 비유한다.

78) 허버트가 케임브리지에 있는 한 창녀에 대해 퀸턴에게 언급하고 있다.

79) Sir Galahad, 아서 왕의 원탁에 등장하는, Launcelot과 Elaine의 아들이자 성배(the holy grail)를 찾는데 성공한, 기사도와 명예를 대변하는 가장 고결한 기사 중 기사이다.

80) (윗사람이 아랫사람에게 친절한 어조로 부르는) brother.

please to the old man wont it dear give us a kiss honey
Oh stop that save that for day after tomorrow
I'll want interest then dont let Quentin do anything he cant finish oh by the way did I tell Quentin the story about the man's parrot and what happened to it a sad story remind me of that think of it yourself[81)] ta-ta see you in the funnypaper
Well
Well
What are you up to now
Nothing
You're meddling in my business again didn' t you get enough of that last summer[82)]
Caddy you've got fever *You're sick how are you sick*[83)]
I'm just sick. I cant ask.
Shot his voice through the
Not that blackguard Caddy

Now and then the river glinted beyond things in sort of swooping glints, across noon and after. Good after now, though we had passed where he was still pulling upstream majestical in the face of god gods. Better. Gods. God would be canaille too in Boston in Massachusetts. Or maybe just not a husband. The wet oars winking him along in bright winks and female palms. Adulant. Adulant if not a husband he'd ignore God. *That blackguard, Caddy* The river glinted away beyond a swooping curve.

---

81) 허버트는 퀸턴에게 (앵무새처럼) 후자가 자신에 대해 들은 이야기(하버드 스캔들이나, 아니면 캐디와의 성행위)를 반복하지 말라고 경고한다.

82) 캐디는 자신의 결혼을 말리는 퀸턴을 두고, 작년 여름 달턴으로부터 그녀를 보호하기 위해 벌인 일처럼, 이번에도 자신의 일에 오빠가 관여한다고 불만을 토로한다.

83) 허버트와의 대화 후 다시 이전의 기억, 즉 캐디의 방에서 가진 그녀와의 대화로 이어지며, 캐디의 "아픈" 상태는 그녀의 임신상태를 말하지만 퀸턴은 아프다는 그녀의 말을 제대로 이해하지 못하고 있다.

I'm sick you'll have to promise

Sick how are you sick

I'm just sick I cant ask anybody yet promise you will

If they need any looking after it's because of you how are sick

Under the window we could hear the car leaving for the station, the 8:10 train. To bring back cousins. Heads. Increasing himself head by head but not barbers. Manicure girls. We had a blood horse once. In the stable yes, but under leather a cur. *Quentin has shot all of their voices through the floor of Caddy's room*

The car stopped. I got off, into the middle of my shadow. A road crossed the track. There was a wooden marquee with an old man eating something out of a paper bag, and then the car was out of hearing too. The road went into trees, where it would be shady, but June foliage in New England not much thicker than April at home. I could see a smoke stack. I turned my back to it, tramping my shadow into the dust. *There was something terrible in me sometimes at night I could see it grinning at me I could see it through them grinning at me through their faces it's gone now and I'm sick*

Caddy

Dont touch me just promise

If you're sick you cant

Yes I can after that it'll be all right it wont matter dont let them send him to Jackson promise

I promise Caddy Caddy

Dont touch me dont touch me

What does it look like Caddy

What

That that grins at you that thing through them

I could still see the smoke stack. That's where the water would be, healing out to the sea and the peaceful grottoes. Tumbling peacefully they would, and when He said Rise only the flat irons. When Versh and I hunted all day we wouldn't take any lunch, and at twelve oclock I'd get hungry. I'd stay hungry until about one, then all of a sudden I'd even forget that I wasn't hungry anymore. *The street lamps go down the hill then heard the car go down the hill. The chair-arm flat cool smooth under my forehead shaping the chair the apple tree leaning on my hair above the eden clothes by the nose seen* You've got fever I felt it yesterday it's like being near a stove.

Dont touch me.

Caddy you cant do it if you are sick. That blackguard.

I've got to marry somebody. *Then they told me the bone would have to be broken again*[84)]

At least I couldn't see the smoke stack. The road went beside a wall. Trees leaned over the wall, sprayed with sunlight. The stone was cool. Walking near it you could feel the coolness. Only our country was not like this country. There was something about just walking through it. A kind of still and violent fecundity that satisfied even bread-hunger like. Flowing around you, not brooding and nursing every niggard stone. Like it were put to makeshift for enough green to go around among the trees and even the blue of distance not that rich chimaera.[85)] *told me the bone would have to be broken again and inside me it began to say Ah Ah Ah and I began to sweat. What do I care I know what a broken leg is all it is it wont be anything I'll just have to stay in the house a little longer that's all and my jaw-muscles getting numb and my mouth saying Wait Wait just a minute through the sweat ah ah ah behind my teeth and Father damn that horse damn that horse. Wait it's my fault. He came along the fence every morning with a basket toward the kitchen dragging a*

---

84) 앞서 캐디의 '아픈' 상태에 대한 기억들은 그 자신이 말에서 떨어져 다리를 부러뜨린 기억과 연결되고 있다.

85) "Only our country"에서 여기까지는, 퀜턴이 (빈곤과 검약으로 대변되는) 뉴잉글랜드 지방과 (부분적으로 사자, 염소, 용의 형상을 모두 가진 괴물 키메라가 상징하듯, 괴기스러울 정도로 과다한 풍요로움으로 넘치는 자연환경을 가진) 남부지방을 비교하고 있다.

stick along the fence every morning I dragged myself to the window cast and all and laid for him with a piece of coal[86] *Dilsey said you goin to ruin yoself aint you got mo mo sense than that not fo days since you bruck hit. Wait I'll get used to it in a minute wait just a minute I'll get*

Even sound seemed to fail in this air, like the air was worn out with carrying sounds so long. A dog's voice carries further than a train, in the darkness anyway. And some people's. Niggers. Louis Hatcher never even used his horn carrying it and that old lantern. I said, "Louis, when was the last time you cleaned that lantern?"

"I cleant hit a little while back. You member when all dat flood-watter wash dem folks away up yonder? I cleant hit dat ve'y day. Old woman and me settin fo de fire dat night and she say 'Louis, whut you gwine do ef dat flood git out dis fur?' and I say 'Dat's a fack. I reckon I had better clean dat lantun up.' So I cleant hit dat night."

"That food was way up in Pennsylvania" , I said. "It couldn't ever have got down this far."

"Dat's whut you says," Louis said. "Watter kin git des ez high en wet in Jefferson ez hit kin in Pennsylvaney, I reckon. Hit's de folks dat says d high watter cant git dis fur dat comes floatin out on de ridge-pole,[87] too."

"Did you and Martha get out that night?"

"We done jest dat. I cleant dat lantun and me and her sot de balance of de night on top o dat knoll back de graveyard. En ef I'd a knowed of aihy[88] one higher, we'd a been on hit instead."

"And you haven't cleaned that lantern since them."

---

86) "He"는 아마 캐디의 첫 애인("pimpled-faced infant")쯤으로 생각할 수 있으며, 퀜틴은 당시 말에서 떨어져 다리가 부러진 상태이지만, 아침마다 누이를 찾아오는 그 녀석을 몰아내기 위해 안간힘을 다하는 퀜틴의 모습을 볼 수 있다.

87) 집 지붕(의 용마루) 위.

88) "ere a"로 해당하는 방언으로 'any' 의 의미이다.

"Whut I want to clean hit when dey aint no need?"

"You mean, until another flood comes along?"

"Hit kep us outen dat un."

"Oh, come on, Uncle Louis," I said.

"Yes, suh. You do yo way en I do mine. Ef all I got to do to keep outen de high watter is to clean dis yere lantun, I wont quoil[89] wid no man."

"Unc'Louis wouldn't ketch nothin wid a light he could see by," Versh said.

"I wuz huntin possums in dis country when dey was still drowndin nits in yo pappy's head wid coal oil, boy," Louis said. "Ketchin um, too."

"Dat's de troof," [90] Versh said. "I reckon Unc' Louis done caught mo possums than aihy man in dis country."

"Yes, suh," Louis said. "I got plenty light fer possums to see, all right. I aint heard none o dem complainin. Hush, now. Dar he. Whooey. Hum awn, dawg." And we'd sit in the dry leaves that whispered a little with the slow respiration of our waiting and with the slow breathing of the earth and the windless October, the rank smell of the lantern fouling the brittle air, listening to the dogs and to the echo of Louis' voice dying away.[91] He never raised it, yet on a still night we have heard it from our front porch. When he called the dogs in he sounded just like the horn he carried slung on his shoulder and never used, but clearer, mellower, as though his voice were a part of darkness and silence, coiling out of it, coiling into it again.

---

89) quarrel.

90) truth.

91) 여기 퀸턴이 묘사하고 있는, 엉클 루이스와의 주머니쥐(possum) 사냥에 대한 기억은 퀸턴이 좋아하는 어린시절 기억 중 하나이다. 퀸턴이 좋아했던 기억에는 캄슨 집안과 가족은 포함되지 않으며, 그것들은 모두 흑인들(딜시, 루이스 해처, 그리고 버지)과 함께한 기억들이다.

WhoOoooo. WhoOoooo. WhoOooooooooooooooo. *Got to marry somebody*

Have there been very many Caddy

I dont know too many will you look after Benjy and Father

You dont know whose it is then does he know[92)]

Dont touch me will you look after Benjy and Father

I began to feel the water before I came to the bridge. The bridge was of gray stone, lichened, dappled with slow moisture where the fungus crept. Beneath it the water was clear and still in the shadow, whispering and clucking about the stone in fading swirls of spinning sky. *Caddy that*

I've got to marry somebody Versh told me about a man who mutilated himself. He went into the woods and did it with a razor, sitting in a ditch. A broken razor flinging them[93)] backward over his shoulder the same motion complete the jerked skein of blood backward not looping. But that's not it. It's not not having them. It's never to have had them then I could say O That That's Chinese I dont know Chinese.[94)] And Father said it's because you are a virgin: dont you see? Women are never virgins. Purity is a negative state and therefore contrary to nature. It's nature is hurting you not Caddy and I said That's just words and he said So is virginity and I said you dont know. You cant know and he said. Yes. On the instant when we come to realise that tragedy is second-hand.

---

92) 퀀틴은 누이의 임신을 인지하면서 그녀의 과거 성적 행각을 캐묻고 있다. "he"는 허버트일 확률이 높으며, 퀀틴은 캐디가 누구의 아이를 가졌는지에 대해 허버트가 얼마나 알고 있는지를 묻고 있다.

93) them = testicles.

94) 퀀틴의 성적 두려움은 급기야 성에 대한 그의 무지에의 욕망과 직결되어 드러나고 있다. 그는 성에 대해 알고 싶지도 않으며, 자신의 세계나 마음속에 성이 존재하지 않기를 바라며, 그의 그러한 욕망은 성을 알지 못할 뿐만 아니라 알고 싶지도 않는 중국어에 비유하게 한다.

Where the shadow of the bridge fell I could see down for a long way, but not as far as the bottom. When you leave a leaf in water a long time after a while the tissue will be gone and the delicate fibers waving slow as the motion of sleep. They dont touch one another, no matter how knotted up they once were, no matter how close they lay once to the bones. And maybe when He says Rise the eyes will come floating up too, out of the deep quiet and the sleep, to look on glory. And after a while the flat irons would come floating up. I hid them under the end of the bridge[95] and went back and leaned on the rail.

I could not see the bottom, but I could see a long way into the motion of the water before the eye gave out, and then I saw a shadow hanging like a fat arrow stemming into the current. Mayflies skimmed in and out of the shadow of the bridge just above the surface. *If it could just be a hell beyond that: the clean flame the two of us more than dead. Then you will have only me then only me then the two of us amid the pointing and the horror beyond the clean flame* The arrow increased without motion, then in a quick swirl the trout lipped a fly beneath the surface with that sort of gigantic delicacy of an elephant picking up a peanut. The fading vortex drifted away down stream and then I saw the arrow again, nose into the current, wavering delicately to the motion of the water above which the May flies slanted and poised. *Only you and me then amid the pointing and the horror walled by the clean flame*

The trout hung, delicate and motionless among the wavering shadows. Three boys with fishing poles came onto the bridge and we leaned on the rail and looked down ay the trout. They knew the fish. He was a neighborhood character.

"They've been trying to catch that trout for twenty-five years. There's a store in Boston offers a twenty-five dollar fishing rod to

---

95) 퀸턴은 아까 철물점에서 산 다리미 두 개("flat irons")를 자신이 나중에 돌아와 익사하게 될 (아마도 같은) 다리 아래 숨기고 있다.

anybody that can catch him."

"Why dont you all catch him, then? Wouldn't you like to have a twenty-five dollar fishing rod?"

"Yes," they said. They leaned on the rail, looking down at the trout. "I sure would," one said.

"I wouldn't take the rod," the second said. "I'd take the money instead."

"Maybe they wouldn't do that," the first said. "I bet he'd make you take the rod."

"Then I'd sell it."

"You couldn't get twenty-five dollars for it."

"I'd take what I could get, then. I can catch just as many fish with this pole as I could with a twenty-five dollar one." Then they talked about what they would do with twenty-five dollars. They all talked at once, their voices insistent and contradictory and impatient, making of unreality a possibility, then a probability, then an incontrovertible fact, as people will when their desires become words.

"I'd buy a horse and wagon," the second said.

"Yes you would," the others said.

"I would. I know where I can buy one for twenty-five dollars. I know the man."

"Who is it?"

"That's all right who it is. I can buy it for twenty-five dollars."

"Yah," the others said. "He dont know any such thing. He's just talking."

"Do you think so?" the boy said. They continued to jeer at him, but he said nothing more. He leaned on the rail, looking down at the trout which he had already spent, and suddenly the acrimony, the conflict, was gone from their voices, as if to them too it was as though he had captured the fish and bought his horse and wagon, they too partaking of that adult trait of being convinced of anything by an assumption of silent superiority. I suppose that people, using themselves and each other so much by words, are at least consistent in attributing wisdom to a still tongue, and for a while I could feel the other two seeking swiftly for some means by which to cope with him, to rob him of his horse and wagon.

"You couldn't get twenty-five dollars for that pole," the first said. "I bet anything you couldn't."

"He hasn't caught that trout yet," the third said suddenly, then they both cried:

"Yah, what'd I tell you? What's the man's name? I dare you to tell. There aint any such man."

"Ah, shut up," the second said. "Look. Here he comes again." They leaned on the rail, motionless, identical, their poles slanting slenderly in the sunlight, also identical, their poles slanting slenderly in the sunlight, also identical. The trout rose without haste, a shadow in faint wavering increase; again the little vortex faded slowly downstream. "Gee," the first one murmured.

"We dont try to catch him anymore," he said. "We just watch Boston folks that come out and try."

"Is he the only fish in this pool?"

"Yes. He ran all the others out. The best place to finish around here is down at the Eddy."

"No it aint," the second said. "It's better at Bigelow's Mill two to one." Then they argued for a while about which was the best fishing and then left off all of a sudden to watch the trout rise again and the broken swirl of water suck down a little of the sky. I asked how far it was to the nearest town. They told me.

"But the closets car line is that way," the second said, pointing back down the road. "Where are you going?"

"Nowhere. Just walking."

"You from the college?"

"Yes. Are there any factories in that town?"

"Factories?" They looked at me.

"No," the second said. "Not there." They looked at my clothes. "You looking for work?"

"How about Bigelow's Mill?" the third said. "That's a factory."

"Factory my eye. He means a sure enough factory."

"One with a whistle," I said. "I haven't heard any one oclock whistles yet."

"Oh," the second said. "There's a clock in the unitarial steeple. You can find out the time from that. Haven't you got a watch on that chain?"

"I broke it this morning." I showed them my watch. They examined it gravely.

"It's still running," the second said. "What does a watch like that cost?"

"It was a present," I said. "My father gave it to me when I graduated from high school."

"Are you a Canadian?" the third said. He had red hair.

"Canadian?"

"He dont talk like them," the second said. "I've heard them talk. He talks like they do in minstrel shows."[96)]

"Say," the third said. "Aint you afraid he' ll hit you?"

"Hit me?"

"You said he talks like a colored man."

"Ah, dry up," the second said. "You can see the steeple when you get over that hill there."

I thanked them. "I hope you have good luck. Only dont catch that old fellow down there. He deserves to be let alone."

"Cant anybody catch that fish," the first said. They leaned on the rail, looking down onto the water, the three poles like three slanting threads of yellow fire in the sun. I walked upon my shadow,

---

96) 퀸턴의 남부 악센트를 지적하는 말이다. minstrel show는 흑인들로 분장한 백인연예인들의 쇼이며, 유럽에서 그 기원을 찾을 수 있다. 미국에서는 1830년대부터 그 모습을 볼 수 있으며, 노동자계층의 백인들이 (남부농장의) 흑인노예들로 분장하여 그들의 음악과 춤을 모방하며, 흑인문화를 즐기는 동시에 패러디하는 쇼 형식이다.

tramping it into the dappled shade of trees again. The road curved, mounting away from the water. It crossed the hill, then descended winding, carrying the eye, the mind on ahead beneath a still green tunnel, and the square cupola above the trees and round eye of the clock but far enough. I sat down at the roadside. The grass was ankle deep, myriad. The shadows on the road were as still as if they had been put there with a stencil, with slanting pencils of sunlight. But it was only a train, and after a while it died away beyond the trees, the long sound, and then I could hear my watch and the train dying away, as though it were running through another month or another summer somewhere, rushing away under the poised gull and all things rushing. Except Gerald. He would be sort of grand too, pulling in lonely state across the noon, rowing himself right out of noon, up the long bright air like an apotheosis, mounting into a drowsing infinity where only he and the gull, the one terrifically motionless, the other in a steady and measured pull and recover that partook of inertia itself, the world punily beneath their shadows on the sun.[97] *Caddy that blackguard that blackguard Caddy*[98]

Their voices came over the hill, and the three slender poles like balanced threads of running fire. They looked at me passing, not slowing.

---

97) "Except Gerald . . . ."에서 여기까지: 노를 젓고 있는 제랄드의 모습은, 갈매기처럼, (퀸턴 자신의 파괴적인 시간과는 달리) 시간의 흐름으로부터 벗어나 있는("rowing himself right out of noon") 이미지이다. 여기 퀸턴은 남봉꾼인 제랄드를 혐오하기도 하지만 동시에 시간과 아주 편안한 관계를 형성해내는 듯한 제랄드를 부러워도 하는 부분이다. 퀸턴은 상상 속에서 제랄드를 위대하면서도 정지된 영원성과도 같은 상징적인 존재로 의미화하면서, 마치 이 허접한 세계를 초월해 있는 신적인 존재("an apotheosis")의 반열에 올리고 있다. 확실한 것은 제랄드가 물 위에서 아주 편안히 움직이고 있다면, 반면 퀸턴에게 그 물은 오직 죽음과 망각만을 상징하고 있는 것이다.

98) 제랄드에 대한 생각은 곧 캐디의 결혼식 전 그녀와 나눈 대화의 기억 속으로 빠져든다. 여기 "blackguard"는 허버트이다.

"Well," I said. "I dont see him."

"We didn't try to catch him," the first said. "You cant catch that fish."

"There's the clock," the second said, pointing. "You can tell the time when you get a little closer."

"Yes," I said. "All right." I got up. "You all going to town?"

"We're going to the Eddy for club," the first said.

"You cant catch anything at the Eddy," the second said.

"I guess you want to go to the mill, with a lot of fellows splashing and scaring all the fish away."

"You cant catch any fish at the Eddy."

"We wont catch none nowhere if we dont go on," the third said.

"I dont see why you keep on talking about the Eddy," the second said.

"You cant catch anything there."

"You dont have to go," the first said. "You're not tied to me."

"Let's go to the mill and go swimming," the third said.

"I'm going to the Eddy and fish," the first said. "You can do as you please."

"Say, how long has it been since you heard of anybody catching a fish at the Eddy?" the second said to the third.

"Let's go to the mill and go swimming," the third said. The cupola sank slowly beyond the trees, with the round face of the clock far enough yet. We went on in the dappled shade. We came to an orchard, pink and white. It was full of bees; already we could heard them.

"Let's go to the mill and go swimming," the third said. A lane turned off besides the orchard. The third boy slowed and halted. The first went on, flecks of sunlight slipping along the pole across his shoulder and down the back of his shirt. "Come on," the third said. The second boy stopped too. *Why must you marry somebody Caddy*

Do you want me to say it do you think that if I say it it wont be

"Let's go up to the mill," he said. "Come on."

The first boy went on. His bare feet made no sound, failing softer than leaves in the thin dust. In the orchard the bees sounded like a wind getting up, a sound caught by a spell just under crescendo and sustained. The lane went along the wall, arched over, shattered with bloom, dissolving into trees. Sunlight slanted into it, sparse and eager. Yellow butterflies flickered along the shade like flecks of sun.

"What do you want to go to the Eddy for?" the second boy said. "You can fish at the mill if you want to."

"Ah, let him go," the third said. They looked after the first boy. Sunlight slid patchily across his walking shoulders, glinting along the pole like yellow ants.

"Kenny," the second said. *Say it to Father will you I will am my fathers Progenitive I invented him created I him Say it to him it will not be for he will say I was not and then you and I since philoprogenitive*

"Ah, come on," the third boy said. "They're already in." They looked after the first boy. "Yah," they said suddenly, "go on then, mamma's boy. If he goes swimming he'll get his head wet and then he'll get a licking." They turned into the lane and went on, the yellow butterfies slanting about them along the shade.

it is because there is nothing else I believe there is something else but there may not be and then I You will find that even injustice is scarcely worthy of what you believe yourself to be He paid me no attention, his jaw set in profile, his face turned a little away beneath his broken hat.

"Why dont you go swimming with them?" I said. that *blackguard Caddy*

Were you trying to pick a fight with him were you

A liar and a scoundrel Caddy was dropped from his club for cheating at cards got sent to Coventry caught cheating at midterm exams and expelled[99]

Well what about it I'm not going to play cards with

"Do you like fishing better than swimming?" I said. The sound of the bees diminished, sustained yet, as though instead of sinking into silence, silence merely increased between us, as water rises. The road curved again and became a street between shady lawns with white houses. *Caddy that blackguard can you think of benjy and Father and do it not of me*

What else can I think about what else have I thought about The boy turned from the street. He climbed a picket fence without looking back and crossed the lawn to a tree and laid the pole down and climbed into the fork of the tree and sat there, his back to the road and the dappled sun motionless at last upon his white shirt. *else have I thought about I cant even cry I died last year I told you I had but I didn't know then what I meant I didn't know what I was saying* Some days in late August at home are like this, the air thin and eager like this, with something in it sad and nostalgic and familiar. Man the sum of his climatic experiences Father said. Man the sum of what have you. A problem in impure properties carried tediously to an unvarying nil: stalmate of dust and desire. *but now I know I'm dead I tell you*

Then why must you listen we can go away you and Benjy and me where nobody knows us where The buggy was drawn by a white horse, his feet clopping in the thin dust; spidery wheels chattering thin and dry, moving uphill beneath a rippling shawl of leaves. Elm. No: ellum. Ellum.

On what on your school money the money they sold the pasture for so you could go to Harvard dont you see you've got to finish now if you dont finish he'll have nothing

Sold the pasture His white shirt was motionless in the fork, in the flickering shade. The wheels were spidery. Beneath the sag of the buggy the hooves neatly rapid like the motion of a lady doing embroidery, diminishing without progress like a figure on a treadmill

---

99) 허버트는 카드게임에서 속임수를 사용해 대학 클럽으로부터 추방당하며("sent to Coventry"), 중간고사 때는 속임수를 써 학교에서 제명되었다.

being drawn rapidly offstage. The street turned again. I could see the white cupola, the round stupid assertion of the clock. *Sold the pasture*

Father will be dead in a year they say if he doesn't stop drinking and he wont stop he cant stop since I since last summer and then they'll send Benjy to Jackson I cant cry I cant even cry one minute she was standing in the door the next minute he was pulling at her dress and bellowing his voice hammered back and forth between the walls in waves and she shrinking against the wall getting smaller and smaller with her white face her eyes like thumbs dug into it until he pushed her out of the room his voice hammering back and forth as though its own momentum would not let it stop as though there were no place for it in silence bellowing

When you opened the door a bell tinkled, but just once, high and clear and small in the neat obscurity above the door, as though it were gauged and tempered to make that single clear small sound so as not to wear the bell out nor to require the expenditure of too much silence in restoring it when the door opened upon the recent warm scent of baking; a little dirty child with eyes like a toy bear's and two patent-leather pig-tails.

"Hello, sister." Her face was like a cup of milk dashed with coffee in the sweet warm emptiness. "Anybody here?"

But she merely watched me until a door opened and the lady came. Above the counter where the ranks of crisp shapes behind the glass her neat gray face her hair tight and sparse from her neat gray skull, spectacles in neat gray rims riding approaching like something on a wire, like a cash box in a store. She looked like a librarian. Something among dusty shelves of ordered certitudes long divorced from reality, desiccating peacefully, as if a breath of that air which sees in justice done

"Two of these, please, ma'am."

From under the counter she produced a square cut from a newspaper and laid it on the counter and lifted the two buns out. The little girl watched them with still and unwinking eyes like two currants floating motionless in a cup of weak coffee Land of the kike home of the wop.[100] Watching the bread, the neat gray hand, a broad gold band on the left forefinger, knuckled there by a blue knuckle.

"Do you do your own baking, ma'am?"

"Sir?" she said. Like that. Sir? Like on the stage. Sir? "Five cents. Was there anything else?"

"No, ma'am. Not for me. This lady wants something." She was not tall enough to see over the case, so she went to the end of the counter and looked at the little girl.

"Did you bring her in here?"

"No, ma'am. She was here when I came."

"You little wretch," she said. She came out around the counter, but she didn't touch the little girl. "Have you got anything in your pockets?"

"She hasn't got any pockets," I said. "She wasn't doing anything. She was just standing here, waiting for you."

"Why didn't the bell ring, then?" She glared at me. She just needed a bunch if switches, a blackboard behind her 2 x 2 e 5. "She'll hide it under her dress and a body'd never know it. You, child. How'd you get in here?"

The little girl said nothing. She looked at the woman, then she gave me a flying black glance and looked at the woman again. "Them foreigners," the woman said. "How'd she get in without the bell ringing?"

"She came in when I opened the door," I said.[101] "It rang once for both of us. She couldn't reach anything from here, anyway. Besides, I dont think she would. Would you, sister?" The little girl looked at

---

100) 북부에 대한 퀸턴의 사회적/인종적 편견을 엿볼 수 있다. "kike"는 유대인, "wop"은 이탈리아인을 지칭하는 인종비하적인 표현이다.

101) 이탈리아 소녀를 위해 엄한 외모와 함께 의심 많고 인종차별적인 가게 여주인을 향해 퀸턴은 거짓말을 하고 있다.

me, secretive, contemplative. "What do you want? bread?"

She extended her fist. It uncurled upon a nickel, moist and dirty, moist dirt ridged into her flesh. The coin was damp and warm. I could smell it, faintly metallic.

"Have you got a five cent loaf, please, ma'am?"

From beneath the counter she produced a square cut from a newspaper sheet and laid it on the counter and wrapped a loaf into it. I laid the coin and another one on the counter. "And another one of those buns, please, ma'am."

She took another bun from the case. "Give me that parcel," she said. I gave it to her and she unwrapped it and put the third bun in and wrapped it and took up the coins and found two coppers in her apron and gave them to me. I handed them to the little girl. Her fingers closed about them, damp and hot, like worms.

"You going to give her that bun?" the woman said.

"Yessum," I said. "I expect your cooking smells as good to her as it does to me."

I took up the two packages and gave the bread to the little girl, the woman all iron-gray behind the counter, watching us with cold certitude. "You wait a minute," she said. She went to the rear. The door opened again and closed. The little girl watched me, holding the bread against her dirty dress.

"What's your name?" I said. She quit looking at me, but she was still motionless. She didn't even seem to breathe. The woman returned. She had a funny looking thing in her hand. She carried it sort of like it might have been a dead pet rat.

"Here," she said. The child looked at her. "Take it," the woman said, jabbing it at the little girl. "It just looks peculiar. I calculate you wont know the difference when you eat it. Here. I cant stand here all day." The child took it, still watching her. The woman rubbed her hands on her apron. "I got to have that bell fixed," she said. She went to the door and jerked it open. The little bell tinkled once, faint and clear and invisible. We moved toward the door and the woman's peering back.

"Thank you for the cake," I said.

"Them foreigners," she said, staring up into the obscurity where the bell tinkled. "Take my advice and stay clear of them, young man."

"Yessum," I said. "Come on, sister." We went out. "Thank you, ma'am."

She swung the door to, then jerked it open again, making the bell give forth its single small note. "Foreigners," she said, peering up at the bell.

We went on. "Well," I said. "How about some ice cream?" She was eating the gnarled cake. "Do you like ice cream?" She gave me a black still look. chewing. "Come on."

We came to the drugstore and had some ice cream. She wouldn't put the loaf down. "Why not put it down so you can eat better?" I said, offering to take it. But she held to it, chewing the ice cream like it was taffy. The bitten cake lay on the table. She ate the ice cream steadily, then she fell to on the cake again, looking about at the showcases. I finished mine and we went out.

"Which way do you live?" I said.

A buggy, the one with the white horse it was. Only Doc Peabody is fat. Three hundred pounds. You ride with him on the uphill side, holding on Children.[102] Walking easier than holding uphill. *Seen the doctor yet have you seen Caddy*

I dont have to I cant ask now afterward it will be all right it wont matter

Because women so delicate so mysterious Father said. Delicate

---

102) 하얀색 말이 끌고 있는 일인승 마차가 지나가는 것을 보자, 퀸턴은 고향의 의사(Doc Peabody)를 기억해내면서, 그 의사가 몸무게가 너무 많이 나가는 바람에, 마차가 기울어져 마치 옆에 탄 아이가 언덕(의사) 위에 앉아 마차를 꽉 잡고 있는 듯한 이미지를 떠올린다.

equilibrium of periodical filth between two moons balanced. Moons he said full and yellow as harvest moons her hips thighs. Outside outside of them always but. Yellow. Feet soles with walking like. Then know that some man that all those mysterious and imperious concealed. With all that inside of them shapes an outward suavity waiting for a touch to. Liquid putrefaction like drowned thing floating like pale rubber flabbily filled getting the odor of honeysuckle all mixed up.[103)]

"You'd better take your bread on home, hadn't you?"

She looked at me. She chewed quietly and steadily; at regular intervals a small distention passed smoothly down her throat. I opened my package and gave her one of the buns. "Goodbye," I said.

I went on. Then I looked back. She was behind me. "Do you live down this way?" She said nothing. She walked beside me, under my elbow sort of, eating. We went on. It was quiet, hardly anyone about *getting the odor of honeysuckle all mixed She would have told me not to let me sit there on the steps hearing her door twilight slamming hearing Benjy still crying Supper she would have to come down then getting honeysuckle all mixed up in it* We reached the corner.

"Well, I've got to go down this way," I said. "Goodbye." She stopped too. She swallowed the last of the cake, then she began on the bun, watching me across it. "Goodbye," I said. I turned into the street and went on, but I went to the next corner before I stopped.

"Which way do you live?" I said. "This way?" I pointed down the

---

103) 이 문단은 퀸턴과 아버지 캄슨씨의 여성관을 특징짓는, 여성과 여성 섹슈얼리티에 대한 놀라움, 공포, 혐오와 불결함 등 많은 감정들이 복잡하게 연결되고 있다. 마지막 문장에서는 특히 여성의 멘스와 성에 대한 퀸턴의 혐오감이 잘 드러나면서, 여성의 성에 대한 그의 개인적인 상징물이라 할 수 있는 인동덩굴의 향기와 연결되고 있다. 그리고 중간 부분의 "Feet soles with walking like"은, 로스와 폴크에 의하면, 성교시 (여성의) 발과 다리의 움직임을 묘사한다고 지적하면서, 이 부분은 아마 퀸턴이 캐디와 달턴의 성관계 장면을 몰래 엿본, 실제 아니면 혼돈된 기억의 일부로 본다.

street. She just looked at me. "Do you live over that way? I bet you live close to the station, where the trains are. Dont you?" She just looked at me, serene and secret and chewing. The street was empty both ways, with quiet lawns and houses neat among the trees, but no one at all except back there. We turned and went back. Two men sat in chairs in front of a store.

"Do you all know this little girl? She sort of took up with me and I cant find where she live."

They quit looking at me and looked at her.

"Must be one of them new Italian families," one said. He wore a rusty frock coat. "I've seen her before. What's your name, little girl?" She looked at them blackly for a while, her jaws moving steadily. She swallowed without ceasing to chew.

"Maybe she cant speak English," the other said.

"They sent her after bread," I said. "She must be able to speak something."

"What's your pa's name?" the first said. "Pete? Joe? name John huh?" She took another bite from the bun.

"What must I do with her?" I said. "She just follows me. I've got to get back to Boston."

"You from the college?"

"Yes, sir. And I've got to get on back."

"You might go up the street and turn her over to Anse. He'll be up at the livery stable. The marshal."

"I reckon that's what I'll have to do," I said. "I've got to do something with her. Much obliged. Come on, sister."

We went up the street, on the shady side, where the shadow of the broken façade blotted slowly across the road. We came to the livery stable. The marshal wasn't there. A man sitting in a chair tilted in the broad low door, where a dark cool breeze smelling of ammonia blew among the ranked stalls, said to look at the postoffice. He didn't know her either.

"Them furriners. I cant tell one from another. You might take her across the tracks where they live, and maybe somebody'll claim her."

We went to the postoffice. It was back down the street. The man in the frock coat was opening a newspaper.

"Anse just drove out of town," he said. "I guess you'd better go down past the station and walk past them houses by the river. Somebody there'll know her."

"I guess I'll have to," I said. "Come on, sister." She pushed the last piece of the bun into her mouth and swallowed it. "Want another?" I said. She looked at me, chewing, her eyes black and unwinking and friendly. I took the other two buns out and gave her one and bit into the other. I asked a man where the station was and he showed me. "Come on, sister."

We reached the station and crossed the tracks, where the river was. A bridge crossed it, and a street of jumbled frame houses followed the river, backed onto it. A shabby street, but with an air heterogeneous and vivid too. In the center of an untrimmed plot enclosed by a fence of gaping and broken pickets stood an ancient lopsided surrey and a weathered house from an upper window of which hung a garment of vivid pink.

"Does that look like your house?" I said. She looked at me over the bun. "This one?" I said, pointing. She just chewed, but it seemed to me that I discerned something affirmative, acquiescent even if it wasn't eager, in her air. "This one?" I said. "Come on, then." I entered the broken gate. I looked back at her. "Here?" I said. "This look like your house?"

She nodded her head rapidly, looking at me, gnawing into the damp halfmoon of the bread. We went on. A walk of broken random flags,[104] speared by fresh coarse blades of grass, led to the broken stoop. There was no movement about the house at all, and the pink garment hanging in no wind from the upper window. There was a

---

104) flagstones.

bell pull with a porcelain knob, attached to about six feet of wire when I stopped pulling and knocked. The little girl had the crust edgeways in her chewing mouth.

A woman opened the door. She looked at me, then she spoke rapidly to the little girl in Italian, with a rising inflexion, then a pause, interrogatory. She spoke to her again, the little girl looking at her across the end of the crust, pushing it into her mouth with a dirty hand.

"She says she lives here," I said. "I met her down town. Is this your bread?"

"No spika," the woman said. She spoke to the little girl again. The little girl just looked at her.

"No live here?" I said. I pointed to the girl, then at her, then at the door. The woman shook her head. She spoke rapidly. She came to the edge of the porch and pointed down the road, speaking.

I nodded violently too. "You come show?" I said. I took her arm, waving my other hand toward the road. She spoke swiftly, pointing. "You come show," I said, trying to lead her down the steps.

"Si, si," she said, holding back, showing me whatever it was. I nodded again.

"Thanks. Thanks. Thanks." I went down the steps and walked toward the gate, not running, but pretty fast. I reached the gate and stopped and looked at her for a while. The crust was gone now, and she looked at me with her black, friendly stare. The woman stood on the stoop, watching us.

"Come on, then," I said. "We'll have to find the right one sooner or later."

She moved along just under my elbow. We went on. The houses all seemed empty. Not a soul in sight. A sort of breathlessness that empty houses have. Yet they couldn't all be empty. All the different rooms, if you could just slice the walls away all of a sudden. Madam, your daughter, if you please. No. Madam, for God's sake, your daughter. She moved along just under my elbow, her shiny tight pigtails, and then the last house played out and the road curved out of sight beyond a wall, following the river. The woman was emerging from the broken gate, with a shawl over her head and clutched under her chin. The road curved on, empty. I found a coin and gave it to the little girl. A quarter. "Goodbye, sister," I said. Then I ran.

I ran fast, not looking back. just before the road curved away I looked back. She stood in the road, a small figure clasping the loaf of bread to her filthy little dress, her eyes still and black and unwinking. I ran on.

A lane turned from the road. I entered it and after a while I slowed to a fast walk. The lane went between back premises—unpainted houses with more of those gay and startling colored garments on lines, a barn broken-backed, decaying quietly among rank orchard trees, unpruned and weed-choked, pink and white and murmurous with sunlight and with bees. I looked back. The entrance to the lane was empty. I slowed still more, my shadow pacing me, dragging its head through the weeds that hid the fence.

The lane went back to a barred gate, became defunctive[105] in grass, a mere path scarred quietly into new grass. I climbed the gate into a wood-lot and crossed it and came to another wall and followed that one, my shadow behind me now. There were vines and creepers where at home would be honeysuckle. Coming and coming especially in the dust when it rained, getting honeysuckle all mixed up in it as though it were not enough without that, not unbearable enough. *What did you let him for kiss kiss*

I didn't let him I made him watching me getting mad What do you think of that? Red print of my hand coming up through her face like turning a light on under your hand her eyes going bright

105) defunct = decreased or died out. "defunctive"는 포크너 작품들에서 "funereal"(장례식의)의 의미로 자주 등장하는 용어이며, defunct(죽은)를 그렇게 사용하고 있다. 여기서 그것은 (길이) "없어진/사라진"의 의미로 해석할 수 있다.

It's not for kissing I slapped you. Girl's elbows at fifteen Father said you swallow like you had a fishbone in your throat what's the matter with you and Caddy across the table not to look at me. It's for letting it be some darn town squirt I slapped you you will will you now I guess you say calf rope. My red hand coming up out of her face. What do you think of that scouring her head into the. Grass sticks criss-crossed into the flesh tingling scouring her head. Say calf rope[106] *say it*

I didn' let kiss a dirty girl like Natalie anyway The wall went into shadow, and then my shadow, I had tricked it again. I had forgot about the river curving along the road. I climbed the wall. And then she watched me jump down, holding the loaf against her dress.

I stood in the weeds and we looked at one another for a while.

"Why didn't you tell me you lived out this way, sister?" The loaf was wearing slowly out of the paper; already it needed a new one. "Well, come on then and show me the house." *not a dirty girl like Natalie. It was raining we could hear it on the roof, sighing through the high sweet emptiness of the barn.*

There? touching her

Not there

There?[107] *not raining hard but we couldn't hear anything but the roof and if it was my blood or her blood*

She pushed me down the ladder and ran off and left me Caddy did

Was it there it hurt you when Caddy did ran off was it there

Oh She walked just under my elbow, the top of her patent leather head, the loaf fraying out of the newspaper.

"If you dont get home pretty soon you're going to wear that loaf

---

106) 누군가에게 "calf rope"을 말하게 하는 것은 항복을 인정하라고 강요하는 것이다.

107) 이 장면은 퀸턴과 나탈리가 함께 하고 있는 장면에 질투난 캐디가 끼어들며 나탈리를 밀쳐낸 후, 상처를 입은 나탈리에게 퀸턴이 일종의 "의사"놀이, 즉 그녀의 몸을 만지고 있다.

out. And then what'll your mamma say?" *I bet I can lift you up*

You cant I'm too heavy

Did Caddy go away did she go to the house you cant see the barn from our house did you ever try to see the barn from

It was her fault she pushed me she ran away

I can lift you up see how I can

Oh her blood or my blood Oh We went on in the thin dust, our feet silent as rubber in the thin dust where pencil of sun slanted in the trees. And I could feel water again running swift and peaceful in the secret shade.[108)]

"You live a long way, dont you. You're mighty smart to go this far to town by yourself." *It's like dancing sitting down did you ever dance sitting down? We could hear the rain, a rat in the crib, the empty barn vacant with horses. How do you hold to dance do you hold like this*

Oh

I used to hold like this you thought I wasn't strong enough didn't you

Oh Oh Oh Oh

I hold to use like this[109)] *I mean did you hear what I said I said*

oh oh oh oh

The road went on, still and empty, the sun slanting more and more. Her stiff little pigtails were bound at the tips with bits of crimson

---

108) 물(죽음)에 대한 퀜틴의 의식/집착은 여기 이탈리아 소녀와 헤어지는 부분에서도 여러 번 반복되고 있으며, "secret shade"는 달턴과 캐디가 만나던 그 비밀스런 숲에 대한 기억을 되살리고 있다 하겠다.

109) 여기 이탤릭체 부분은 퀜턴과 나탈리 간의 아이들 장난 놀음을 묘사하는 부분으로, 이미지화하기는 힘들지만 둘이 앉아 서로 만지며 껴안고 있는 (다분히 성적인) 모습이라 하겠다. "오 오 . . ." 소리는 나탈리의 신음소리이며, 이어지는 "I hold to use like this"는 "I used to hold like this"를 퀜턴이 잘못 사용하면서 코믹한 효과뿐만 아니라 나탈리와의 성적 놀음을 방해하는 효과 또한 엿볼 수 있다.

cloth. A corner of the wrapping flapped a little as she walked, the nose of the loaf naked. I stopped.

"Look here. Do you live down this road? We haven't passed a house in a mile, almost."

She looked at me, black and secret and friendly.

"Where do you live, sister? Dont you live back there in town?"

There was a bird somewhere in the woods, beyond the broken and infrequent slanting of sunlight.

"Your papa's going to be worried about you. Dont you reckon you' ll get a whipping for not coming straight home with that bread?"

The bird whistled again, invisible, a sound meaningless and profound, inflexionless, ceasing as though cut off with the blow of a knife, and again, and that sense of water swift and peaceful above secret places, felt, not seen not heard.

"Oh, hell, sister." About half the paper hung limp. "That's not doing any good now." I tore it off and dropped it beside the road. "Come on. We'll have to go back to town. We'll go back along the river."

We left the road. Among the moss little pale flowers grew, and the sense of water mute and unseen. *I hold to use like this I mean I use to hold She stood in the door looking at us her hands on her hips*[110)]

You pushed me it was your fault it hurt me too

We were dancing sitting down I bet Caddy cant dance sitting down

Stop that stop that

I was just brushing the trash off the back of your dress

You keep your nasty old hands off of me it was your fault you pushed me down I'm mad at you

I don't care she looked at us stay mad she went away We began to

---

110) 캐디가 마구간 문 앞에 서서 퀸턴과 나탈리가 하는 짓을 못마땅하게 쳐다보고 있는 장면이다. 어쩌면 언급된 캐디의 동네 애숭이와의 첫 키스 사건은 나탈리와 퀸턴 간의 사건을 두고 캐디가 오빠를 향해 '복수전' 을 벌이고 있는 것인지도 모른다.

hear the shouts, the splashing; I saw a brown body gleam for an instant.

Stay mad. My shirt was getting wet and my hair. Across the roof hearing the roof loud now I could see Natalie going through the garden among the rain. Get wet I hope you catch pneumonia go on home Cowface. I jumped hard as I could into the hogwallow the mud yellowed up to my waist stinking I kept on plunging until I fell down and rolled over in it "Hear them in swimming, sister? I wouldn't mind doing that myself." If I had time. When I have time. I could hear my watch. *mud was warmer than the rain it smelled awful. She had her back turned I went around in front of her. You know what I was doing? She turned her back I went around in front of her the rain creeping into the mud flatting her bodice through her dress it smelled horrible. I was hugging her that's what I was doing. She turned her back I went around in front of her. I was hugging her I tell you.*

I dont give a damn what you were doing

You dont you dont I'll make you I'll make you give a damn. She hit my hands away I smeared mud on her with the other hand I couldn't feel the wet smacking of her hand I wiped mud from my legs smeared it on her wet hard turning body hearing her fingers going into my face but I couldn't feel it even when the rain began to taste sweet on my lips[111)]

They saw us from the water first, heads and shoulders. They yelled and one rose squatting and sprang among them. They looked like beavers, the water lipping about their chins, yelling.

"Take that girl away! What did you want to bring a girl here for? Go on away!"

"She wont hurt you. We just want to watch you for a while."

111) 캐디가 퀀턴의 얼굴을 할퀴어 피가 나고 있는 상황이며, 비를 맞으며 흘러내리는 피는 입술에서 "달콤하게" 느껴지기 시작한다.

They squatted in the water. Their heads drew into a clump, watching us, then they broke and rushed toward us, hurling water with their hands. We moved quick.

"Look out, boys; she wont hurt you."

"Go on away, Harvard!" It was the second boy, the one that thought[112)] the horse and wagon back there at the bridge. "Splash them, fellows!"

"Let's get out and throw them in," another said. "I aint afraid of any girl."

"Splash them! Splash them!" They rushed toward us, hurling water. We moved back. "Go on away!" they yelled. "Go on away!"

We went away. They huddled just under the bank, their slick heads in a row against the bright water. We went on. "That's not for us, is it." The sun slanted through to the moss here and there, leveller. "Poor kid, you're just a girl." Little flowers grew among the moss, littler than I had ever seen. "You're just a girl. Poor kid." There was a path, curving along beside the water. Then the water was still again, dark and still and swift. "Nothing but a girl. Poor sister." *We lay in the wet grass panting the rain like cold shot on my back. Do you care now do you do you*

My Lord we sure are in a mess get up. Where the rain touched my forehead it began to smart my hand came red away streaking off pink in the rain. Does it hurt

Of course it does what do you reckon

I tried to scratch your eyes out my Lord we sure do stink we better try to wash it off in the branch "There's town again, sister. You'll have to go home now. I've got to get back to school. Look how late it's getting. You'll go home now, wont you?" But she just looked at me with her black, secret, friendly gaze, the half-naked loaf clutched to her breast. "It's wet. I thought we jumped back in time." I took my

---

112) thought = imagined or thought up.

handkerchief and tried to wipe the loaf, but the crust began to come off, so I stopped. "We'll just have to let it dry itself. Hold it like this." She held it like that. It looked kind of like rats had been eating it now. *and the water building and building up the squatting back the sloughed mud stinking surfaceward pocking the pattering surface like grease on a hot stove. I told you I'd make you*

I dont give a goddam what you do

Then we heard the running and we stopped and looked back and saw him coming up the path running, the level shadows flicking upon his legs.

"He's in a hurry. We'd —" then I saw another man, an oldish man running heavily, clutching a stick, and a boy naked from the waist up, clutching his pants as he ran.

"There's Julio," the little girl said, and then I saw his Italian face and his eyes as he sprang upon me. We went down. His hands were jabbing at my face and he was saying something and trying to bite me, I reckon, and then they hauled him off and held him heaving and thrashing and yelling and they held his arms and he tried to kick me until they dragged him back. The little girl was howling, holding the loaf in both arms. The half naked boy was darting and jumping up and down, clutching his trousers and someone pulled me up in time to see another stark naked figure come around the tranquil bend in the path running and change direction in midstride and leap into the woods, a couple of garments rigid as boards behind it. Julio still struggled. The man who had pulled me up said, "Whoa, now. We got you." He wore a vest but no coat. Upon it was a metal shield. In his other hand he clutched a knotted, Polished stick.

"You're Anse, aren't you?" I said. "I was looking for you. What's the matter?"

"I warn you that anything you say will be used aganst you," he said. "You're under arrest."

"I killa heem," Julio said. He struggled. Two men held him. The little girl howled steadily, holding the bread. "You steala my seester,"

Julio said. "Let go, meesters."

"Steal his sister?" I said. "Why I've been —"

"Shet up," Anse said. "You can tell that to Squire."

"Steal his sister?" I said. Julio broke from the men and sprang at me again, but the marshal met him and they struggled until the other two pinioned his arms again. Anse released him, panting.

"You durn furriner," he said. "I've a good mind to take you up too, for assault and battery." He turned to me again. "Will you come peaceable, or do I handcuff you?"

"I'll come peaceable," I said. "Anything, just so I can find someone—do something with—Stole his sister," I said. "Stole his—"

"I've warned you," Anse said. "He aims to charge you with meditated criminal assault. Here, you, make that gal shut up that noise."

"Oh," I said. Then I began to laugh. Two more boys with plastered heads and round eyes came out of the bushes, buttoning shirts that had already dampened onto their shoulders and arms, and I tried to stop the laughter, but I couldn't.

"Watch him, Anse, he's crazy, I believe."

"I'll h-have to qu-quit," I said. "It'll stop in a mu-minute. The other time it said ah ah ah." [113] I said, laughing. "Let me sit down a while." I sat down, they watching me, and the little girl with her streaked face and the gnawed looking loaf, and the water swift and peaceful below the path. After a while the laughter ran out. But my throat wouldn't quit trying to laugh, like retching after your stomach is empty.

"Whoa, now," Anse said. "Get a grip on yourself."

"Yes," I said, tightening my throat. There was another yellow butterfly, like one of the sunflecks had come loose. After a while I

---

113) 이 부분은 아마 부러진 다리 때문에 내는 퀸턴의 고통스런 신음소리일 수 있다.

didn't have to hold my throat so tight. I got up. "I'm ready. Which way?"

We followed the path, the two others watching Julio and the little girl and the boys somewhere in the rear. The path went along the river to the bridge. We crossed it and the tracks, people coming to the doors to look at us and more boys materialising from somewhere until when we turned into the main street we had quite a procession. Before the drug store stood an auto, a big one, but I didn't recognise them until Mrs Bland said,

"Why, Quentin! Quentin Compson!" Then I saw Gerald, and Spoade in the back seat, sitting on the back of his neck. And Shreve. I didn't know the two girls.

"Quentin Compson!" Mrs Bland said.

"Good afternoon," I said, raising my hat. "I'm under arrest. I'm sorry I didn't get your note. Did Shreve tell you?"

"Under arrest?" Shreve said. "Excuse me," he said. He heaped himself up and climbed over their feet and got out. He had on a pair of my flannel pants, like a glove. I didn't remember forgetting them. I didn't remember how many chins Mrs Bland had, either. The prettiest girl was with Gerald in front, too. They watched me through veils, with a kind of delicate horror. "Who's under arrest?" Shreve said. "What's this, mister?"

"Gerald," Mrs Bland said. "Send these people away. You get in this car, Quentin."

Gerald got out. Spoade hadn't moved.

"What's he done, Cap?" he said. "Robbed a hen house?"

"I warn you," Anse said. "Do you know the prisoner?"

"Know him," Shreve said. "Look here—"

"Then you can come along to the squire's. You're obstructing justice. Come along." He shook my arm.

"Well, good afternoon," I said. "I'm glad to have seen you all. Sorry I couldn't be with you."

"You, Gerald," Mrs Bland said.

"Look here, constable," Gerald said.

"I warn you you're interfering with an officer of the law," Anse said. "If you've anything to say, you can come to the squire's and make cognizance of the prisoner." [114] We went on. Quite a procession now, Anse and I leading. I could hear them telling them what it was, and Spoade asking questions, and then Julio said something violently in Italian and I looked back and saw the little girl standing at the curb, looking at me with her friendly, inscrutable regard.

"Git on home," Julio shouted at her. "I beat hell outa you."

We went down the street and turned into a bit of lawn in which, set back from the street, stood a one storey building of brick trimmed with white. We went up the rock path to the door, where Anse halted everyone except us and made them remain outside. We entered, a bare room smelling of stale tobacco. There was a sheet iron stove in the center of a wooden frame filled with sand, and a faded map on the wall and the dingy plat of a township. Behind a scarred littered table a man with a fierce roach of iron gray hair peered at us over steel spectacles.

"Got him, did ye, Anse?" he said.

"Got him, Squire."

He opened a huge dusty book and drew it to him and dipped a foul pen into an inkwell filled with what looked like coal dust.

"Look here, mister," Shreve said.

"The prisoner's name," the squire said. I told him. He wrote it slowly into the book, the pen scratching with excruciating deliberation.

"Look here, mister," Shreve said. "We know this fellow. We——"

"Order in the court," Anse said.

"Shut up, bud," Spoade said. "Let him do it his way. He's going to

---

114) 안스는 여기서 법적 용어를 잘못 사용하고 있다. 실제 죄인의 공지 권한을 가진 것은 법정이지, 증인이나 친구들이 될 수 없다.

anyhow."

"Age," the squire said. I told him. He wrote that, his mouth moving as he wrote. "Occupation." I told him. "Harvard student, hey?" he said. He looked up at me, bowing his neck a little to see over the spectacles. His eyes were clear and cold, like a goat's. "What are you up to, coming out here kidnapping children?"

"They're crazy, Squire," Shreve said. "Whoever says this boy's kidnapping —"

Julio moved violently. "Crazy?" he said. "Dont I catcha heem, eh? Dont I see weetha my own eyes—"

"You're a liar," Shreve said. "You never—"

"Order, order," Anse said, raising his voice.

"You fellers shet up," the squire said. "If they dont stay quiet, turn'em out, Anse." They got quiet. The squire looked at Shreve, then at Spoade, then at Gerald. "You know this young man?" he said to Spoade.

"Yes, your honor," Spoade said. "He's just a country boy in school up there. He dont mean any harm. I think the marshal'll find it's a mistake. His father's a congregational minister."

"H'm," the squire said. "What was you doing, exactly?" I told him, he watching me with his cold, pale eyes. "How about it, Anse?"

"Might have been," Anse said. "Them durn furriners."

"I American," Julio said. "I gotta da pape," [115)]

"Where's the gal?"

"He sent her home," Anse said.

"Was she scared or anything?"

"Not till Julio there jumped on the prisoner. They were just walking along the river path, towards town. Some boys swimming told us which way they went."

"It's a mistake, Squire," Spoade said. "Children and dogs are

---

115) 훌리오는 자신의 미국 시민권을 증명할 서류를 가지고 있다고 말한다.

always taking up with him like that. He cant help it."

"H'm," the squire said. He looked out of the window for a while. We watched him. I could hear Julio scratching himself. The squire looked back.

"Air you satisfied the gal aint took any hurt, you, there?"

"No hurt now," Julio said sullenly.

"You quit work to hunt for her?"

"Sure I quit. I run. I run like hell. Looka here, looka there, then man tella me he seen him giva her she eat. She go weetha."

"H'm," the squire said. "Well, son, I calculate you owe Julio something for taking him away from his work."

"Yes, sir," I said. "How much?"

"Dollar, I calculate."

I gave Julio a dollar.

"Well," Spoade said. "If that's all—I reckon he's discharged, your honor?"

The squire didn't look at him. "How far'd you run him, Anse?"

"Two miles, at least. It was about two hours before we caught him."

"H'm," the squire said. He mused a while. We watched him, his stiff crest, the spectacles riding low on his nose. The yellow shape of the window grew slowly across the floor, reached the wall, climbing. Dust motes whirled and slanted. "Six dollars."

"Six dollars?" Shreve said. "What's that for?"

"Six dollars," the squire said. He looked at Shreve a moment, then at me again.

"Look here," Shreve said.

"Shut up," Spoade said. "Give it to him, bud, and let's get out of here. The ladies are waiting for us. You got six dollars?"

"Yes," I said. I gave him six dollars.

"Case dismissed," Shreve said.

"You get a receipt," Shreve said. "You get a signed receipt for that money."

The squire looked at Shreve mildly. "Case dismissed," he said without raising his voice.

"I'll be damned—" Shreve said.

"Come on here," Spoade said, taking his arm. "Good afternoon, Judge. Much obliged." As we passed out the door Julio's voice rose again, violent, then ceased. Spoade was looking at me, his brown eyes quizzical, a little cold. "Well, bud, I reckon you'll do your girl chasing in Boston after this."

"You damned fool," Shreve said. "What the hell do you mean anyway, straggling off here, fooling with these damn wops?"

"Come on," Spoade said. "They must be getting impatient."

Mrs Bland was talking to them. They were Miss Holmes and Miss Daingerfield[116)] and they quit listening to her and looked at me again with that delicate and curious horror, their veils turned back upon their little white noses and their eyes fleeing and mysterious beneath the veils.

"Quentin Compson," Mrs Bland said. "What would your mother say. A young man naturally gets into scrapes, but to be arrested on foot by a country policeman. What did they think he'd done, Gerald?"

"Nothing," Gerald said.

"Nonsense. What was it, you, Spoade?"

"He was trying to kidnap that little dirty girl, but they caught him in time," Spoade said.

"Nonsense," Mrs Bland said, but her voice sort of died away and she stared at me for a moment, and the girl drew their breaths in with a soft concerted sound. "Fiddlesticks," Mrs Bland said briskly. "If that isn't just like these ignorant lowclass Yankees. Get in, Quentin."

Shreve and I sat on two small collapsible seats. Gerald cranked the

---

116) 여기 두 이름은 작가의 언어유희를 짐작할 수 있는 부분으로, 퀀턴의 기억 속에 집(home)은 위험한 장소(dangerous field)임을 강조하려는 의도를 엿볼 수 있다.

car and got in and we started.

"Now, Quentin, you tell me what all this foolishness is about," Mrs Bland said. I told them, Shreve hunched and furious on his little seat and Spoade sitting again on the back of his neck beside Miss Daingerfield.

"And the joke is, all the time Quentin had us all fooled," Spoade said. "All the time we thought he was the model youth that anybody could trust a daughter with, until the police showed him up at his nefarious work."

"Hush up, Spoade," Mrs Bland said. We drove down the street and crossed the bridge and passed the house where the pink garment hung in the window. "That's what you get for not reading my note. Why didn't you come and get it? Mr MacKenzie says he told you it was there."

"Yessum. I intended to, but I never went back to the room."

"You'd have let us sit there waiting I dont know how long, if it hadn't been for Mr MacKenzie. When he said you hadn't come back, that left an extra place, so we asked him to come. We're very glad to have you anyway, Mr MacKenzie." Shreve said nothing. His arms were folded and he glared straight ahead past Gerald's cap. It was a cap for motoring in England. Mrs Bland said so. We passed that house, and three others, and another yard where the little girl stood by the gate. She didn't have the bread now, and her face looked like it had been streaked with coaldust. I waved my hand, but she made no reply, only her head turned slowly as the car passed, following us with her unwinking gaze. Then we ran beside the wall, our shadows running along the wall, and after a while we passed a piece of torn newspaper lying beside the road and I began to laugh again. I could feel it in my throat and I looked off into the trees where the afternoon slanted, thinking of afternoon and of the bird and the boys in swimming. But still I couldn't stop it and then I knew that if I tried too hard to stop it I'd be crying and I thought about how I'd thought about I could not be a virgin, with so many of them walking along in the shadows and whispering with their soft girlvoices lingering in the shadowy places and the words coming out and perfume and eyes you could feel not see, but if it was that simple to do it wouldn't be anything and if it wasn't anything, what was I[117] and then Mrs Bland said, "Quentin? Is he sick, Mr MacKenzie?" and then Shreve's fat hand touched my knee and Spoade began talking and I quit trying to stop it.

"If that hamper is in his way, Mr MacKenzie, move it over on your side. I brought a hamper of wine because I think young gentlemen should drink wine, although my father, Gerald's grandfather" *ever do that Have you ever done that In the gray darkness a little light her hands locked about*

"They do, when they can get it," Spoade said. "Hey, Shreve?" *her knees her face looking at the sky the smell of honeysuckle upon her face and throat*

"Beer, too," Shreve said. His hand touched my knee again. I moved my knee again. *like a thin wash of lilac colored paint talking about him bringing*

"You're not a gentlemen," Spoade said. *him between us until the shape of her blurred not with dark*

"No, I'm canadian," Shreve said. *talking about him the oar blades winking him along winking the Cap made for motoring in England and all time rushing beneath and they two blurred within the other forever more he had been in the army had killed men*[118]

---

117) "I thought about how I'd thought about I could not be a virgin . . ." 에서 여기까지: 퀸턴은 세상은 너무도 많은 여자들로 가득 차 있어 남자가 순결을 지키기 힘들며, 때문에 순결 상실은 "단순하고" 일상적인 것이며 별로 중요하지 않은 것으로 결론짓는다. 하지만 그는 다시 생각을 계속하면서, 만약 그것이 그다지 중요한 것이 아니라면 자신의 순결성이나 그의 존재 또한 아무런 의미를 가질 수 없는 것이 아니냐고 스스로에게 질문을 제기하고 있다. 왜냐면 작품에서 그의 정체성은 바로 캐디의 순결성을 보호하는 데 달려 있다고 해도 과장되지 않기 때문이다.

"I adore Canada," Miss Daingerfield said. "I think it's marvellous."

"Did you ever drink perfume?" Spoade said. *with one hand he could lift her his shoulder and run with her running Running*

"No," Shreve said. *running the beast with two backs and she blurred in the winking oars running the swine of Euboeleus running coupled within*[119] *how many Caddy*

"Neither did I," Spoade said. *I dont know too many there was something terrible in me terrible in me Father I have committed Have you ever done that We didnt we didnt do that did we do that*

"and Gerald's grandfather always picked his own mint before breakfast, while the dew was still on it. He wouldn't even let old Wilkie touch it do you remember Gerald but always gathered it himself and made his own julep.[120] He was as crotchety about his julep as an old made, measuring everything by a recipe in his head. There was only one man he ever gave that recipe to; that was" *we did how can you not know it if youll just wait Ill tell you how it was it was a crime we did a terrible crime it cannot be hid you think it can but wait   Poor Quentin youve never done that have you   and Ill tell*

---

118) 퀸턴이 과거 캐디와의 대화 속에서 달턴을 끌어들이고 있는 캐디를 기억해내면서, 그는 달턴과 제랄드를 혼돈하여 서술하고 있는 부분이다. 달턴이나 제랄드는 캐디에게 남성적이면서도 낭만적이고 매력적인 남성성을 대변한다면, 퀸턴에게 그들은 위협적인 인물인 것이다.

119) 셰익스피어 비극 『오델로』, 1막 1장(118)에서 이야고가 오델로와 데스데모나의 성행위를 묘사하는 것("making the beast with two backs")과 거의 비슷하게 여기서 표현하고 있다. 무장으로서의 오델로의 용맹과 힘 그리고 세계에 대한 그의 견문에 현혹된 데스데모나는 비슷한 차원에서 달턴에게 매료된 캐디를 연상시킨다. 이어지는 문장은 지하세계의 왕(Hades)에게 납치된 페르세포네(Persephone)의 전설과 관련되어 있다. 하계의 왕이 페르세포네를 납치하기 위해 하계의 문을 열 때 균열된 땅의 틈새에 빨려 들어간 인물이 Euboeleus(돼지를 기르는 자)이다. 이 전설에서 암흑세계로 납치된 페르세포네는 캐디와, Hades는 달턴과 비교할 수 있다.

120) mint julep, 버번위스키, 민트, 설탕, 빙수를 함께 섞어 만든 남부음료.

you how it was Ill tell Father then itll have to be because you love Father then well have to go away amid the pointing and the horror the clean flame Ill make you say we did Im stronger than you Ill make you know we did you thought it was them but it was me listen I fooled you all the time it was me you thought I was in the house where that damn honeysuckle trying not to think the swing the cedars the secret surges the breathing locked drinking the wild breath the yes Yes Yes yes "never be got to drink wine himself, but he always said that a hamper what book did you read that in the one where Gerald's rowing suit of wine was a necessary part of any gentlemen's picnic basket" *did you love them Caddy did you love them When they touched me I died*

one minute she was standing there the next he was yelling and pulling at her dress they went into the hall and up the stairs yelling and shoving at her up the stairs to the bathroom door and stopped her back against the door and her arm across her face yelling and trying to shove her into the bathroom when she came in to supper T.P. was feeding him he started again just whimpering at first until she touched him then he yelled she stood there her eyes like cornered rats then I was running in the gray darkness it smelled of rain and all flower scents the damp warm air released and crickets sawing away in the grass pacing me with a small travelling island of silence Fancy watched me across the fence blotchy like a quilt on a line I thought damn that nigger he forgot to feed her again I ran down the hill in that vacuum of crickets like a breath travelling across a mirror she was lying in the water her head on the sand spit the water flowing about her hips there was a little more light in the water her skirt half saturated flopped along her flanks to the waters motion in heavy ripples going nowhere renewed themselves of their own movement I stood on the bank I could smell the honeysuckle on the water gap the air seemed to drizzle with honeysuckle and with the rasping of crickets a substance you could feel on the flesh

is Benjy still crying

I dont know yes I dont know
poor Benjy
I sat down on the bank the grass was damp a little then I found my shoes wet
get out of that water are you crazy
but she didnt move her face was a white blur framed out of the blur of the sand by her hair
get out now
she sat up then she rose her skirt flopped against her draining she climbed the bank her clothes flopping sat down
why dont you wring it out do you want to catch cold
yes
the water sucked and gurgled across the sand spit and on it the dark among the willows across the shallow the water rippled like a piece of cloth holding still a little light as water does
hes crossed all the oceans all around the world
then she talked about him clasping her wet knees her face tilted back in the gray light the smell of honeysuckle there was a light in mothers room and in Benjys where T.P. was putting him to bed
do you love him
her hand came out I didnt move it fumbled down my arm and she held my hand flat against her chest her heart thudding
no no
did he make you then he made you do it let him he was stronger than you and he tomorrow Ill kill him I swear I will father neednt know until afterward and then you and I nobody need ever know we can take my school money we can cancel my matriculation Caddy you hate him
dont you dont you
she held my hand against her chest her heart thudding I turned and caught her arm
Caddy you hate him dont you
she moved my hand up against her throat her heart was hammering

there

poor Quentin

her face looked at the sky it was low so low[121] that all smells and sounds of night seemed to have been crowded down like under a slack tent especially the honeysuckle it had got into my breathing it was on her face and throat like paint her blood pounded against my hand I was leaning on my other arm it began to jerk and jump and I had to pant to get any air at all out of that thick gray honeysuckle

yes I hate him I would die for him Ive already died for him I die for him over and over again everytime this goes[122]

when I lifted my hand I could still feel crisscrossed twigs and grass burning into the palm

poor Quentin

she leaned back on her arms her hands locked about her knees

youve never done that have you

what done what

that what I have what I did

yes yes lots of times with lots of girls

then I was crying her hand touched me again and I was crying against her damp blouse then she lying on her back looking past my head into the sky I could see a rim of white under her irises I opened my knife

do you remember the day damuddy died when you sat down in the water in your drawers

yes

I held the point of the knife at her throat

it wont take but a second just a second then I can do mine I can do mine then

all right can you do yours by yourself

---

121) 하늘이 낮아 보이는 이유는 비구름과 여름날 숨 막힐 정도의 습도와 열기 때문이다.

122) "this goes" = Caddy' s heart "thudding."

yes the blades long enough Benjy in bed by now
yes
it wont take but a second Ill try not to hurt
all right
will you close your eyes
no like this youll have to push it harder
touch your hand to it
but she didnt move her eyes were wide open looking past my head at the sky
Caddy do you remember how Dilsey fussed at you because your drawers were muddy
dont cry
Im not crying Caddy
push it are you going to
do you want me to
yes push it
touch your hand to it
dont cry poor Quentin
but I couldnt stop she held my head against her damp hard breast I could hear her heart going firm and slow now not hammering and the water gurgling among the willows in the dark and waves of honeysuckle coming up the air my arm and shoulder were twisted under me
what is it what are you doing
her muscles gathered I sat up
its my knife I dropped it
she sat up
what time is it
I dont know
she rose to her feet I fumbled along the ground
Im going let it go
to the house
I could feel her standing there I could smell her damp clothes feeling

her there
its right here somewhere
let it go you can find it tomorrow come on
wait a minute Ill find it
are you afraid to
here it is it was right here all the time
was it come on
I got up and followed we went up the hill the crickets hushing before us its funny how you can sit down and drop something and have to hunt all around for it
the gray it was gray with dew slanting up into the gray sky then the trees beyond
damn that honeysuckle I wish it would atop
you used to like it
we crossed the crest and went on toward the trees she walked into me[123) she gave over a little the ditch was a black scar on the gray grass she walked into me again she looked at me and gave over we reached the ditch
lets go this way
what for
lets see if you can still see Nancys bones I havent thought to look in a long time have you
it was matted with vines and briers dark
they were right here you cant tell whether you see them or not can you stop Quentin
come on
the ditch narrowed closed she turned toward the trees
stop Quentin

---

123) 이 문장은 달턴을 만나러가는 캐디와 헤어져야 하는 상황에서, 퀀턴은 그들의 행보를 의도적으로 늦추며 걸음을 천천히 하거나 다른 방향으로 걸으면서 캐디의 진로와 엇갈리고 있는 모습이다.

Caddy
I got in front of her again
Caddy
stop it
I held her
Im stronger than you
she was motionless hard unyielding but still
I wont fight stop youd better stop
Caddy dont Caddy
it wont do any good dont you know it wont let me go
the honeysuckle drizzled and drizzled I could hear the crickets watching us in a circle she moved back went around me on toward the trees
you go on back to the house you neednt come
I went on
why dont you go on back to the house
damn that honeysuckle
we reached the fence she crawled through I crawled through when I rose from stooping he was coming out of the trees into gray toward us coming toward us tall and flat and still even moving like he was still she went to him
this is Quentin Im wet Im wet all over you dont have to if you dont want to[124)]
their shadows one shadow her head rose it was above his on the sky higher their two heads[125)]
you dont have to if you dont want to
then not two heads the darkness smelled of rain of damp grass and leaves the gray light drizzling like rain the honeysuckle coming up in damp waves I could see her face a blur against his shoulder he held

124) 캐디는 몸이 젖었기 때문에 달턴을 향해 자신을 들어 안을 필요가 없다고 말한다.
125) 달턴이 캐디를 안아 위로 들어 올리고 있는 모습이다.

her in one arm like she was no bigger than a child[126) he extended his hand

glad to know you

we shook hands then we stood there her shadow high against his shadow one shadow

whatre you going to do Quentin

walk a while I think Ill go through the woods to the road and come back through town

I turned away going

goodnight

Quentin

I stopped

what do you want

in the woods the tree frogs were going smelling rain in the air they sounded like toy music boxes that were hard to turn and the honeysuckle come here

what do you want

come here Quentin

I went back she touched my shoulder leaning down her shadow the blur of her face leaning down from his high shadow I drew back

look out

you go on home

Im not sleepy Im going to take a walk

wait for me at the branch

Im going for a walk

Ill be there soon wait for me you wait

no Im going through the woods

I didnt look back the tree frogs didnt pay me any mind the gray light like moss in the trees drizzling but still it wouldnt rain after a while I

---

126) 남자다운 힘을 과시해 보이는 달턴과 함께 있는 캐디의 모습이 퀸턴의 눈에는 아이에 비교되고 있다.

turned went back to the edge of the woods as soon as I got there I began to smell honeysuckle again[127)] I could see the lights on the courthouses clock and the glare of town the square on the sky and the dark willows along the branch and the light in mothers windows the light still on in Benjys room and I stopped through the fence[128)] and went across the pasture running I ran in the gray grass among the crickets the honeysuckle getting stronger and stronger and the smell of water then I could see the water the color of gray honeysuckle I lay down on the bank with my face close to the ground so I couldnt smell the honeysuckle I couldnt smell it then and I lay there feeling the earth going through my clothes listening to the water and after a while I wasnt breathing so hard and I lay there thinking that if I didnt move my face I wouldnt have to breathe hard and smell it and then I wasnt thinking about anything at all she came along the bank and stopped I didnt move

its late you go on home

what

you go on home its late

all right

her clothes rustled I didnt move they stopped rustling

are you going in like I told you

I didnt hear anything

Caddy

yes I will if you want me to I will

I sat up she was sitting on the ground her hands clasped about her knee go on to the house like I told you

---

127) 퀸턴은 결국 캐디가 오지 말기를 원하던 그 숲으로 발길을 향하고 있으며, 그 숲에서 캐디와 달턴이 성행위를 하고 있음은 마지막 문장("as soon as . . . smell honeysuckle again")에서 암시되고 있다.

128) 퀸턴은 둘이 있는 그 숲을 벗어나, 캐디가 시키는 대로 아까 그녀와 자신이 있던 강가로 되돌아가고 있다.

yes Ill do anything you want me to anything yes
she didnt even look at me I caught her shoulder and shook her hard
you shut up
I shook her
you shut up you shut up
yes
she lifted her face then I saw she wasnt even looking at me at all I could
see that white rim
get up
I pulled her she was limp I lifted her to her feet
go on now
was Benjy still crying when you left
go on
we crossed the branch the roof came in sight then the windows upstairs hes asleep now
I had to stop and fasten the gate she went on in the gray light the smell of rain and still it wouldnt rain and honeysuckle beginning to come from the garden fence beginning she went into the shadow I could hear her feet then
Caddy
I stopped at the steps I couldnt hear her feet
Caddy
I heard her feet then my hand touched her not warm not cool just still her clothes a little damp still
do you love him now
not breathing except slow like far away breathing
Caddy do you love him now
I dont know
outside the gray light the shadows of things like dead things in stagnant water
I wish you were dead
do you you coming in now

are you thinking about him now
I dont know
tell me what youre thinking about tell me
stop stop Quentin
you shut up you shut up you hear me you shut up are you going to shut up
all right I will stop well[129] make too much noise
Ill kill you do you hear
lets go out to the swing theyll hear you here
Im not crying do you say Im crying
no hush now well wake Benjy up
you go on into the house go on now
I am dont cry Im bad anyway you cant help it
theres a curse on us its not our fault is it our fault
hush come on and go to bed now
you cant make me theres a curse on us
finally I saw him he was just going into the barbershop he looked out
I went on and waited
Ive been looking for you two or three days
you wanted to see me
Im going to see you
he rolled the cigarette quickly with about two motions he struck the match with his thumb
we cant talk here suppose I meet you somewhere
Ill come to your room are you at the hotel
no thats not so good you know that bridge over the creek in there back of
yes all right
at one oclock right
yes

---

129) we'll

I turned away
Im obliged to you
look
I stopped looked back
she all right
he looked like he was made out of bronze his khaki shirt
she need me for anything now
Ill be there at one
she heard me tell T.P. to saddle Prince at one oclock she kept watching me not eating much she came
too
what are you going to do
nothing cant I go for a ride if I want to
youre going to do something what is it
none of your business whore whore
T.P. had Prince at the side door
I wont want him Im going to walk
I went down the drive and out the gate I turned into the lane then I ran before I reached the bridge I saw him leaning on the rail the horse was hitched in the woods he looked over his shoulder then he turned his back he didnt look up until I came onto the bridge and stopped he had a piece of bark in his hands breaking pieces from it and dropping them over the rail into the water
I came to tell you to leave town
he broke a piece of bark deliberately dropped it carefully into the water watched it float away
I said you must leave town
he looked at me
did she send you to me
I say you must go not my father not anybody I say it
listen save this for a while I want to know if shes all right have they been bothering her up there
thats something you dont need to trouble yourself about

then I heard myself saying Ill give you until sundown to leave town
he broke a piece of bark and dropped it into the water then he laid the bark on the rail and rolled a cigarette with those two swift motions spun the match over the rail
what will you do if I dont leave
Ill kill you dont think that just because I look like a kid to you
the smoke flowed in two jets from his nostrils across his face
how old are you
I began to shake my hands were on the rail I thought if I hid them hed know why
Ill give you until tonight
listen buddy whats your name Benjys the natural isnt he
you are
Quentin
my mouth said it I didnt say it at all
Ill give you till sundown[130)]
Quentin
he raked the cigarette ash carefully off against the rail he did it slowly and carefully like sharpening a pencil my hands had quit shaking
listen no good taking it so hard its not your fault kid it would have been some other fellow
did you have a sister did you
no but theyre all bitches
I hit him my open hand beat the impulse to shut it to his face[131)] his hand moved as fast as mine the cigarette went over the rail I swung with the other hand he caught it too before the cigarette reached the

---

130) 퀸턴은 여기 자신이 한 말이 얼마나 허황되고 멜로드라마적인가를 스스로 의식하면서, 캐디의 명예를 보호하려는 낭만주의적 바보처럼 행동하는 자신을 향해 그리고 스스로도 통제할 수 없는 행위들에 빠져 헤어나지 못하는 자신을 이런 식으로 연출하고 있다 하겠다.

water he held both my wrists in the same hand his other hand flicked to his armpit under his coat behind him the sun slanted and a bird singing somewhere beyond the sun we looked at one another while the bird singing he turned my hands loose

look here

he took the bark from the rail and dropped it into the water it bobbed up the current took it floated away his hand lay on the rail holding the pistol loosely we waited

you cant hit it now

no

it floated on it was quite still in the woods I heard the bird again and the water afterward the pistol came up he didnt aim at all the bark disappeared[132] then pieces of it floated up spreading he hit two more of them pieces of bark no bigger than silver dollars

thats enough I guess

he swung the cylinder out and blew into the barrel a thin wisp of smoke dissolved he reloaded the three chambers shut the cylinder he handed it to me butt first

what for I wont try to beat that

youll need it from what you said Im giving you this one because youve seen what itll do

to hell with your gun

I hit him I was still trying to hit him long after he was holding my wrists but I still tried then it was like I was looking at him through a piece of colored glass I could hear my blood and then I could see the sky again[133] and branches against it and the sun slanting through

---

131) 비록 퀸턴은 주먹을 불끈 쥐고 달턴의 얼굴을 갈기고 싶은 충동에도 불구하고, 여자아이처럼 손바닥을 벌린 채("open hand") 달턴의 빰을 치고 있다.

132) 달턴이 훌륭한 명사수임을 보여주는데, 하지만 이런 문장은 퀸턴의 낭만주의적, 멜로드라마적 상상력의 산물로 보기도 한다.

133) 달턴과의 '대결'에서 퀸턴이 기절하는 순간이다.

them and he holding me on my feet
did you hit me
I couldnt hear
what
yes how do you feel
all right let go
he let me go I leaned against the rail
do you feel all right
let me alone Im all right
can you make it home all right
go on let me alone
youd better no try to walk take my horse
no you go on
you can hang the reins on the pommel and turn him loose hell go back to the stable
let me alone you go on and let me alone
I leaned on the rail looking at the water[134)] I heard him untie the horse and ride off and after a while I couldnt hear anything but the water and then the bird again I left the bridge and sat down with my back against a tree and leaned my head against the tree and shut my eyes a patch of sun came through and fell across my eyes and I moved a little further around the tree I heard the bird again and the water and then everything sort of rolled away and I didnt feel anything at all I felt almost good after all those days and the nights with honeysuckle coming up out of the darkness into my room where I was trying to sleep even when after a while I knew that he hadnt hit me that he had lied about that for her sake too and that I had just

---

134) 고향에서 그리고 하버드에서, 다리 위에서 "물을 쳐다보고 있는" 퀸턴의 모습은 퀸턴 장에서 그를 특징짓는 중요한 이미지라 하겠다. 그것은 그의 자아도취적 입장을 반영하고 있을 뿐만 아니라 물과 관련된 여성성 공간 그리고 궁극적으로 그의 죽음과도 직결되기 때문이다.

passed out like a girl but even that didnt matter anymore and I sat there against the tree with little flecks of sunlight brushing across my face like yellow leaves on a twig listening to the water and not thinking about anything at all even when I heard the horse coming fat I sat there with my eyes closed and heard its feet bunch scuttering the hissing sand and feet running and her hard running hands fool fool are you hurt

I opened my eyes her hands running on my face

I didnt know which way until I heard the pistol I didnt know where I didnt think he and you running off slipping

I didnt think he would have

she held my face between her hands bumping my head against the tree stop stop that

I caught her wrists

quit that quit it

I knew he wouldnt I knew he wouldnt

she tried to bump my head against the tree

I told him never to speak to me again I told him

she tried to break her wrists free

let me go

stop it Im stronger than you stop it now

let me go Ive got to catch him and ask his let me go Quentin please let me go let me go

all at once she quit her wrists went lax

yes I can tell him I can make him believe anytime I can make him

Caddy

she hadnt hithced Prince he was liable to strike out for home if the notion took him

anytime he will believe me

do you love him Caddy

do I what

she looked at me then everything emptied out of her eyes and they looked like the eyes in statues blank and unseeing and serene

put your hand against my throat
she took my hand and held it flat against her throat
now say his name
Dalton Ames
I felt the first surge of blood there it surged in strong accelerating beats
say it again
her face looked off into the trees where the sun slanted and where the bird
say it again
Dalton Ames
her blood surged steadily beating and beating against my hand

It kept on running[135)] for a long time, but my face felt cold and sort of dead, and my eye, and the cut place on my finger was smarting again. I could hear Shreve working the pump, then he came back with the basin and a round blob of twilight wobbling in it, with a yellow edge like a fading balloon, then my reflection. I tred to see my face in it.

"Has it stopped?" Shreve said. "Give me the rag." He tried to take it from my hand.

"Look out," I said. "I can do it. Yes, it's about stopped now." I dipped the rag again, breaking the balloon. The rag stained the water. "I wish I had a clean one."

"You need a piece of beefsteak for that eye," Shreve said. "Damn if you wont have a shiner tomorrow. The son of a bitch," he said.

"Did I hurt him any?" I wrung out the handkerchief and tried to clean the blood off of my vest.

"You cant get that off," Shreve said. "You'll have to send it to the cleaner's. Come on, hold it on your eye, why dont you."

"I can get some of it off," I said. But I wan't doing much good.

135) 퀸턴이 시작한 싸움에서 제랄드가 퀸턴의 눈가를 찢어 피가 흐르고 있는 상황이다.

"What sort of shape is my collar in?"

"I dont know," Shreve said. "Hold it against your eye. Here."

"Look out," I said. "I can do it. Did I hurt him any?"

"You may have hit him. I may have looked away just then or blinked or something. He boxed the hell out of you. He boxed you all over the place. What did you want to fight him with your fists for? You goddam fool. How do you feel?"

"I feel fine," I said. "I wonder if I can get something to clean my vest."

"Oh, forget your damn clothes. Does your eye hurt?"

"I feel fine," I said. Everything was sort of violet and still, the sky green paling into gold beyond the gable of the house and a plume of smoke rising from the chimney without any wind. I heard the pump again. A man was filling a pail, watching us across his pumping shoulder. A woman crossed the door, but she didn't look out. I could hear a cow lowing somewhere.

"Come on," Shreve said. "Let your clothes alone and put that rag on your eye. I'll send your suit out first thing tomorrow."

"All right. I'm sorry I didn't blee on him a little, at least."

"Son of a bitch," Shreve said. Spoade came out of the house, talking to the woman I reckon, and crossed the yard. He looked at me with his cold, quizzical eyes.

"Well, bud," he said, looking at me, "I'll be damned if you dont go to a lot of trouble to have your fun. Kidnapping, then fighting. What do you do on your holidays? burn houses?"

"I'm all right," I said. "What did Mrs Bland say?"

"She's giving Gerald hell for bloodying you up. She'll give you hell for letting him, when she sees you. She dont object to the fighting, it's the blood that annoys her. I think you lost caste with her a little by not holing your blood better. How do you feel?"

"Sure," Shreve said. "If you cant be a Bland, the next best thing is to commit adultery with one or get drunk and fight him, as the case may be."

"Quite right," Spoade said. "But I didn't know Quentin was drunk."

"He wasn't," Shreve said. "Do you have to be drunk to want to hit that son of a bitch?"

"Well, I think I'd have to be pretty drunk to try it, after seeing how Quentin came out. Where'd he learn to box?"

"He's been going to Mike's every day, over in town," I said.

"He has?" Spoade said. "Did you know that when you hit him?"

"I dont know," I said. "I guess so. Yes."

"Wet it again," Shreve said. "Want some fresh water?"

"This is all right," I said. I dipped the cloth again and held it to my eye. "Wish I had something to clean my vest." Spoade was still watching me.

"Say," he said. "What did you hit him for? What was it he said?"

"I dont know. I dont know why I did."

"The first I knew was when you jumped up all of a sudden and said, 'Did you ever have a sister? did you?' and when he said No, you hit him. I noticed you kept on looking at him, but you didn't seem to be paying any attention to what anybody was saying until you jumped up and asked him if he had any sisters."

"Ah, he was blowing off a usual," Shreve said, "about his women. You know: like he does, before girls, so they dont know exactly what he's saying. All his damn innuendo and lying and a lot of stuff that dont make sense even. Telling us about some wench that he made a date with to meet at a dance hall in Atlantic City and stood her up and went to the hotel and went to bed and how he lay there being sorry for her waiting on the pier for him, without him there to give her what she wanted. Talking about the body's beauty and the sorry ends thereof and how tough women have it, without anything else they can do except lie on their backs. Leda lurking in the bushes, whimpering and moaning for the swan, see.[136] The son of a bitch. I'd hit him myself. Only I'd grabbed up her damn hamper of wine and done it if it had been me."

"Oh," Spoade said, "the champion of dames. Bud, you excite not only admiration, but horror." He looked at me, cold and quizzical. "Good God," he said.

"I'm sorry I hit him," I said. "Do I look too bad to go back and get it over with?"

"Apologies, hell," Shreve said. "Let them go to hell. We're going to town."

"He ought to go back so they'll know he fights like a gentleman," Spoade said. "Gets licked like one, I mean."

"Like this?" Shreve said. "With his clothes all over blood?"

"Why, all right," Spoade. "You know best."

"He cant go around in his undershirt," Shreve said. "He's not a senior yet. Come on, let's go to town."

"You needn't come," I said. "You go on back to the picnic."

"Hell with them," Shreve said. "Come on here."

"What'll I tell them?" Spoade said. "Tell them you and Quentin had a fight too?"

"Tell them nothing," Shreve said. "Tell her her option expired at sunset. Come on, Quentin. I'll ask that woman where the nearest interurban—"

"No," I said. "I'm not going back to town."

Shreve stopped, looking at me. Turning his glasses looked like small yellow moons.

"What are you going to do?"

"I'm not going back to town yet. You go back to the picnic. Tell them I wouldn't come back because my clothes were spoiled."

"Look here," he said. "What are you up to?"

"Nothing. I'm all right. You and Spoade go on back. I'll see you tomorrow." I went on across the yard, toward the road.

---

136) 그리스 신화에서 Leda(인간)는 백조로 변신한 제우스신에게 강간당한(/사랑받은) 여인이다. 그리고 이들의 결합에서 트로이의 Helen이 탄생한다.

"Do you know where the station is?" Shreve said.

"I'll find it. I'll see you all tomorrow. Tell Mrs Bland I'm sorry I spoiled her party." They stood watching me. I went around the house. A rock path went down to the road. Roses grew on both sides of the path. I went through the gate, onto the road. It dropped downhill, toward the woods, and I could make out the auto beside the road. I went up the hill. The light increased as I mounted, and before I reached the top I heard a car. It sounded far away across the twilight and I stopped and listened to it. I couldn't make out the auto any longer, but Shreve was standing in the road before the house, looking up the hill. Behind him the yellow light lay like a wash of paint on the roof of the house. I lifted my hand and went on over the hill, listening to the car. Then the house was gone and I stopped in the green and yellow light and heard the car growing louder and louder, until just as it began to die away it ceased all together. I waited until I heard it start again. Then I went on.

As I descended the light dwindled slowly, yet at the same time without altering its quality, as if I and not light were changing, decreasing, though even when the road ran into trees you could have read a newspaper. Pretty soon I came to a lane. I turned into it. It was closer and darker than the road, but when it came out at the trolley stop—another wooden marquee—the light was still unchanged. After the lane it seemed brighter, as though I had walked through night in the lane and come out into morning again. Pretty soon the car came. I got on it, they turning to look at my eye, and found a seat on the left side.

The lights were on in the car, so while we ran between trees I couldn't see anything except my own face and a woman across the aisle with a hat sitting right on top of her head, with a broken feather in it, but when we ran out of the trees I could see the twilight again, that quality of light as if time really had stoppped for a while, with the sun hanging just under the horizon, and then we passed the marquee where the old man had been eating out of the sack, and the road going on under the twilight, into twilight and the sense of water peaceful and swift beyond. Then the car went on, the draft building steadily up in the open door until it was drawing steadily through the car with the odor of summer and darkness except honeysuckle. Honeysuckle was the saddest odor of all, I think. I remember lots of them. Wistaria was one. On the rainy days when Mother wasn't feeling quite bad enough to stay away from the windows we used to play under it. When Mother stayed in bed Dilsey would put old clothes on us and let us go out in the rain because she said rain never hurt young folks. But if Mother was up we always began by playing on the porch until she said we were making too much noise, then we went out and played under wistaria frame.

This was where I saw the river for the last time this morning, about here. I could feel water beyond the twilight, smell. When it bloomed in the spring and it rained the smell was everywhere you didn't notice it so much at other times but when it rained the smell began to come into the house at twilight either it would rain more at twilight or there was something in the light itself but it always smelled strongest then until I would lie in bed thinking when will it stop when will it stop. The draft in the door smelled of water, a damp steady breath. Sometimes I could put myself to sleep saying that[137)] over and over until after the honeysuckle got all mixed up in it the whole thing came to symbolise night and unrest I seemed to be lying neither asleep nor awake looking down a long corridor of gray halflight where all stable things had become shadowy paradoxical all I had done shadows all I had felt suffered taking visible from antic and perverse mocking without relevance inherent themselves with the denial of the significance they should have affirmed thinking I was I was not who was not was not who.

I could smell the curves of the river beyond the dusk and I saw the

---

137) "when will it stop when will it stop."

last light supine and tranquil upon tideflats like pieces of broken mirror, then beyond them lights began in the pale clear air, trembling a little like butterflies hovering a long way off. Benjamin the child of. How he used to sit before that mirror. Refuge unfailing in which conflict tempered silenced reconciled.[138] Benjamin the child of mine old age held hostage into Egypt. O Benjamin. Dilsey said it was because Mother was too proud for him.[139] They come into white people's lives like that in sudden sharp black trickles that isolate white facts for an instant in unarguable truth like under a microscope; the rest of the time just voices that laugh when you see nothing to laugh at, tears when no reason for tears. They will bet on the odd or even number of mourners at a funeral. A brothel full of them in Memphis went into a religious trance ran naked into the street. It took three policemen to subdue one of them. Yes Jesus O good man Jesus O that good man.

The car stopped. I got out, with them looking at my eye. When the trolley came it was full. I stopped on the back platform.

"Seats up front," the conductor said. I looked into the car. There were no seats on the left side.[140]

---

138) 앞 문장과 연결하여 거울 앞에 앉은 벤지의 이미지에서, 거울이 벤지에게 "피난처"처럼 어떤 위안이 되고 있다면, 이 순간 퀸턴에게 벤지의 그 기억이 위안이 되고 있다 할 수 있다. 그것은 곧 퀸턴이 자살을 열망함을 암시한다. 즉 그는 지금 수면이라는 또 다른 종류의 거울 위에 드러나는 자신의 그림자 속에서 자신의 모든 "갈등"이 "침묵되고 화해되는" 그의 피난처를 찾고 있는 것이다. 이어지는 문장에서 벤자민, 야콥 그리고 이집트의 조셉과의 관계는 성경(Genesis 42-44) 참고.

139) 벤지의 이름이 모리에서 벤자민/벤지로 바뀐 이유를 엿볼 수 있는 부분으로, 캄슨 부인은 벤지가 저능아란 사실을 안 후 자신의 동생(Maury)/바스콤 가문의 이름을 더 이상 사용하길 원치 않는다.

140) 퀸턴은 차를 탈 때도 자신의 왼쪽 눈이 찢어진 것을 의식하며 차 뒤 칸으로 오르고 있으며, 차 안에서도 피가 얼룩진 왼쪽 눈을 의식하며 왼쪽 창문가 좌석을 찾고 있다(물론 좌석은 없지만). 그리고 조금 뒤 퀸턴은 기숙사 건물을 들어서면서도 왼

"I'm not going far," I said. "I'll just stand here."

We crossed the river. The bridge, that is, arching slow and high into space, between silence and nothingness where lights—yellow and red and green—trembled in the clear air, repeating themselves.

"Better go up front and get a seat," the conductor said.

"I get off pretty soon," I said. "A couple of blocks."

I got off before we reached the postoffice. They'd all be sitting around somewhere by now though, and then I was hearing my watch and I began to listen for the chimes and I touched Shreve's letter through my coat, the bitten shadows of the elms flowing upon my hand. And then as I turned into quad the chimes did begin and I went on while the notes came up like ripples on a pool and passed me and went on, saying Quarter to what? All light. Quarter to what.

Our windows were dark. The entrance was empty. I walked close to the left wall when I entered, but it was empty: just the stairs curving up into shadows echoes of feet in the sad generations like light dust upon the shadows, my feet waking them like dust, lightly to settle again.

I could see the letter[141] before I turned the light on, propped against a book on the table so I would see it. Calling him my husband. And then Spoade said they were going somewhere, would not be back until late, and Mrs Bland would need another cavalier.[142] But I would have seen him and he cannot get another car for an hour because after six oclock. I took out my watch and listened to it clicking away, not knowing it[143] couldn't even lie. Then I laid it face up on the table and took Mrs Bland's letter and tore it across and dropped the pieces into the waste basket and took off my coat, vest,

---

쪽 벽 가까이서 걸음을 옮기고 있음을 알 수 있다.

141) 퀸턴을 피크닉에 초대하는 블랜드 부인의 편지.

142) Shreve.

143) 시계바늘들이 부러진 퀸턴의 손목시계.

collar, tie and shirt. The tie was spoiled too, but then niggers.[144)] Maybe a pattern of blood he could call that the one Christ was wearing. I found the gasoline in Shreve's room and spread the vest on the table, where it would be flat, and opened the gasoline.[145)]

the first car in town a girl Girl that's what Jason couldn't bear smell of gasoline making him sick then got madder than ever because a girl Girl had no sister but Benjamin Benjamin the child of my sorrowful if I'd just had a mother so I could say Mother Mother It took a lot of gasoline, and then I couldn't tell if it was still the stain or just the gasoline. It had started the cut to smarting again so when I went to wash I hung the vest on a chair and lowered the light cord so that the bulb would be drying the splotch. I washed my face and hands, but even then I could smell it within the soap stinging, constricting the nostrils a little. Then I opened the bag and took the shirt and collar an tie out and put the bloody ones in and closed the bag, and dressed. While I was brushing my hair the half hour went. But there was until the tree quarters anyway, except suppose *seeing on the rushing darkness only his own face no broken feather unless two of them but not two like that going to Boston the same night then my face his face for an instant across the crashing when out of darkness two lighted windows in rigid fleeing crash gone his face and mine just I see saw did I see*[146)] *not goodbye the marquee empty of eating the road empty in darkness in silence the bridge arching*

---

144) 인종차별적 편견을 드러내는 퀜턴의 모습이다. 퀜턴은 자신의 옷가지들을 디콘에게 남기는데, 제랄드와의 싸움에서 피가 묻은 넥타이일지라도 흑인들은 가리지 않고 입을 것이기에, 그것을 디콘에게 주어도 된다고 생각한다.

145) 피를 지우기 위한 소독용으로 휘발유를 사용하고 있다.

146) 이 장면은 퀜턴이 다가올 순간을 예측하며, 자살을 위해 다시 다리를 향하는 차 속의 자신의 모습과 시내에서 다시 학교로 돌아오는 차 속의 쉬리브("his own face")의 모습이 서로 교차하며 어둠 속에서 마주치는 순간을 상상하면서, 궁극적으로 암흑, 침묵, 깊은 잠, 강물 속에서의 영원한/평화로운 자신의 죽음을 생각하고 있다.

into silence darkness sleep the water peaceful and swift not goodbye

I turned out the light and went into my bedroom, out of the gasoline but I could still smell it. I stood at the window the curtains moved slow out of the darkness touching my face like someone breathing asleep, breathing slow into the darkness again, leaving the touch. *After they had gone up stairs Mother lay back in her chair, a camphor handkerchief to her mouth. Father hasn't moved he still sat beside her holding her hand the bellowing hammering away like no place for it in silence* When I was little there was a picture in one of our books, a dark place into which a single weak ray of light came slanting upon two faces lifted out of the shadow. *You know what I'd do if I were King?* she never was a queen or a fairy she was always a king or a giant or a general *I'd break that place open and drag them out and I'd whip them good* It was torn out, jagged out. I was glad. I'd have to turn back to it until the dungeon was Mother herself she and Father upward into weak light holding hands and us lost somewhere below even them without even a ray of light. Then the honeysuckle got into it. As soon as I turned off the light and tried to go to sleep it would begin to come into the room in waves building and building up until I would have to pant to get any air at all out of it until I would have to get up and feel my way like when I was a little boy *hands can see touching in the mind shaping unseen door Door now nothing hands can see* My nose could see gasoline, the vest on the table, the door. The corridor was still empty of all the feet in sad generations seeking water. *yet the eyes unseeing clenched like teeth not disbelieving doubting even the absence of pain shin ankle knee the long invisible flowing of the stair-railing where a misstep in the darkness filled with sleeping Mother Father Caddy Jason Maury door I am not afraid only Mother Father Caddy Jason Maury geting so far ahead sleeping I will sleep fast when I door Door door* It was empty too, the pipes, the porcelain, the stained quiet wall, the throne of contemplation. I had forgotten the glass, but I could *hands can see cooling fingers invisible swan-throat where less than Moses rod*[147] *the glass touch tentative not to drumming lean cool throat drumming cooling the metal the glass full overfull cooling the glass the fingers flushing sleep leaving the taste of dampened sleep in the long silence of the throat* I returned up the corridor, waking the lost feet in whispering battalions in the silence, into the gasoline, the watch telling its furious lie on the dark table. Then the curtains breathing out of the dark upon my face, leaving the breathing upon my face. A quarter hour yet. And then I'll not be. The peacefullest words. Peacefullest words. *Non fui. Sum. Fui. Non sum.*[148] Somewhere I heard bells once. Mississippi or Massachusetts. I was. I am not. Massachusetts or Mississippi. Shreve has a bottle in his trunk. *Aren't you even going to open it* Mr and Mrs Jason Richmond Compson announce the *Three times. Days. Aren't you even going to open it* marriage of their daughter Candace *that liquor teaches you to confuse the means with the end* I am. Drink. I was not. Let us sell Benjy's pasture so that Quentin may go to Harvard and I may knock my bones together and together. I will be dead in. Was it one year Caddy said. Shreve has a bottle in his trunk. Sir I will not need Shreve's I have sold Benjy's pasture and I can be dead in Harvard Caddy said in the caverns and the grottoes of the sea tumbling peacefully to the wavering tides because Harvard is such a fine sound forty acres is no high price for a fine sound. A fine dead sound we will swap Benjy's pasture for a fine dead sound. It will last him a long time because he cannot hear it unless he can smell it *as soon as she came in the door he began to cry* I thought all the time it was just one of those town squirts that Father was always teasing her about until. I didn't notice him any more than any other stranger

---

147) 성경(Exodus 17:6; Numbers 20:11)에서 모세가 바위로부터 시원한 물을 끌어내던 그의 지팡이처럼, 퀸턴은 어린시절 집에서 찬물이 나오던 ("백조의 목"처럼 생긴) 물꼭지의 느낌을 기억해내고 있다.

148) I was not. I am. I was. I am not.

drummer or what thought they were army shirts until all of a sudden I knew he wasn't thinking of me at all as a potential source of harm but was thinking of her when he looked at me was looking at me through her like through a piece of colored glass *why must you meddle with me dont you know it wont do any good I thought you'd have left that for Mother and Jason*

did Mother set Jason to spy on you I wouldn't have.

Women only use other people's codes of honor it's because she loves Caddy staying downstairs even when she was sick so Father couldn't kid Uncle Maury before Jason Father said Uncle Maury was too poor a classicist to risk the blind immortal boy in person[149)] he should have chosen Jason because Jason would have made only the same kind of blunder Uncle Maury himself would have made not one to get him a black eye the Patterson boy was smaller than Jason too they sold the kites for a nickel a piece until the trouble over finances[150)] Jason got a new partner still smaller one small enough anyway because T. P. said Jason still treasurer but Father said why should Uncle Maury work if he Father could support five or six niggers that did nothing at all but sit with their feet in the oven he certainly could board and lodge Uncle Maury now and then and lend him a little money who kept his Father's belief in the celestial derivation of his own species at such a fine heat then Mother would cry and say that Father believed his people were better than hers that he was ridiculing Uncle Maury to teach us the same thing she couldn't see that Father was teaching us that all men are just

---

149) "blind immortal boy" = Cupid (사랑의 메신저). 캄슨씨는 처남(모리 삼촌)을 놀리며 그와 패터슨 부인 간의 사랑의 메신저는 벤지임을 꼬집고 있다.

150) 어린시절 자신보다 어린 친구(패터슨집 아들)에게 속임수를 써, 연들을 팔아 더 많은 이득을 챙긴 제이슨의 모습과 함께, 훗날 캐디의 돈을 훔치는 제이슨의 모습을 예고한다. 제이슨 역시, 모리 삼촌과 마찬가지로, 패터슨가의 남자들에게 속임수를 쓰고 있음을 엿볼 수 있다.

accumulations dolls stuffed with sawdust swept up from the trash heaps where all previous dolls had been thrown away the sawdust flowing from what wound in what side that not for me died not. It used to be I thought of death as a man something like Grandfather a friend of his a kind of private and particular friend like we used to think of Grandfather's desk not to touch it not even to talk loud in the room where it was I always thought of them as being together somewhere all the time waiting for old Colonel Sartoris to come down and sit with them waiting on a high place beyond cedar trees Colonel Sartoris was on a still higher place looking out across at something[151)] and they were waiting for him to get done looking at it and come down Grandfather wore his uniform and we could hear the murmur of their voices from beyond the cedar they were always talking and Grandfather was always right

The three quarters began. The first note sounded, measured and tranquil, serenely peremptory, emptying the unhurried silence for the next one and that's it if people could only change one another forever that way merge like a flame swirling up for an instant then blown cleanly out along the cool eternal dark instead of lying there trying not to think of the swing until all cedars came to have that vivid dead smell of perfume that Benjy hated so. Just by imagining the clump it seemed to me that I could hear whispers secret surges smell the beating of hot blood under wild unsecret flesh watching against red eyelids the swine untethered in pairs rushing coupled into the sea and

---

151) "waiting for old Colonel Sartoris . . ."에서 여기까지는, 어린시절 퀸턴이 할아버지를 죽음과 함께 연상시키면서, 할아버지와 친구 사토리스 대령이 삼나무 너머 저 높은 곳에서 서로 얘기 나누는 모습을 상상하던 자신을 기억해낸다. 그리고 조금 아래 연결되는 곳에서("the swing until all the cedars came to have that vivid dead smell of perfume . . .") 더 명료히 드러나지만, 캐디가 연인들을 만나던 그네도 바로 이 삼나무 숲 안에 있다는 점에서 캐디의 섹슈얼리티와 죽음의 이미지는 이 삼나무들과도 연관되어 상상되고 있다.

he we must just stay awake and see evil done for a little while its not always and i it doesnt have to be even that long for a man of courage and he do you consider that courage and i yes sir dont you and he every man is the arbiter of his own virtues whether or not you consider it courageous is of more importance than the act itself than any act otherwise you could not be in earnest and i you dont believe i am serious and he i think you are too serious to give me any cause for alarm you wouldnt have felt driven to the expedient of telling me you had committed incest otherwise and i i wasnt lying i wasnt lying and he you wanted to sublimate a piece of natural human folly into a horror and then exorcise it with truth and i it was to isolate her out of the loud world so that it would have to flee us of necessity and then the sound of it would be as though it had never been and he did you try to make her do it and i i was afraid to i was afraid she might and then it[152) wouldnt have done any good but if i could tell you we did it would have been so and then the others wouldnt be so and then the world would roar away and he and now this other you are not lying now either but you are still blind to what is in yourself to that part of general truth the sequence of natural events and their causes which shadows every mans brow even benjys you are not thinking of finitude you are contemplating an apotheosis in which a temporary state of mind will become symmetrical above the flesh and aware both of itself and of the flesh it will not quite discard you will not even be dead and i temporary and he you cannot bear to think that someday it will no longer hurt you like this now were getting at it you seem to regard it merely as an experience that will whiten your hair overnight so to speak without altering your appearance at all you wont do it under these conditions it will be a gamble and the strange thing is that man who is conceived by accident and whose every breath is a fresh cast with dice already loaded against him will not

152) 퀸턴과 캐디의 근친상간이 실제 일어나는 경우를 말한다.

face that final main which he knows before hand he has assuredly to face without essaying expedients ranging all the way from violence to petty chicanery that would not deceive a child until someday in very disgust he risks everything on a single blind turn of a card no man ever does that under the first fury of despair or remorse or bereavement he dose it only when he has realised that even the despair or remorse or bereavement is not particularly important to the dark diceman and i temporary and he it is hard believing to think that a love or a sorrow is a bond purchased without design and which matures willynilly and is recalled without warning to be replaced by whatever issue the gods happen to be floating at the time no you will not do that until you come to believe that even she was not quite worth despair perhaps and i i will never do that nobody knows what i know and he i think youd better go on up to cambridge right away you might go up into maine[153] for a month you can afford it if you are careful it might be a good thing watching pennies has healed more scars than jesus and i suppose i realise what you believe i will realise up there next week or next month and he then you will remember that for you to go to harvard has been your mothers dream since you were born and no compson has ever disappointed a lady and i temporary it will be better for me for all of us and he every man is the arbiter of his own virtues but let no man prescribe for another mans wellbeing and i temporary and he was the saddest word of all there is nothing else in the world its not despair until time its not even time until it was[154]

---

153) 아버지는 퀀턴에게 절망감을 극복하기 위해서라도 북부(Maine)로 갈 것을 제안하고 있다.

154) 포크너 작품세계에서 시간개념, 즉 과거의 중요성을 엿볼 수 있는 부분이다. 이 세상에서 가장 "슬픈 말"은 과거("was")인데, 그 이유는 세상의 모든 것은 과거 속으로 들어가 버린 후에야 존재성이 부여되기 때문이다. 절망도 어떤 과거의 사건이며, 시간 그 자체도 과거 속으로 들어가 버린 후가 아니면 존재 의미를 측정할

The last note sounded.[155] At last it stopped vibrating and the darkness was still again. I entered the sitting room and turned on the light. I put my vest on. The gasoline was faint now, barely noticeable, and in the mirror the stain didn't show. Not like my eye did, anyway. I put on my coat. Shreve's letter[156] crackled through the cloth and I took it out and examined the address, and put it in my pocket. Then I carried the watch into Shreve's room and put it in his drawer and went to my room and got a fresh handkerchief and went to the door and put my hand on the light switch. Then I remembered I hadn't brushed my teeth, so I had to open the bag again. I found my toothbrush and got some of Shreve's paste and went out and brushed my teeth. I squeezed the brush as dry as I could and put it back in the bag and shut it, and went to the door again. Before I snapped the light out I looked around to see if there was anything else, then I saw that I had forgotten my hat. I'd have to go by the postoffice and I'd be sure to meet some of them, and they'd think I was a Harvard Square student making like he was a senior. I had forgotten to brush it too, but Shreve had a brush, so I didin't have to open the bag any more.

수 없는 것이다. 우리가 느끼는 모든 현재는 과거이며, 그 또한 과거가 된 후에야 비로소 그 존재성이 생성되기에 과거라는 말이 가장 슬픈 말인 것이다.

155) 시간의 45분대(the third quarter of the hour)를 알리는 교회 종소리의 마지막 음을 말하는 것일 수도 있지만, 동시에 그 음은 퀸턴 기억속의 마지막 종소리일 수도 있다.

156) 쉬리브에게 남긴 퀸턴의 자살 편지.

April Sixth, 1928

Once a bitch always a bitch, what I say. I says you're lucky if her playing out of school is all that worries you.[1] I says she ought to be down there in that kitchen right now, instead of up there in her room, gobbing paint on her face and waiting for six niggers that cant even stand up out of a chair unless they've got a pan full of bread and meat to balance them, to fix breakfast for her. And Mother says,

"But to have the school authorities think that I have no control over her, that I cant——"

"Well," I says. "You cant can you? You never have tried to do anything with her," I says. "How do you expect to begin this late, when she's seventeen years old?"

She thought about that for a while.

"But to have them think that . . . I didn't even know she had a report card. She told me last fall that they had quit using them this year. And now for Professor Junkin to call me on the telephone and tell me if she's absent one more time, she will have to leave school. How does she do it? Where does she go? You're down town all day; you ought to see her if she stays on the streets."

"Yes," I says. "If she stayed on the streets. I dont reckon she'd be playing out of school just to do something she could do in public," I says.

"What do you mean?" she says.

---

1) "you"는 캄슨 부인, "her"는 캐디의 딸 미스 퀸틴이다.

"I dont mean anything," I says. "I just answered your question." Then she begun to cry again, talking about how her own flesh and blood rose up to curse her.

"You asked me," I says.

"I dont mean you," she says. "You are the only one of them that isn't a reproach to me."

"Sure," I says. "I never had time to be. I never had time to go to Harvard or drink myself into the ground. I had to work. But of course if you want me to follow her around and see what she does, I can quit the store and get a job where I can work at night. Then I can watch her during the day and you can use Ben for the night shift."

"I know I'm just a trouble and a burden to you," she says, crying on the pillow.

"I ought to know it," I says. "You've been telling me that for thirty years. Even Ben ought to know it now. Do you want me to say anything to her about it?"

"Do you think it will do any good?" she says.

"Not if you come down there interfering just when I get started," I says. "If you want me to control her, just say so and keep your hands off. Everytime I try to, you come butting in and then she gives both of us the laugh."

"Remember she's your own flesh and blood," she says.

"Sure," I says, "that's just what I'm thinking of—flesh. And a little blood too, if I had my way. When people act like niggers, no matter who they are the only thing to do is treat them like a nigger."

"I'm afraid you'll lose your temper with her," she says.

"Well," I says. "You haven't had much luck with your system. You want me to do anything about it, or not? Say one way or the other; I' ve got to get on to work."

"I know you have to slave your life away for us," she says. "You know If I had my way, you'd have an office of your own to go to, and hours that became a Bascomb. Because you are a Bascomb, despite your name. I know that if your father could have foreseen—"

"Well," I says, "I reckon he's entitled to guess wrong and then, like anybody else, even a Smith or a Jones." She begun to cry again.

"To hear you speak bitterly of your dead father," she says.

"All right," I says, "all right. Have it your way. But as I haven't got an office, I'll have to get on to what I have got. Do you want me to say anything to her?"

"I'm afraid you'll lose your temper with her," she says.

"All right," I says. " I wont say anything, then."

"But something must be done," she says. "To have people think I permit her to stay out of school and run about the streets, or that I cant prevent her doing it . . . Jason, Jason,"[2] she says. "How could you. How could you leave me with these burdens."

"Now, now," I says. "You'll make yourself sick. Why dont you either lock her up all day too, or turn her over to me and quit worrying over her?"

"My own flesh and blood," she says, crying. So I says,

"All right. I'll tend to her. Quit crying, now."

"Dont lose your temper," she says. "She's just a child, remember."

"No," I says. "I wont." I went out, closing the door.

"Jason," she says. I didn't answer. I went down the hall. "Jason," she says beyond the door. I went on down stairs. There wasn't anybody in the diningroom, then I heard her in the kitchen. She was trying to make Dilsey let her have another cup of coffee. I went in.

"I reckon that's your school costume, is it?" I says. "Or maybe today's a holiday?"

"Just a half a cup, Dilsey," she says. "Please."

"No, suh," Dilsey says. "I aint gwine[3] do it. You aint got no business wid mo'n one cup, a seventeen year old gal, let lone whut Miss Cahline say. You go on and git dressed for school, so you kin

---

2) 고인이 된 남편의 이름을 부르고 있다.

3) going to.

ride to town wid Jason. You fixin to be late again."

"No she's not," I says. "We're going to fix that right now." She looked at me, the cup in her hand. She brushed her hair back from her face, her kimono slipping off her shoulder. "You put that cup down and come in here a minute," I says.

"What for?" she says.

"Come on," I says. "Put that cup in the sink and come in here."

"What you up to now, Jason?" Dilsey says.

"You may think you can run over me like you do your grandmother and everybody else," I says. "But you'll find out different. I'll give you ten seconds to put that cup down like I told you."

She quit looking at me. She looked at Dilsey. "What time is it, Dilsey?" she says. "When it's ten seconds, you whistle. Just a half a cup. Dilsey, pl—"

I grabbed her by the arm. She dropped the cup. It broke on the floor and she jerked back, looking at me, but I held her arm. Dilsey got up from her chair.

"You, Jason," she says.

"You turn me loose," Quentin says. "I'll slap you."

"You will, will you?" I says. "You will will you?" She slapped at me. I caught that hand too and held her like a wildcat. "You will, will you?" I says. "You think you will?"

"You, Jason!" Dilsey says. I dragged her into the diningroom. Her kimono came unfastened, flapping about her, dam[4)] near naked. Dilsey came hobbling along. I turned and kicked the door shut in her face.

"You keep out of here," I says.

Quentin was leaning against the table, fastening her kimono. I looked at her.

---

4) damn.

"Now," I says. "I want to know what you mean, playing out of school and telling your grandmother lies and forging her name on your report and worrying her sick. What do you mean by it?"

She didn't say anything. She was fastening her kimono up under her chin, pulling it tight around her, looking at me. She hadn't got around to painting herself yet and her face looked like she had polished it with a gun rag. I went and grabbed her wrist. "What do you mean?" I says.

"None of your damn business," she says. "You turn me loose."

Dilsey came in the door. "You, Jason," she says.

"You get out of here, like I told you," I says, not even looking back. "I want to know where you go when you play out of school," I says. "You keep off the streets, or I'd see you. Who do you play out with? Are you hiding out in the woods with one of those dam slick-headed jellybeans?[5] Is that where you go?"

"You—you old goddam!" she says. She fought, but I held her. "You damn old goddam!" she says.

"I'll show you," I says. "You may can scare an old woman off, but I'll show you who's got hold of you now." I held her with one hand, then she quit fighting and watched me, her eyes getting wide and black.

"What are you going to do?" she says.

"You wait until I get this belt out and I'll show you," I says, pulling my belt out. Then Dilsey grabbed my arm.

"Jason," she says. "You, Jason! Aint you shamed of yourself."

"Dilsey," Quentin says. "Dilsey."

"I aint gwine let him," Dilsey says. "Dont you worry, honey." She held to my arm. Then the belt came out and I jerked loose and flung her away. She stumbled into the table. She was so old she couldn't do

---

5) "jellybean"은 1920년대 사용되던 은어로, 머리를 매끈하게 빗어 넘기고 외모와 멋 부리기에 신경 쓰던 젊은이를 두고 나온 말이다.

any more than move hardly. But that's all right: we need somebody in the kitchen to eat up the grub the young ones cant tote off. She came hobbling between us, trying to hold me again. "Hit me, den," she says, "ef nothin else but hittin somebody wont do you. Hit me," she says.

"You think I wont?" I says.

"I dont put no devilment beyond you," she says. Then I heard Mother on the stairs. I might have known she wasn't going to keep out of it. I let go. She stumbled back against the wall, holding her kimono shut.

"All right," I says. "We'll just put this off a while. But dont think you can run it over me. I'm not an old woman, nor an old half dead nigger, either. You dam little shut," I says.

"Dilsey," she says. "Dilsey, I want my mother."

Dilsey went to her. "Now, now," she says. "He aint gwine so much as lay his hand on you while Ise[6)] here." Mother came on down the stairs.

"Jason," she says. "Dilsey."

"Now, now," Dilsey says. "I aint gwine let him tech[7)] you." She put her hand on Quentin. She knocked it down.

"You damn old nigger," she says. She ran toward the door.

"Dilsey," Mother says on the stairs. Quentin ran up the stairs, passing her. "Quentin," Mother says. "You, Quentin." Quentin ran on. I could hear her when she reached the top, then in the hall. Then the door slammed.

Mother had stopped. Then she came on. "Dilsey," she says.

"All right," Dilsey says. "Ise comin. You go on and git dat car and wait now," she says, "so you kin cahy[8)] her to school."

---

6) I is = I am.

7) touch.

8) carry.

"Dont you worry," I says. "I'll take her to school and I'm going to see that she stays there. I've started this thing, and I'm going through with it."

"Jason," Mother says on the stairs.

"Go on, now," Dilsey says, going toward the door. "You want to git her started too? Ise comin, Miss Cahline."

I went on out. I could hear them on the steps. "You go on back to bed now," Dilsey was saying. "Dont you know you aint feeling well enough to git up yet? Go on back, now. I'm gwine to see she gits to school in time."

I went on out the back to back the car out, then I had to go all the way round to the front before I found them.

"I thought I told you to put that tire on the back of the car," I says.

"I aint had time," Luster says. "Aint nobody to watch him till mammy git done in de kitchen."

"Yes," I says. "I feed a whole dam kitchen full of niggers to follow around after him, but if I want an automobile tire changed, I have to do it myself."

"I aint had nobody to leave him wid," he says. Then he begun moaning and slobbering.

"Take him on round to the back," I says. "What the hell makes you want to keep him around here where people can see him? I made them go on, before he got started bellowing good. It's bad enough on Sundays, with that dam field full of people that haven't got a side show and six niggers to feed, knocking a dam oversize mothball around.[9] He's going to keep on running up and down that fence and bellowing every time they come in sight until first thing I know they're going to begin charging me golf dues, then Mother and Dilsey'll have to get a couple of china door knobs and a walking stick

---

9) 한때는 캄슨 집안의 땅이었던 골프장에서 골프를 즐기는, 돈과 여가시간을 가진 골퍼들을 향해 제이슨은 반감을 토로하고 있다.

and work it out, unless I play at night with a lantern. Then they'd send us all to Jackson, maybe. God knows, they'd hold Old Home week when that happened.

I went on back to the garage. There was the tire, leaning against the wall, but be damned if I was going to put it on. I backed out and turned around. She was standing by the drive. I says,

"I know you haven't got any books: I just want to ask you what you did with them, if it's any of my business. Of course I haven't got any right to ask," I says. "I'm just the one that paid $11.65 for them last September."

"Mother buys my books," she says. "There's not a cent of your money on me. I'd starve first."

"Yes?" I says. "You tell your grandmother that and see what she says. You dont look all the way naked," I says, "even if that stuff on your face does hide more of you than anything else you've got on."

"Do you think your money or hers either paid for a cent of this?" she says.

"Ask your grandfather," I says. "Ask her what became of those checks. You saw her burn one of them,[10] as I remember." She wasn't even listening, with her face all gummed up with paint and her eyes hard as a fice dog's.[11]

"Do you know what I'd do if I thought your money or hers either bought one cent of this?" she says, putting her hand on her dress.

"What would you do?" I says. "Wear a barrel?"

"I'd tear it right off and throw it into the street," she says. "Dont you believe me?"

---

10) "them"="those checks." 매달 캐디는 딸을 위해 캄슨 부인에게 수표를 보내고 있지만, 제이슨은 어머니를 설득해—캐디가 보내주는 돈이 비도덕적이라고 믿게 함으로써—보내준 수표를 불태우게 한다. 하지만 뒤에 밝혀지듯이, 제이슨은 캐디가 보내준 수표를 자기 몫으로 챙기고, 어머니에게는 매번 가짜 수표를 불태우게 하고 있다.

11) "fice"는 작은 잡종 개이다.

"Sure you would," I says. "You do it every time."

"See if I wouldn't," she says. She grabbed the neck of her dress in both hands and make like she would tear it.

"You tear that dress," I says. "and I'll give you a whipping right here that you'll remember all your life."

"See if I dont," she says. Then I saw that she rally was trying to tear it, to tear it right off of her. By the time I got the car stopped and grabbed her hands there was about a dozen people looking. It made me so mad for a minute it kind of blinded me.

"You do a thing like that again and I'll make you sorry you ever drew breath," I says.

"I'm sorry now," she says. She quit, then her eyes turned kind of funny and I says to myself if you cry here in this car, on the street, I'll whip you. I'll wear you out. Lucky for her she didn't, so I turned her wrists loose and drove on. Luckily we were near an alley, where I could turn into the back street and dodge the square. They were already putting the tent up in Beard's lot. Earl[12)] had already given me the two passes for our show windows. She sat there with her face turned away, chewing her lip. "I'm sorry now," she says. "I dont see why I was ever born."

"And I know of at least one other person that dont understand all he knows about that," I says. I stopped in front of the school house. The bell had rung, and the last of them were just going in. "You're on time for once, anyway," I says. "Are you going in there and stay there, or am I coming with you and make you?" She got out and banged the door. "Remember what I say," I says. "I mean it. Let me hear one more time that you are slipping up and down back alleys with one of those dam squirts."

She turned back at that, "I dont slip around," she says, "I dare anybody to know everything I do."

12) 제이슨이 일하고 있는 철물점 주인.

"And they all know it, too," I says. "Everybody in this town knows what you are. But I wont have it anymore, you hear? I dont care what you do, myself," I says. "But I've got a position in this town, and I'm not going to have any member of my family going on like a nigger wench. You hear me?"

"I dont care," she says. "I'm bad and I'm going to hell, and I dont care. I'd rather be in hell than anywhere where you are."

"If I hear one more time that you haven't been to school, you'll wish you were in hell," I says. She turned and ran on across the yard. "One more time, remember," I says. She didn't look back.

I went to the postoffice and got the mail and drove on to the store and parked. Earl looked at me when I came in. I gave him a chance to say something about my being late, but he just said,

"Those cultivators have come. You'd better help Uncle Job[13] put them up."

I went on to the barn, where old Job was uncrating them, at the rate of about there bolts to the hour.

"You ought to be working for me," I says. "Every other no-count nigger in town eats in my kitchen."

'I works to suit de man whut pays me Sat'dy night," he says. "When I does dat, it dont leave me a whole lot of time to please other folks." He screwed up a nut. "Aint nobody works much in dis country cep de boll-weevil,[14] noways," he says.

"You'd better be glad you're not a boll-weevil waiting on those cultivators," I says. "You'd work yourself to death before they'd be ready to prevent you."

"Dat's de troof," [15] he says. "Boll-weevil got tough time. Work ev' y day in de week out in de hot sun, rain er shine. Aint got no front

---

13) 당시 흑인들 사이에서는 흔한 이름.

14) 목화 깍지(boll)를 갉아먹는 해충.

15) truth.

porch to set on en watch de wattermilyuns growin and Sat'dy dont mean nothin a-tall to him."

"Saturday wouldn't mean nothing to you, either," I says, "if it depended on me to pay you wages. Get those things out of the crates now and drag them inside."

I opened her letter[16] first and took the check out. Just like a woman. Six days late. Yet they try to make men believe that they're capable of conducting a business. How long would a man that thought the first of the month came on the sixth last in business. And like as not, when they sent the bank statement out, she would want to know why I never deposited my salary until the sixth. Things like that never occur to a woman.

> "I had no answer to my letter about Quentin's easter dress. Did it arrive all right? I've had no answer to the last two letters I wrote her, though the check in the second one was cashed with the other check. Is she sick? Let me know at once or I'll come there and see for myself. You promised you would let me know when she needed things. I will expect to hear from you before the 10th. No you'd better wire me at once. You are opening my letters to her. I know that as well as if I were looking at you. You'd better wire me at once about her to this address."

About that time Earl started yelling at Job, so I put them away and went over to try to put some life into him. What this country needs is white labor. Let these dam trifling niggers starve for a couple of years, then they'd see what a soft thing they have.

Along toward ten oclock I went up front. There was a drummer[17]

16) 캐디의 편지.

17) 출장 세일즈맨.

there. It was a couple of minutes to ten, and I invited him up the street to get a dope.[18)] We got to talking about crops.

"There's nothing to it," I says. "Cotton is a speculator's crop. They fill the farmer full of hot air and get him to raise a big crop for them to whipsaw on the market, to trim the suckers with. Do you think the farmer gets anything out of it except a red neck and a hump in his back? You think the man that sweats to put it into the ground gets a red cent more than a bare living," I says. "Let him make a big crop and it wont be worth picking; let him make a small crop and he wont have enough to gin. And what for? so a bunch of dam eastern jews I' m not talking about men of the jewish religion," I says. "I've known some jews that were fine citizens. You might be one yourself," I says.

"No," he says. "I'm an American."

"No offense," I says. "I give every man his due, regardless of religion or anything else. I have nothing against jews as an individual," I says. "It's just the race. You'll admit that they produce nothing. They follow the pioneers into a new country and sell them clothes."

"You're thinking of Armenians," he says, "aren't you. A pioneer wouldn't have any use for new clothes."

"No offense," I says. "I dont hold a man's religion against him."

"Sure," he says. "I'm an American. My folks have some French blood, why I have a nose like this. I'm an American, all right."

"So am I," I says. "Not many of us left. What I'm talking about is the fellows that sit up there in New York and trim the sucker gamblers."[19)]

---

18) 코카콜라(Coca Cola)를 당시 남부에서는 "dope"(마약)이라고 불렀는데, 아마 음료 속에 코카인과 중독성 자극제가 섞여 있다고 믿던 통념 때문이라 하겠다. 1880년대 나온 원조 코카콜라 속에는 실제로 코카인 성분이 상당량 포함되어 있었으며, 그 마약 성분은 1890년대에 제거되었다고 하지만, 그 후에도 시비는 계속되었다.

"That's right," he says. "Nothing to gambling, for a poor man. There ought to be a law against it."

"Dont you think I'm right?" I says.

"Yes," he says. "I guess you're right. The farmer catches it coming and going."

"I know I'm right," I says. "It's a sucker game, unless a man gets inside information from somebody that knows what's going on. I happen to be associated with some people who're right there on the ground. They have one of the biggest manipulators in New York for an adviser. Way I do it," I says, "I never risk much at a time. It's the fellow that thinks he knows it all and is trying to make a killing with three dollars that they're laying for. That's why they are in the business."

Then it struck ten.[20] I went up to the telegraph office. It opened up a little, just like they said. I went into the corner and took out the telegram again, just to be sure. While I was looking at it a report came in. It was up two points. They were all buying. I could tell that from what they were saying. Getting aboard. Like they didn't know it could go but one way. Like there was a law or something against doing anything but buying. Well, I reckon those eastern jews have got to live too. But I'll be damned if it hasn't come to a pretty pass when any dam foreigner that cant make a living in the country where God put him, can come to this one and take money right out of an American's pockets. It was up two points more. Four points. But hell, they were right there and knew what was going on. And if I wasn't going to take the advice, what was I paying them ten dollars a month

---

19) "the fellows"는 뉴욕의 주식거래를 자문해주는 유대인들이며, 여기 제이슨은 그들을 두고 불평을 토로하고 있다. 실제 그들은 제이슨에게 목화시장 주를 두고 제대로 조언을 하였지만 그는 그것을 받아들이지 않을 뿐이다.

20) 제이슨도 퀀턴처럼 시간을 의식하는 모습이다. 하지만 시간에 대한 제이슨의 집착은 자신이 투자한 목화시장 시세에 대한 관심에서 비롯된다.

for. I went out, then I remembered and came back and sent the wire. "All well. Q writing today." [21]

"Q?" the operator says.

"Yes," I says. "Q. Cant you spell Q?"

"I just asked to be sure," he says.

"You send it like I wrote it and I'll guarantee you to be sure," I says. "Send it collect."

"What you sending, Jason?" Doc Wright says, looking over my shoulder. "Is that a code message to buy?"

"That's all right about that," I says. "You boys use your own judgment. You know more about it than those New York folks do."

"Well, I ought to," Doc says. "I'd a saved money this year raising it at two cents a pound."

Another report came in. It was down a point.

"Jason's selling," Hopkins says. "Look at his face."

"That's all right about what I'm doing," I says. "You boys follow your own judgement. Those rich New York jews have got to live like everybody else," I says.

I went on back to the store. Earl was busy up front. I went on back to the desk and read Lorraine's[22] letter. "Dear daddy wish you were here. No good parties when daddys out of town I miss my sweet daddy." I reckon she does. Last time I gave her forty dollars. Gave it to her. I never promise a woman anything nor let her know what I'm going to give her. That's the only way to manage them. Always keep them guessing. If you cant think of any other way to surprise them, give them a bust in the jaw.

I tore it up and burned it over the spittoon. I make it a rule never to keep a scrap of paper bearing a woman's hand, and I never write them at all. Lorraine is always after me to write to her but I says

---

21) Q는 목화주가와 관련된 특수 전보 코드 문자 중 하나로 볼 수 있다.

22) 로레인은 제이슨이 멤피스에 두고 있는 여자(창녀)이다.

anything I forgot to tell you will save till I get to Memphis again but I says I dont mind you writing me now and then in a plain envelope, but if you ever try to call me up on the telephone, Memphis wont hold you I says. I says when I'm up there I'm one of the boys, but I'm not going to have any woman calling me on the telephone. Here I says, giving her the forty dollars. If you ever get drunk and take a notion to call me on the phone, just remember this and count ten before you do it.

"When'll that be?" she says.

"What?" I says.

"When you're coming back," she says.

"I'll let you know," I says. Then she tried to buy a beer, but I wouldn't let her. "Keep your money," I says. "Buy yourself a dress with it." I gave the maid a five, too. After all, like I say money has no value; it's just the way you spend it. It dont belong to anybody, so why try to hoard it. It just belongs to the man that can get it and keep it. There's a man right here in Jefferson made a lot of money selling rotten goods to niggers, lived in a room over the store about the size of a pigpen, and did his own cooking. About four or five years ago he was taken sick. Scared the hell out of him so that when he was up again he joined the church and bought himself a Chinese missionary,[23)] five thousand dollars a year. I often think how mad he'll be if he was to die and find out there's not any heaven, when he thinks about that five thousand a year. Like I say, he'd better go on and die now and save money.

When it was burned good I was just about to shove the others into my coat when all of a sudden something told me to open Quentin's before I went home, but about that time Earl started yelling for me up front, so I put them away and went and waited on the dam redneck while he spent fifteen minutes deciding whether he wanted a

---

23) 중국에서 선교활동을 하는 종교기관을 도우기 위해 돈을 기부.

twenty cent hame[24)] string or a thirty-five cent one.

"You'd better take that good one," I says, "How do you fellows ever expect to get ahead, trying to work with cheap equipment?"

"If this one aint any good," he says, "why have you got it on sale?"

"I didn't say it wasn't any good," I says. "I said it's not as good as that other one."

"How do you know it's not," he says. "You ever use airy one of them?"

"Because they dont ask thirty-five cents for it," I says. "That's how I know it's not as good."

He held the twenty cent one in his hands, drawing it through his fingers. "I reckon I'll take this hyer one," he says. I offered to take it and wrap it, but he rolled it up and put it in his overalls. Then he took out a tobacco sack and finally got it untied and shook some coins out. He handed me a quarter. "That fifteen cents will buy me a snack of dinner," he says.

"All right," I says. "You're the doctor. But dont come complaining to me next year when you have to buy a new outfit."

"I aint makin next year's crop yit," he says. Finally I got rid of him, but every time I took that letter out something would come up. They were all in town for the show, coming in in droves to give their money to something that brought nothing to the town and wouldn't leave anything except what those grafters in the Mayor's office will split among themselves, and Earl chasing back and forth like a hen in a coop, saying "Yes, ma'am, Mr Compson will wait on you. Jason, show this lady a churn or a nickel's worth of screen hooks."

Well, Jason likes work. I says no I never had university advantages because at Harvard they teach you how to go for a swim at night without knowing how to swim and at Sewanee they dont even teach

---

24) hames.

you what water is.[25] I says you might send me to the state University; maybe I'll learn how to stop my clock with a nose spray[26] and then you can send Ben to the Navy I says or to the cavalry anyway, they use geldings in the cavalry. Then when she sent Quentin home for me to feed too I says I guess that's right too, instead of me having to go way up north for a job they sent the job down here to me and then Mother begun to cry and I says it's not that I have any objection to having it[27] here; if it's any satisfaction to you I'll quit work and nurse it myself and let you and Dilsey keep the flour barrel full, or Ben. Rent him out to a sideshow; there must be folks somewhere that would pay a dime to see him, then she cried more and kept saying my poor afflicted baby and I says yes he'll be quite a help to you when he gets his growth not being more than one and a half times as high as me now and she says she'd be dead soon and then we'd all be better off and so I says all right, all right, have it your way. It's your grandchild, which is more than any other grandparents it's got can say for certain. Only I says it's only a question of time. If you believe she'll do what she says and not try to see it, you fool yourself because the first time that was the Mother kept on saying thank God you are not a Compson except in name, because you are all I have left now, you and Maury and I says well I could spare Uncle Maury myself and then they came and said they were ready to start. Mother stopped crying then. She pulled her veil

---

25) 물론 앞부분은 퀸턴이 하버드에서 익사한 사건을 제이슨이 비아냥대고 있다면, 뒷부분은 아버지 캄슨씨가 졸업한 학교(Sewanee)에서 위스키를 물이나 다른 음료로 희석하지 않고 그대로 마시는 법을 배웠을 것이라고 농담하면서, 아버지가 술독에 빠져 죽은 사실을 조롱하고 있다.

26) 역시 비아냥대는 투로 제이슨은 자신이 동부의 일류대학은 아니라도 주립대학 정도의 교육만 받았더라도, 자신이 끊임없이 코에다 뿌려대는 두통 치료제들로 자살하는 방법을 스스로 터득할 수 있었을 것이라고 농담하고 있다.

27) Miss Quentin.

down and we went down stairs. Uncle Maury was coming out of the diningroom, his handkerchief to his mouth.[28] They kind of made a lane and we went out the door just in time to see Dilsey driving Ben and T. P. back around the corner. We went down the steps and got in. Uncle Maury kept saying Poor little sister, poor litter sister, talking around his mouth and patting Mother's hand. Talking around whatever it was.

"Have you got your band[29] on?" she says. "Why dont they go on, before Benjamin comes out and makes a spectacle. Poor litter boy. He doesn't know. He cant even realise."

"There, there," Uncle Maury says, patting her hand, talking around his mouth. "It's better so. Let him be unaware of bereavement until he has to."

"Other women have their children to support them in times like this." Mother says.

"You have Jason and me," he says.

"It's so terrible to me," she says. "Having the two of them like this, in less than two years."

"There, there." he says. After a while he kind of sneaked his hand to his mouth and dropped them out the window. Then I knew what I had been smelling. Clove stems.[30] I reckon he thought that the least he could do at Father's or maybe the sideboard thought it was still Father and tripped him up when he passed. Like I say, if he had to sell something to send Quentin to Harvard we'd all been a dam sight better off if he'd sold that sideboard and bought himself a one-armed strait jacket with part of the money.[31] I reckon the reason all the

---

28) 모리 삼촌이 술을 몰래 마시고 나와 들키지 않기 위해 입을 손수건으로 가리고 있는 모습이다.

29) mourning band.

30) 구강 청강제, 모리 삼촌이 술 냄새를 숨기기 위해 씹는 것이다.

31) 여기서도 아버지에 대한 제이슨의 반감은 노골적으로 드러나는데, 만약 아버지가

Compson gave out before it got to me like Mother says, is that he drank it up. At least I never heard of him offering to sell anything to send me to Harvard.

So he kept on patting her hand and saying "Poor litter sister," patting her hand with one of the black gloves that we got the bill for four days later because it was the twenty-sixth because it was the same day one month[32] that Father went up there and got it and brought it home and wouldn't tell anything about where she was or anything and Mother crying and saying "And you didn't even see him? You didn't even try to get him to make any provision for it?" and Father says "No she shall not touch his money not one cent of it" and Mother says "He can be forced to by law. He can prove nothing, unless— Jason Compson," she says. "Were you fool enough to tell—"

"Hush, Caroline," Father says, then he sent me to help Dilsey get that old cradle out of the attic and I says,

"Well, they brought my job home tonight"[33] because all the time we kept hoping they'd get things straightened out and he'd keep her because Mother kept saying she would at least have enough regard for the family not to jeopardise my chance after she and Quentin had

---

퀸턴을 하버드에 보내기 위해 집안 소유의 목초지(지금은 골프장)를 파는 대신 자신의 술병들을 보관하는 찬장(sideboard)을 팔았더라면 훨씬 더 나았을 것이라고, 뿐만 아니라 아버지 스스로 "strait jacket"(폭력적일 수 있는 위험한 정신이상자를 통제하는 장치)을 사 입어 술을 마시는 아버지의 한쪽 팔("one-armed")만이라도 통제하는 편이 더 나았을 것이라고 통렬한 농담을 퍼붓고 있다.

32) 미스 퀸턴이 캄슨 집에 도착한 시점.

33) 제이슨이 여기 언급하고 있는 "my job"은 두 가지 차원으로 이해할 수 있는데, 먼저 그 "일"은 허버트가 캐디와의 결혼을 통해 약속되어 있던 제이슨의 은행 일자리로, 둘 간의 이혼으로 그것이 무산되어 집으로 되돌아왔다는 것을 냉소적으로 말하고 있으며, 이와 연관되어 그것은 앞으로 조카 미스 퀸턴을 키우는 일이 자신의 일거리가 될 것임을 예고하고 있는 발언이기도 하다.

had theirs.

"And whar else do she belong?" Dilsey says. "Who else gwine raise her cep me? Aint I raised ev'y one of y'all?"

"And a dam fine job you made of it," I says. "Anyway it'll give her something to sure enough worry over now." So we carried the cradle down and Dilsey started to set it up in her old room. Then Mother started sure enough.

"Hush," Miss Cahline," Dilsey says. "You gwine wake her up."

"In there?" Mother says. "To be contaminated by that atmosphere? It'll be hard enough as it is, with the heritage she already has."

"Hush," Father says. "Dont be silly."

"Why aint she gwine sleep in here," Dilsey says. "In the same room whar I put her maw to bed ev'y night of her life since she was big enough to sleep by herself."

"You dont know," Mother says. "To have my own daughter cast off by her husband. Poor little innocent baby," she says, looking at Quentin. "You will never know the suffering you've caused."

"Hush, Caroline," Father says.

"What you want to go on like that fo Jason fer?" [34)] Dilsey says.

"I've tried to protect him," Mother says. "I've always tried to protect him from it. At least I can do my best to shield her."

"How sleepin in dis room gwine hurt her, I like to know," Dilsey says.

"I cant help it," Mother says. "I know I'm just a troublesome old woman. But I know that people cannot flout God's laws with impunity."

"Nonsense," Father says. "Fix it in Miss Caroline's room then, Dilsey."

"You can say nonsense," Mother says. "But she must never know. She must never even learn that name. Dilsey, I forbid you ever to

---

34) before [in front of] Jason for.

speak that name in her hearing. If she could grow up never to know that she had a mother, I would thank God."

"Dont be a fool," Father says.

"I have never interfered with the way you brought them up," Mother says. "But now I cannot stand anymore. We must decide this now, tonight. Either that name is never to be spoken in her hearing, or she must go, or I will go. Take your choice."

"Hush," Father says. "You're just upset. Fix it in here, Dilsey."

"En you's about sick too,"[35] Dilsey says. "You looks like a hant.[36] You git in bed and I'll fix you a toddy and see kin you sleep. I bet you aint had a full night's sleep since you lef."

"No," Mother says." Dont you know what the doctor says? Why must you encourage him to drink? That's what's the matter with him now. Look at me, I suffer too, but I'm not so weak that I must kill myself with whiskey."

"Fiddlesticks," Father says. "What do doctors know? They make their livings advising people to do whatever they are not doing at the time, which is the extent of anyone's knowledge of the degenerate ape. You'll have a minister in to hold my hand next." Then Mother cried, and he went out. Went down stairs, and then I heard the sideboard.[37] I woke up and heard him going down again. Mother had gone to sleep or something, because the house was quiet at last. He was trying to be quiet too, because I couldn't hear him, only the bottom of his nightshirt and his bare legs in front of the sideboard.

Dilsey fixed the cradle and undressed her and put her in it. She never had waked up since he brought her in the house.

"She pretty near too big fer hit," Dilsey says. "Dar now. I gwine spread me a pallet right acrost de hall, so you wont need to git up in

---

35) 한 달 정도 후면 사망하게 될, 악화되고 있는 캄슨씨의 건강 상태를 암시한다.

36) haunt or ghost.

37) 아버지가 술 마시는 모습을 암시한다.

de night."

"I wont sleep," Mother says. "You go on home. I wont mind. I'll be happy to give the rest of my life to her, if I can just prevent——"

"Hush, now," Dilsey says. "We gwine take keer of her. En you go on to bed too," she says to me. "You got to go to school tomorrow."

So I went out, then Mother called me back and cried on me a while.

"You are my only hope," she says. "Every night I thank God for you." While we were waiting there for them to start she says Thank God if he had to be taken too, it is you left me and not Quentin. Thank God you are not a Compson, because all I have left now is you and Maury and I says, Well I could spare Uncle Maury myself. Well, he kept on patting her hand with his black glove, talking away from her. He took them off when his turn with the shovel came. He got up near the first, where they were holding the umbrellas over them, stamping every now and then and trying to kick the mud off their feet and sticking to the shovels so they'd have to knock it off, making a hollow sound when it fell on it,[38] and when I stepped back around the hack I could see him behind a tombstone, taking another one out of a bottle.[39] I thought he never was going to stop because I had on my new suit too, but it happened that there wasn't much mud on the wheels yet, only Mother saw it and says I dont know when you'll ever have another one and Uncle Maury says, "Now, now. Dont you worry at all. You have me to depend on, always."

And we have. Always. The fourth letter was from him. But there wasn't any need to open it. I could have written it myself, or recited it to her from memory, adding ten dollars just to be safe. But I had a hunch about that other letter.[40] I just felt that it was about time she

---

38) 캄슨씨의 장례식으로 시점이 변경되면서 그날 비가 오고 있음을 알 수 있다. 마지막 문장에서 앞의 "it"은 진흙이며, 두 번째 "it"는 캄슨씨의 관이다.

39) 모리 삼촌이 묘비 뒤에서 술을 한 모금씩 마시는 모습이다.

was up to some of her tricks again. She got pretty wise after that first time. She found out pretty quick that I was a different breed of cat from Father. When they begun to get it filled up toward the top Mother started crying sure enough, so Uncle Maury got in with her and drove off. He says You can come in with somebody: they'll be glad to give you a lift. I'll have to take your mother on and I thought about saying, Yes you ought to brought two bottles instead of just one only I thought about where we were, so I let them go on. Little they cared how wet I got, because then Mother could have a whale of a time being afraid I was taking pneumonia.

Well, I got to thinking about that and watching them throwing dirt into it, slapping it on anyway like they were making mortar or something or building a fence, and I began to feel sort of funny and so I decided to walk around a while. I thought that if I went toward town they'd catch up and be trying to make me get in one of them, so I went on back toward the nigger graveyard. I got under some cedars, where the rain didn't come much, only dripping now and then, where I could see when they got through and went away. After a while they were all gone and I waited a minute and came out.

I had to follow the path to keep out of the wet grass so I didn't see her until I was pretty near there, standing there in a black cloak, looking at the flowers. I knew who it[41] was right off, before she turned and looked at me and lifted up her veil.

"Hello, Jason," she says, holding out her hand. We shook hands.

"What are you doing here?" I says. "I thought you promised her you wouldn't come back here. I thought you had more sense than that."

"Yes?" she says. She looked at the flowers again. There must have been fifty dollars' worth. Somebody had put one bunch on Quentin's.

40) 캐디가 딸에게 보낸 편지.

41) Caddy.

"You did?" she says.

"I'm not surprised though," I says. "I wouldn't put anything past you. You dont mind anybody. You dont give a dam about anybody."

"Oh," she says, "that job." She looked at the grave. "I' m sorry a' bout that, Jason."

"I bet you are," I says. "You'll talk mighty meek now. But you needn't have come back. There's not anything left. Ask Uncle Maury, if you dont believe me."

"I dont want anything," she says. She looked at the grave. "Why didn't they let me know?"[42] she says. "I just happened to see it in the paper. On the back page. Just happened to."

I didn't say anything. We stood there, looking at the grave, and then I got to thinking about when we were little and one thing and another and I got to feeling funny again, kind of mad or something, thinking about now we'd have Uncle Maury around the house all the time,[43] running things like the way he left me to come home in the rain by myself. I says,

"A fine lot you care, sneaking in here soon as he's dead. But it wont do you any good. Dont think that you can take advantage of this to come sneaking back. If you cant stay on the horse you've got, you'll have to walk," I says. "We dont even know your name at that house," I says. "Do you know that? We dont even know your name. You'd be better off if you were down there with him and Quentin," I says. "Do you know that?"

---

42) 캐디의 이러한 물음에서 가족들은 캄슨씨의 죽음을 캐디에게 알리지 않았음을 알 수 있다.

43) 제이슨은 아버지의 죽음에 대한 자신의 감정을 반복하여 "이상한 느낌"(feeling funny)이 든다고 표현하고 있는데, 이러한 모습은 자신의 감정을 느끼고 솔직히 표현해내는데 문제가 있는 제이슨의 모습이라 하겠다. 여기 제이슨은 자신의 슬픔을 토로하기보다는 도리어 캄슨가에 빌붙어 살고 있는 삼촌을 향한 분노로 전이시키고 있다.

"I know it," she says. "Jason," she says, looking at the grave, "if you'll fix it so I can see her a minute I'll give you fifty dollars."

"You haven't got fifty dollars," I says.

"Will you?" she says, not looking at me.

"Let's see it," I says. "I dont believe you've got fifty dollars."

I could see where her hands were moving under her cloak, then she hold her hand out. Dam if it wasn't full of money. I could see two or three yellow ones.[44)]

"Does he still give you money?" I says. "How much does he send you?"

"I'll give you a hundred," she says. "Will you?"

"Just a minute," I says. "And just like I say. I wouldn't have her know it for a thousand dollars."

"Yes," she says. "Just like you say do it. Just so I see her a minute. I wont beg or do anything. I'll go right on away."

"Give me the money," I says.

"I'll give it to you afterward," she says.

"Dont you trust me?" I says.

"No," she says. "I know you. I grew up with you."

"You're a fine one to talk about trusting people," I says. "Well," I says. "I got to get on out of the rain. Goodbye." I made to go away.

"Jason," she says. I stopped.

"Yes?" I says. "Hurry up. I'm getting wet."

"All right," she says. "Here." There wasn't anybody in sight. I went back and took the money. She still held to it. "You'll do it?" she says, looking at me from under the veil. "You promise?"

"Let go," I says. "You want somebody to come along and see us?"

She let go. I put the money in my pocket. "You'll do it, Jason?"

---

44) "yellowbacks, gold certificates," 1882년에서 1922년 사이에 통용되던 지폐로(뒷면이 밝은 노란색을 띤), 가장 작은 단위가 10달러짜리였기 때문에, 여기 언급된 액수는 실제로 큰 금액을 암시할 수 있다.

she says. "I wouldn't ask you, if there was any other way."

"You dam right there's no other way," I says. "Sure I'll do it. I said I would, didn't I? Only you'll have to do just like I say, now."

"Yes," she says. "I will." So I told her where to be, and went to the livery stable. I hurried and got there just as they were unhitching the hack. I asked if they had paid for it yet and he said No and I said Mrs Compson forgot something and wanted it again, so they let me take it. Mink was driving. I bought him a cigar, so we drove around until it begun to get dark on the back streets where they wouldn't see him. Then Mink said he'd have to take the team on back and so I said I'd buy him another cigar and so we drove into the lane and I went across the yard to the house. I stopped in the hall until I could hear Mother and Uncle Maury upstairs, then I went on back to the kitchen. She and Ben were there with Dilsey. I said Mother wanted her and I took her into the house. I found Uncle Maury's raincoat and put it around her and picked her up and went back to the lane and got in the hack. I told Mink to drive to the depot. He was afraid to pass the stable, so we had to go the back way and I saw her standing on the corner under the light and I told Mink to drive close to the walk and when I said Go on, to give the team a bat. Then I took the raincoat off of her and held her to the window and Caddy saw her and sort of jumped forward.

"Hit'em, Mink!" I says, and Mink gave them a cut and we went past her like a fire engine. "Now get on that train like you promised," I says. I could see her running after us through the back window. "Hit'em again," I says. "Let's get on home." When we turned the corner she was still running.

And so I counted the money again that night and put it away, and I didn't feel so bad. I says I reckon that'll show you. I reckon you'll know now that you cant beat me out of a job and get away with it. It never occurred to me she wouldn't keep her promise and take that train. But I didn't know much about them then; I didn't have any more sense than to believe what they said, because the next morning dam if she didn't walk right into the store, only she had sense enough to wear the veil and not speak to anybody. It was Saturday morning, because I was at the store, and she came right on back to the desk where I was, walking fast.

"Liar," she says. "Liar."

"Are you crazy?" I says. "What do you mean? coming in here like this?" She started in, but I shut her off. I says, "You already cost me one job; do you want me lose this one too? If you've got anything to say to me, I'll meet you somewhere after dark. What have you got to say to me?" I says. "Didn't I do everything I said? I said see her a minute, didn't I? Well, didn't you?" She just stood there looking at me, shaking like an ague-fit, her hands clenched and kind of jerking. "I did just what I said I would," I says. "You're the one that lied. You promised to take that train. Didn't you? Didn't you promise? If you think you can get that money back, just try it," I says. "If it'd been a thousand dollars, you'd still owe me after the risk I took. And if I see or hear you're still in town after number 17 runs," I says, "I'll tell Mother and Uncle Maury. Then hold your breath until you see her again." She just stood there, looking at me, twisting her hands together.

"Damn you," she says. "Damn you."

"Sure," I says. "That's all right too. Mind what I say, now. After number 17, and I tell them."

After she was gone I felt better. I says I reckon you'll think twice before you deprive me of a job that was promised me. I was a kid then. I believed folks when they said they'd do things. I've learned better since. Besides, like I say I guess I dont need any man's help to get along I can stand on my own feet like I always have. Then all of a sudden I thought of Dilsey and Uncle Maury. I thought how she'd get around Dilsey and that Uncle Maury would do anything for ten dollars. And there I was, couldn't even get away from the store to protect my own Mother. Like she says, if one of you had to taken, thank God it was you left me I can depend on you and I says well I dont reckon I'll ever get far enough from the store to get out of your reach. Somebody's got to hold on to what little we have left, I reckon.

So as soon as I got home I fixed Dilsey. I told Dilsey she had leprosy and I got the bible and read where a man's flesh rotted off[45)] and I told her that if she ever looked at her or Ben or Quentin they'd catch it too. So I thought I had everything all fixed until that day when I came home and found Ben bellowing.[46)] Raising hell and nobody could quiet him. Mother said, Well, get him the slipper then. Dilsey made out she didn't hear. Mother said it again and I says I'd go I couldn't stand that dam noise. Like I say I can stand lots of things I dont expect much from them but if I have to work all day long in a dam store dam if I dont think I deserve a little peace and quiet to eat dinner in. So I says I'd go and Dilsey says quick, "Jason!"

Well, like a flash I knew what was up, but just to make sure I went and got the slipper and brought it back, and just like I thought, when he saw it you'd thought we were killing him. So I made Dilsey own up, then I told Mother. We had to take her up to bed then, and after things got quieted down a little I put the fear of God into Dilsey. As much as you can into a nigger, that is. That's the trouble with nigger servants, when they've been with you for a long time they get so full of self importance that they're not worth a dam. Think they run the whole family.

"I like to know whut's de hurt in lettin dat po chile see her own baby," Dilsey says. "If Mr Jason was still here hit ud be different."

"Only Mr Jason's not here," I says. "I know you wont pay me any mind, but I reckon you'll do what Mother says. You keep on worrying her like this until you get her into the graveyard too, then

45) 성경(Zechariah 14:12) 참고.

46) 다음 문단에서 드러나듯, 딜시가 식구들 몰래 캐디에게 딸 미스 퀸틴을 보게 하였음을 알 수 있기에, 캐디는 딸아이와 함께 벤지도 보았음을 알 수 있다.

you can fill the whole house full of ragtag and bobtail. But what did you want to let that dam boy see her for?"

"You's a cold man, Jason, if man you is," she says. "I think de Lawd I got mo heart dan dat, even ef hit is black."

"At least I'm man enough to keep that flour barrel full," I says. "And if you do that again, you wont be eating out of it either."

So the next time I told her that if she tried Dilsey again, Mother was going to fire Dilsey and send Ben to Jackson and take Quentin and go away. She looked at me for a while. There wasn't any street light close and I couldn't see her face much. But I could feel her looking at me. When we were little when she'd get mad and couldn't do anything about it her upper lip would begin to jump. Everytime it jumped it would leave a little more of her teeth showing, and all the time she'd be as still as a post, not a muscle moving expect her lip jerking higher and higher up her teeth. But she didn't say anything. She just said,

"All right. How much?"

"Well, if one look through a hack window was worth a hundred," I says. So after that she behaved pretty well, only one time she asked to see a statement of the bank account.

"I know they have Mother's indorsement on them," she says. "But I want to see the bank statement. I want to see myself where those checks go."

"That's in Mother's private business," I says. "If you think you have any right to pry into her private affairs I'll tell her you believe those checks are being misappropriated and you want an audit because you dont trust her."

She didn't say anything or move. I could hear her whispering Damn you oh damn you oh damn you.

"Say it out," I says. "I dont reckon it's any secret what you and I think of one another. Maybe you want the money back," I says.

"Listen, Jason," she says. "Dont lie to me now. About her. I wont ask to see anything. If that isn't enough, I'll send more each month.

Just promise that she'll—that she—You can do that. Things for her. Be kind to her. Little things that I cant, they wont let . . . . But you wont. You never had a drop of warm blood in you. Listen," she says. "If you'll get Mother to let me have her back, I'll give you a thousand dollars."

"You haven't got a thousand dollars," I says. "I know you're lying now."

"Yes I have. I will have. I can get it."

"And I know how you'll get it," I says. "You'll get it the same way you got her. And when she gets big enough—" Then I thought she really was going to hit at me, and then I didn't know what she was going to do. She acted for a minute like some kind of a toy that's wound up too tight and about to burst all to pieces.

"Oh, I'm crazy," she says. "I'm insane. I cant take her. Keep her. What am I thinking of. Jason," she says, grabbing my arm. Her hands were hot as fever. "You'll have to promise to take care of her, to—She's kin to you; your own flesh and blood. Promise, Jason. You have Father's name: do you think I'd have to ask him twice? once, even?"

"That's so," I says. "He did leave me something. What do you want me to do," I says. "Buy an apron and a go-cart?[47] I never got you into this," I says. "I run more risk than you do, because you haven't got anything at stake. So if you expect—"

"No," she says, then she begun to laugh and try to hold it back all at the same time. "No. I have nothing at stake," she says, making that noise, putting her hands to her mouth. "Nuh-nuh-nothing," she says.

"Here," I says. "Stop that!"

"I'm tr-trying to," she says, holding her hands over her mouth. "Oh God, oh God."

---

47) pushcart, hand-cart, 제이슨 생각에는 캐디가 자신이 돈 한 푼 없는 거리 장사꾼이 되기를 바란다고 생각하며 하는 말이다.

"I'm going away from here," I says. "I cant be seen here. You get on out of town now, you hear?"

"Wait," she says, catching my arm. "I've stopped. I wont again. You promise, Jason?" she says, and me feeling her eyes almost like they were touching my face. "You promise? Mother—that money—if sometimes she needs things—If I send checks for her to you, other ones besides those, you'll give them to her? You wont tell? You'll see that she has things like other girls?"

"Sure," I says, "As long as you behave and do like I tell you."

And so when Earl came up front with his hat on he says, "I'm going to step up to Rogers' and get a snack. We wont have time to go home to dinner, I reckon."

What's the matter we wont have time?" I says.

"With this show in town and all," he says. "They're going to give an afternoon performance too, and they'll all want to get done trading in time to go to it. So we'd better just run up to Rogers'."

"All right," I says. "It's your stomach. If you want to make a slave of yourself to your business, it's all right with me."

"I reckon you'll never be a slave to any business," he says.

"Not unless it's Jason Compson's business," I says.

So when I went back and opened it the only thing that surprised me was it was a money order not a check. Yes, sir. You cant trust a one of them. After all the risk I'd taken, risking Mother finding out about her coming down here once or twice a year sometimes, and me having to tell Mother lies about it. That's gratitude for you. And I wouldn't put it past her to try to notify the postoffice not to let anyone expect her cash it. Giving a kid like that fifty dollars. Why I never saw fifty dollars until I was twenty-one years old, with all the other boys with the afternoon off and all day Saturday and me working in a store. Like I say, how can they expect anybody to control her, with her giving her money behind our backs. She has the same home you had I says, and the same raising. I reckon Mother is better judge of what she needs then you are, that haven't even got a home. "If you want to give her money," I says, "you send it to Mother, dont be giving it to her. If I've got to run this risk every few months, you'll have to do like I say, or it's out."

And just about the time I got ready to begin on it because if Earl thought I was going to dash up the street and gobble two bits worth of indigestion on his account he was bad fooled. I may not be sitting with my feet on a mahogany desk but I am being payed for what I do inside this building and if I cant manage to live a civilised life outside of it I'll go where I can. I can stand on my own feet; I dont need any man's mahogany desk to prop me up. So just about the time I got ready to start I'd have to drop everything and run to sell some redneck a dime's worth of nails or something, and Earl up there gobbling a sandwich and half way back already, like as not, and then I found that all the blanks[48)] were gone. I remembered then that I had aimed to get some more, but it was too late now, and then I looked up and there she came. In the backdoor. I heard her asking old Job if I was there. I just had time to stick them in the drawer and close it.

She came around to the desk. I looked at my watch.

"You been to dinner already?" I says. "It's just twelve; I just heard it strike. You must have flown home and back."

"I'm not going home to dinner," she says. "Did I get a letter today?"

"Were you expecting one?" I says. "Have you got a sweetie that can write?"

"From Mother," she says. "Did I get a letter from Mother?" she says, looking at me.

"Mother got one from her," I says. "I haven't opened it. You'll have to wait until she opens it. She'll let you see it, I imagine."

"Please, Jason," she says, not paying any attention." Did I get

---

48) blank checks, 제이슨이 캐디의 서명을 날조하여, 캐디가 보내줬다고 생각하고 어머니에게 매달 태우게 하는 빈 수표들이다.

one?"

"What's the matter?" I says. "I never knew you to be this anxious about anybody. You must expect some money from her."

"She said she—" she says. "Please, Jason," she says. "Did I?"

"You must have been to school today, after all," I say. "Somewhere where they taught you to say please. Wait a minute, while I wait on that customer."

I went and waited on him. When I turned to come back she was out of sight behind the desk. I ran. I ran around the desk and caught her as she jerked her hand out of the drawer. I took the letter away from her, beating her knuckles on the desk until she let go.

"You would, would you?" I says.

"Give it to me," she says. "You've already opened it. Give it to me. Please, Jason. It's mine. I saw the name."

"I'll take a hame string to you," I says. "That's what I'll give you. Going into my papers."

"Is there some money in it?" she says, reaching for it. "She said she would send me some money. She promised she would. Give it to me."

"What do you want with money?" I says.

"She said she would," she says. "Give it to me. please, Jason. I wont ever ask you anything again, if you'll give it to me this time."[49)]

"I'm going to, if you'll give me time," I says. I took the letter and the money order out and gave her the letter. She reached for the

---

49) 미스 퀸턴이 삼촌 제이슨에게 캐디가 보내준 전신환을 자신에게 온전히 주라고 필사적으로("다시는 부탁하지 않을게", "이번만은") 부탁하고 있는데, 이러한 그녀의 말투에서도 곧 그녀가 집으로부터 도망을 계획하고 있음을 암시한다. 조금 뒤에 드러나지만, 캐디가 상당한 돈을 자신에게 보냈다("She said she would send me some money . . . she' s sent a lot of money here")고 삼촌에게 말하는 부분에서, 캐디와 딸이 서로 연락하고 있음을 알 수 있고, 이번 미스 퀸턴의 도망도 캐디가 알고 있으면서 그것을 도우고 있을지도 모른다고 추정할 수 있다.

money order, not hardly glancing at the letter. "You'll have to sign it first," I says.

"How much is it?" she says.

"Read the letter," I says. "I reckon it'll say."

She read it fast, in about two looks.

"It dont say," she says, looking up. She dropped the letter to the floor. "How much is it?"

"It's ten dollars," I says.

"Ten dollars?" she says, staring at me.

"And you ought to be dam glad to get that," I says. "A kid like you. What are you in such a rush for money all of a sudden for?"

"Ten dollars?" she says, like she was talking in her sleep. "Just ten dollars?" She made a grab at the money order. "You're lying," she says. "Thief!" she says. "Thief!"

"You would, would you?" I says, holding her off.

"Give it to me!" she says. "It's mine. She sent it to me. I will see it. I will."

"You will?" I says, holding her. "How're you going to do it?"

"Just let me see it, Jason," she says. "Please. I wont ask you for anything again."

"Think I'm lying, do you?" I says. "Just for that you wont see it."

"But just ten dollars," she says. "She told me she—she told me—Jason, please please please. I've got to have some money. I've just got to. Give it to me, Jason. I'll do anything if you will."

"Tell me what you've got to have money for," I says.

"I've got to have it," she says. She was looking at me. Then all of a sudden she quiet looking at me without moving her eyes at all. I knew she was going to lie. "It's some money I owe," she says. "I've got to pay it. I've got to pay it today."

"Who to?" I says. Her hands were sort of twisting. I could watch her trying to think of a lie to tell. "Have you been charging things at stores again?" I says. "You needn't bother to tell me that. If you can find anybody in this town that'll charge anything to you after what I told them, I'll eat it."

"It's a girl," she says. "It's a girl. I borrowed some money from a girl. I've got to pay it back. Jason, give it to me. Please. I'll do anything. I've got to have it. Mother will pay you. I'll write to her to pay you and that I wont ever ask her for anything again. You can see the letter. Please, Jason. I've got to have it."

"Tell me what you want with it, and I'll see about it," I says. "Tell me." She just stood there, with her hands working against her dress. "All right," I says. "If ten dollars is too little for you, I'll just take it home to Mother, and you know what'll happen to it then. Of course, if you're so rich you dont need ten dollars——"

She stood there, looking at the floor, kind of mumbling to herself. "She said she would send me some money. She said she sends money here and you say she dont send any. She said she's sent a lot of money here. She says it's for me. That it's for me to have some of it. And you say we haven't got any money."

"You know as much about that as I do," I says. "You've seen what happens to those checks."

"Yes," she says, looking at the floor. "Ten dollars," she says. "Ten dollars."

"And you'd better thank your stars it's ten dollars," I says. "Here," I says. I put the money order face down on the desk, holding my hand on it. "Sign it."

"Will you let me see it?" she says. "I just want to look at it. Whatever it says, I wont ask for but ten dollars. You can have the rest. I just want to see it."

"Not after the way you've acted," I says. "You've got to learn one thing, and that is that when I tell you to do something, you've got it to do. You sign your name on that line."

She took the pen, but instead of signing it she just stood there with her head bent and the pen shaking in her hand. Just like her mother. "Oh, God," she says, "oh, God."

"Yes," I says. "That's one thing you'll have to learn if you never learn anything else. Sign it now, and get on out of here."

She signed it. "Where's the money?" she says. I took the order and blotted it and put it in my pocket. Then I gave her the ten dollars.

"Now you go on back to school this afternoon, you here?" I says. She didn't answer. She crumpled the bill up in her hand like it was a rag or something and went on out the front door just as Earl came in. A customer came in with him and they stopped up front. I gathered up the things and put on my hat and went up front.

"Been much busy?" Earl says.

"Not much," I says. He looked out the door.

"That your car over yonder?" he says. "Better not try to go out home to dinner. We'll likely have another rush just before the show opens. Get you a lunch at Rogers' and put a ticket in the drawer."

"Much obliged," I says. "I can still manage to feed myself, I reckon."

And right there he'd stay, watching that door like a hawk until I came through it again. Well, he'd just have to watch it for a while; I was doing the best I could. The time before I says that's the last one now; you'll have to remember to get some more right away. But who can remember anything in all this hurrah. And now this dam show had to come here the one day I'd have to hunt all over town for a blank check, besides all the other things I had to do to keep the house running, and Earl watching the door like a hawk.

I went to the printing shop and told him I wanted to play a joke on a fellow, but he didn't have anything. Then he told me to have a look in the old opera house, where somebody had stored a lot of papers and junk out of the old Merchants' and Farmers' Bank when it failed, so I dodged up a few more alleys so Earl couldn't see me and finally found old man Simmons and got the key from him and went up there and dug around. At last I found a pad on a Saint Louis bank. And of course she'd pick this one time to look at it close. Well, it would have to do. I couldn't waste any more time now.

I went back to the store. "Forgot some papers Mother wants to go to the bank," I says. I went back to the desk and fixed the check. Trying to hurry and all, I says to myself it's a good thing her eyes are giving out, with that little whore in the house, a Christian forbearing woman like Mother. I says you know just as well as I do what she's going to grow up into but I says that's your business, if you want to keep her and raise her in your house just because of Father. Then she would begin to cry and say it was her own flesh and blood so I just says All right. Have it your way. I can stand it if you can.

I fixed the letter up again and glued it back[50] and went out.

"Try not to be gone any longer than you can help," Earl says.

"All right," I says. I went to the telegraph office. The smart boys were all there.

"Any of you boys made your million yet?" I says.

"Who can do anything, with a market like that?" Doc says.

"What's it doing?" I says. I went in and looked. It was three points under the opening. "You boys are not going to let a little thing like the cotten market beat you, are you?" I says. "I thought you were too smart for that."

"Smart, hell," Doc says. "It was down twelve points at twelve oclock. Cleaned me out."

"Twelve points?" I says. "Why the hell didn't somebody let me know? Why didn't you let me know?" I says to the operator.

"I take it as it comes in," he says. "I'm not running a bucket shop."[51]

"You're smart, aren't you?" I says. "Seems to me, with the money I spend with you, you could take time to call me up. Or maybe your dam company's in a conspiracy with those dam eastern sharks."

He didn't say anything. He made like he was busy.

---

50) 캐디의 서명을 날조한 수표를 진짜와 바꿔치기 한 후, 그 수표를 그녀가 매달 집에 보내는 편지 속에다 다시 넣고 있다.

51) "bucket shop"은 부정직한 증권거래 중개점이다.

"You're getting a little too big for your pants," I says. "First thing you know you'll be working for a living."

"What's the matter with you?" Doc says. "You're still three points to the good."

"Yes," I says. "If I happened to be selling. I haven't mentioned that yet, I think. You boys all cleaned out?"

"I got caught twice," Doc says. "I switched just in time."

"Well," I. O. Snopes says, "I've picked hit; I reckon taint no more than fair fer hit to pick me once in a while."

So I left them buying and selling among themselves at a nickel a point. I found a nigger and sent him for my car and stood on the corner and waited. I couldn't see Earl looking up and down the street, with one eye on the clock, because I couldn't see the door from here. After about a week he got back with it.

"Where the hell have you been?" I says. "Riding around where the wenches could see you?"

"I come straight as I could," he says. "I had to drive clean around the square, wid all dem wagons."

I never found a nigger yet that didn't have an airtight alibi for whatever he did. But just turn one loose in a car and he's bound to show off. I got in and went on around the square. I caught a glimpse of Earl in the door across the square.

I went straight to the kitchen and told Dilsey to hurry up with dinner.

"Quentin aint come yit," she says.

"What of that?" I says. "You'll be telling me next that Luster's not quite ready to eat yet. Quentin knows when meals are served in this house. Hurry up with it, now."

Mother was in her room. I gave her the letter. She opened it and took the check out and sat holding it in her hand. I went and got the shovel from the corner and gave her a match. "Come on," I says. "Get it over with. You'll be crying in a minute."

She took the match, but she didn't strike it. She sat there, looking at the check. Just like I said it would be.

"I hate to do it," she says. "To increase your burden by adding Quentin . . ."

"I guess we'll get along," I says. "Come on. Get it over with."

But she just sat there, holding the check.

"This one is on a different bank," she says. "They have been on an Indianapolis bank."

"Yes," I says. "Women are allowed to do that too."

"Do what?" she says.

"Keep money in two different banks," I says.

"Oh," she says. She looked at the check a while. "I'm glad to know she's so . . . she has so much. . . . God sees that I am doing right," she says.

"Come on," I says. "Finish it. Get the fun over."

"Fun?" she says. When I think—"

"I thought you were burning this two hundred dollars a month for fun," I says. "Come on, now. Want me to strike the match?"

"I could bring myself to accept them," she says. "For my children's sake. I have no pride."

"You'd never be satisfied," I says. "You know you wouldn't. You' ve settled that once, let it stay settled. We can get along."

"I leave everything to you," she says. "But sometimes I become afraid that in doing this I am depriving you all of what is rightfully yours. Perhaps I shall be punished for it. If you want me to, I will smother my pride and accept them."

"What would be the good in beginning now, when you've been destroying them for fifteen year?" I says. "If you keep on doing it, you have lost nothing, but if you'd begin to take them now, you'll have lost fifty thousand dollars. We've got along so far, haven't we?" I says. "I haven't seen you in the poorhouse yet."

"Yes," she says. "We Bascombs need nobody's charity. Certainly not that of a fallen woman."

She struck the match and lit the check and put it in the shovel, and then the envelope, and watched them burn.

"You dont know what it is," she says. "Thank God you will never know what a mother feels."

"There are lots of women in this world no better than her," I says. "But they are not my daughters," she says. "It's not myself," she says. "I'd gladly take her back, sins and all, because she is my flesh and blood. It's for Quentin's sake."

Well, I could have said it wasn't much chance of anybody hurting Quentin much, but like I say I dont expect much but I do want to eat and sleep without a couple of women squabbling and crying in the house.

"And your," she says. "I know how you feel toward her."

"Let her come back," I says, "far as I'm concerned."

"No," she says. "I owe that to your father's memory."

"When he was trying all the time to persuade you to let her come home when Herbert threw her out?" I says.

"You dont understand," she says. "I know you dont intend to make it more difficult for me. But it's my place to suffer for my children," she says. "I can bear it."

"Seems to me you go to a lot of unnecessary trouble doing it," I says. The paper burned out. I carried it to the grate and put it in. "It just seems a shame to me to burn up good money," I says.

"Let me never see the day when my children will have to accept that, the wages of sin," she says. "I'd rather see even you dead in your coffin first."

"Have it your way," I says. "Are we going to have dinner soon?" I says. "Because if we're not, I'll have to go on back. We're pretty busy today." She got up. "I've told her once," I says. "It seems she's waiting on Quentin or Luster or somebody. Here, I'll call her. Wait." But she went to the head of the stairs and called.

"Quentin aint come yit," Dilsey says.

"Well, I'll have to get on back," I says. "I can get a sandwich downtown. I dont want to interfere with Dilsey's arrangements," I says. Well, that got her started again, with Dilsey hobbling and mumbling back and forth, saying,

"All right, all right, Ise puttin hit on fast as I kin."

"I try to please you all," Mother says. "I try to make things as easy for you as I can."

"I'm not complaining, am I?" I says. "Have I said a word except I had to go back to work?"

"I know," she says. "I know you haven't had the chance the others had, that you've had to bury yourself in a little country store. I wanted you to get ahead. I knew your father would never realise that you were the only one who had any business sense, and then when everything else failed I believed that when she married, and Herbert . . . after his promise—"

"Well, he was probably lying too," I says. "He may not have even had a bank. And if he had, I dont reckon he'd have to come all the way to Mississippi to get a man for it."

We ate a while. I could hear Ben in the kitchen, where Luster was feeding him. Like I say, if we've got to feed another mouth and she wont take that money, why not send him down to Jackson. He'll be happier there, with people like him. I says God knows there's little enough room for pride in this family, but it dont take much pride to not like to see a thirty year old man playing around the yard with a nigger boy, running up and down the fence and lowing like a cow whenever they play golf over there. I says if they'd sent him to Jackson at first we'd all be better off today. I says, you've done your duty by him; you've done all anybody can expect of you and more than most folks would do, so why not send him there and get that much benefit out of the taxes we pay. Then she says, "I'll be gone soon. I know I'm just a burden to you" and I says "You've been saying that so long that I'm beginning to believe you" only I says you'd better be sure and not let me know you're gone because I'll sure have him on number seventeen that night and I says I think I know a place where they'll take her too and the name of it's not Milk street and Honey avenue[52] either. Then she begun to cry and I says All right all right I have as much pride about my kinfolks as anybody even if I dont always know where they come from.

We ate for a while. Mother sent Dilsey to the front to look for Quentin again.

"I keep telling you she's not coming to dinner," I says.

"She knows better than that," Mother says. "She knows I dont permit her to run about the streets and not come home at meal time. Did you look good, Dilsey?"

"Dont let her, then," I says.

"What can I do," she says. "You have all of you flouted me. Always."

"If you wouldn't come interfering, I'd make her mind," I says. "It wouldn't take me but about one day to straighten her out."

"You'd be too brutal with her," she says. "You have your Uncle Maury's temper."

That reminded me of the letter. I took it out and handed it to her. "You wont have to open it," I says. "The bank will let you know how much it is this time."

"It's addressed to you," she says.

"Go on and open it," I says. She opened it and read it and handed it to me.

> " 'My dear young nephew,' it says,
>
> 'You will be glad to learn that I am now in a position to avail myself of an opportunity regarding which, for reasons which I shall make obvious to you, I shall not to go into details until I have an opportunity to divulge it to you in a more secure manner. My business experience has taught me to

52) 제이슨은 조카 퀸턴의 앞날을 내다보며, 그곳은 결코 성경에 나오는 약속의 땅("the Land of Milk and Honey," Exodus 3.8)이 아니라고 말한다.

be chary of committing anything of a confidential nature to any more concrete medium than speech, and my extreme precaution in this instance should give you some inkling of its value. Needless to say, I have just completed a most exhaustive examination of all its phases, and I feel no hesitancy in telling you that it is that sort of golden chance that comes but once in a lifetime, and I now see clearly before me that goal toward which I have long and unflaggingly striven: i.e., the ultimate solidification of my affairs by which I may restore to its rightful position that family of which I have the honor to be the sole remaining male descendant; that family in which I have ever included your lady mother and her children.

'As it so happens, I am not quiet in a position to avail myself of this opportunity to the uttermost which it warrants, but rather than go out of the family to do so, I am today drawing upon your Mother's bank for the small sum necessary to complement my own initial investment, for which I herewith enclose, as a matter of formality, my note of hand at eight percent. per annum. Needless to say, this is merely a formality, to secure your Mother in the event of that circumstance of which man is ever the plaything and sport. For naturally I shall employ this sum as though it were my own and so permit your Mother to avail herself of this opportunity which my exhaustive investigation has shown to be a bonanza—if you will permit the vulgarism—of the first water and purest ray serene.

'This is in confidence, you will understand, from one business man to another; we will harvest our own vineyards, eh? And knowing your Mother's delicate health and that timorousness which such delicately nurtured Southern ladies would naturally feel regarding matters of business, and their charming proneness to divulge unwittingly such matters in conversation, I would suggest that you do not mention it to her at all. On second thought, I advise you not to do so. It might be better to simply restore this sum to the bank at some future date, say, in a lump sum with the other small sums for which I am indebted to her, and say nothing about it at all. It is our duty to shield her from the crass material world as much as possible.

'Your affectionate Uncle,
'Maury L. Bascomb.' "

"What do you want to do about it?" I says, flipping it across the table.

"I know you grudge what I give him," she says.

"It's your money," I says. "If you want to throw it to the birds even, it's your business."

"He's my own brother," Mother says. "He's the last Bascomb. When we are gone there wont be any more of them."

"That'll be hard on somebody, I guess," I says. "All right, all right," I says. "It's your money. Do as you please with it. You want me to tell the bank to pay it?"

"I know you begrudge him," she says. "I realise the burden on your shoulders. When I'm gone it will be easier on you."

"I could make it easier right now," I says. "All right, all right, I wont mention it again. Move all bedlam[53] in here if you want to."

"He's your own brother," she says. "Even if he is afflicted."

"I'll take your bank book," I says. "I'll draw my check today."

"He kept you waiting six days,"[54] she says. "Are you sure the business is sound? It seems strange to me that a solvent business

---

53) "Bedlam"은 '베들레헴의 성 메리' 병원의 약칭이며, 병원이 되기 전 그곳은 광인들의 요양소였다. 일반적으로는 정신이상자 요양소이나 난장판(무질서가 난무하는 곳)을 의미한다.

54) "He"는 제이슨이 일하는 철물점 주인 얼이며, 그가 제이슨의 월급을 제때 주지 않는다고 어머니는 생각한다(사실은 캐디의 수표가 늦게 도착하여 입금이 늦어짐).

cannot pay its employees promptly."

"He's all right," I says. "Safe as a bank. I tell him not to bother about mine until we get done collecting every month. That's why it's late sometimes."

"I just couldn't bear to have you lose the little I had to invest for you," she says. "I've often thought that Earl is not a good business man. I know he doesn't take you into his confidence to the extent that your investment in the business should warrant. I'm going to speak to him."

"No, you let him alone," I says. "It's his business."

"You have a thousand dollars in it." [55]

"You let him alone," I says. "I'm watching things. I have your power of attorney. It'll be all right."

"You dont know what a comfort you are to me," she says. "You have always been my pride and joy, but when you came to me of your own accord and insisted on banking your salary each month in my name, I thanked God it was you left me if they had to be taken."

"They were all right," I says. "They did the best they could, I reckon."

"When you talk that way I know you are thinking bitterly of your father's memory," she says. "You have a right to, I suppose. But it breaks my heart to hear you."

I got up. "If you've got any crying to do," I says, "you'll have to do it alone, because I've got to get on back. I'll get the bank book."

"I'll get it," she says.

"Keep still," I says. "I'll get it." I went up stairs and got the bank book out of her desk and went back to town. I went to the bank and deposited the check and the money order and the other ten, and stopped at the telegraph office. It was one point above the opening. I

---

55) 제이슨이 얼의 사업 파트너가 될 수 있게 캄슨 부인이 투자한 천 달러를 말한다. 하지만 나중에 드러나듯 그는 그 돈을 어머니 몰래 빼내 차를 샀다.

had already lost thirteen points, all because she had to come helling in there at twelve, worrying me about that letter.

"What time did that report come in?" I says.

"About an hour ago," he says.

"An hour ago?" I says. "What are we paying you for?" I says. "Weekly reports? How do you expect a man to do anything? The whole dam top could blow off and we'd not know it."

"I dont expect you to do anything," he says. "They changed that law making folks play the cotton market."

"They have?" I says. "I hadn't heard. They must have sent the news out over the Western Union."

I went back to the store. Thirteen points. Dam if I believe anybody knows anything about the dam thing except the ones that sit back in those New York offices and watch the country suckers come up and beg them to take their money. Well, a man that just calls shows he has no faith in himself, and like I say if you aren't going to take the advice, what's the use in paying money for it. Besides, these people are right up there on the ground; they know everything that's going on. I could feel the telegram in my pocket. I'd just have to prove that they were using the telegraph company to defraud. That would constitute a bucket shop. And I wouldn't hesitate that long, either. Only be damned if it doesn't look like a company as big and rich as the Western Union could get a market report out on time. Half as quick as they'll get a wire to you saying Your account closed out. But what the hell do they care about the people. They're hand in glove with that New York crowd. Anybody could see that.

When I came in Earl looked at his watch. But he didn't say anything until the customer was gone. Then he says,

"You go home to dinner?"

"I had to go to the dentist," I says because It's not any of his business where I eat but I've got to be in the store with him all the afternoon. And with his jaw running off after all I've stood. You take a little two by four country storekeeper like I say it takes a man with just five hundred dollars to worry about it fifty thousand dollars' worth.

"You might have told me," he says. "I expected you back right away."

"I'll trade you this tooth and give you ten dollars to boot, any time," I says. "Our agreement was an hour for dinner," I says," and if you dont like the way I do, you know what you can do about it."

"I've known that some time," he says. "If it hadn't been for your mother I'd have done it before now, too. She's a lady I've got a lot of sympathy for, Jason. Too bad some other folks I know cant say as much."

"Then you can keep it," I says. "When we need any sympathy I'll let you know in plenty of time."

"I've protected you about that business a long time, Jason," he says.

"Yes?" I says, letting him go on. Listening to what he would say before I shut him up.

"I believe I know more about where that automobile came from than she does."

"You think so, do you?" I says. "When are you going to spread the news that I stole it from my mother?"

"I dont say anything," he says. "I know you have her power of attorney. And I know she still believes that thousand dollars is in this business."

"All right," I says. "Since you know so much, I'll tell you a little more: go to the bank and ask them whose account I've been depositing a hundred and sixty dollars on the first of every month for twelve years."

"I dont say anything," he says. "I just ask you to be a little more careful after this."

I never said anything more. It doesn't do any good. I've found that when a man gets into a rut the best thing you can do is let him stay there. And when a man gets it in his head that he's got to tell something on you for your own good, goodnight. I'm glad I haven't got the sort of conscience I've got to nurse like a sick puppy all the time. If I'd ever be as careful over anything as he is to keep his little shirt tail full of business from making him more than eight percent. I reckon he thinks they'd get him on the usury law if he netted more than eight percent. What the hell chance has a man got, tied down in a town like this and to a business like this. Why I could take his business in one year and fix him so he'd never have to work again, only he'd give it all away to the church or something. If there's one thing gets under my skin, It's a dam hypocrite. A man that thinks anything he dont understand all about must be crooked and that first chance he gets he's morally bound to tell the third party what's none of his business to tell. Like I say if I thought every time a man did something I didn't know all about he was bound to be a crook, I reckon I wouldn't have any trouble finding something back there on those books that you wouldn't see any use for running and telling somebody I thought ought to know about it, when for all I knew they might know a dam sight more about it now than I did, and if they didn't it was dam little of my business anyway and he says, "My books are open to anybody. Anybody that has any claim or believes she has any claim on this business can go back there and welcome."

"Sure, you wont tell," I says. "You couldn't square your conscience with that. You'll just take her back there and let her find it. You wont tell, yourself."

"I'm not trying to meddle in your business," he says. "I know you missed out on some things like Quentin had. But your mother has had a misfortunate life too, and if she was to come in here and ask me why you quit, I'd have to tell her. It aint that thousand dollars. You know that. It's because a man never gets anywhere if fact and his ledgers dont square. And I'm not going to lie to anybody, for myself or anybody else."

"Well, then," I says. "I reckon that conscience of yours is a more valuable clerk than I am; it dont have to go home at noon to eat.

Only dont let it interfere with my appetite," I says, because how the hell can I do anything right, with that dam family and her not making any effort to control her nor any of them like that time when she happened to see one of them kissing Caddy and all next day she went around the house in a black dress and a veil and even Father couldn't get her to say a word except crying and saying her little daughter was dead and Caddy about fifteen then only in three years she'd been wearing haircloth or probably sandpaper at that rate. Do you think I can afford to have her running about the streets with every drummer that comes to town, I says, and them telling the new ones up and down the road where to pick up a hot one when they made Jefferson. I haven't got much pride, I cant afford it with a kitchen full of niggers to feed and robbing the state asylum of its star freshman. Blood, I says governors and generals. It's a dam good thing we never had any kings and presidents; we'd all be down there at Jackson chasing butterflies. I says It'd be bad enough if it was mine;[56] I'd at least be sure it was a bastard to begin with, and now even the Lord doesn't know that for certain probably.

So after a while I heard the band start up, and then they begun to clear out. Headed for the show, every one of them. Haggling over a twenty cent hame string to save fifteen cents, so they can give it to a bunch of Yankees that come in and pay maybe ten dollars for the privilege. I went on out to the back.

"Well," I says. "If you dont look out, that bolt will grow into your hand. And then I'm going to take an axe and chop it out. What do you reckon the boll-weevils'll eat if you dont get those cultivators in shape to raise them a crop?" I says, "sage grass?"

"Dam folks sho do play dem horns," he says. "Tell me man in dat show kin play a tune on a handsaw. Pick hit like a banjo."

---

56) Miss Quentin, 제이슨은 여기서 캐디와 자신간의 근친상간을 상상해 온 듯한 말을 하고 있다.

"Listen," I says. "Do you know how much that show'll spend in this town? About ten dollars," I says. "The ten dollars Buck Turpin has in his pocket right now."

"Whut dey give Mr Buck ten dollars fer?" he says.

"For the privilege of showing here," I says. "You can put the balance of what they'll spend in your eye."

"You mean dey pays ten dollars just to give dey show here?" he says.

"That's all," I says," And how much do you reckon—"

"Gret day," he says. "You mean to tell me dey chargin um to let um show here? I'd pay ten dollars to see dat man pick dat saw, ef I had to. I figures dat tomorrow mawnin I be still owin um nine dollars and six bits at dat rate."

And then a Yankee will talk your head off about niggers getting ahead. Get them ahead, what I say. Get them so far ahead you cant find one south of Louisville with a blood hound. Because when I told him about how they'd pick up Saturday night and carry off at least a thousand dollars out of the county, he says,

"I dont begridge[57)] um. I kin sho afford my two bits."

"Two bits hell," I says. "That dont begin it. How about the dime or fifteen cents you'll spend for a dam two cent box of candy or something. How about the time you're wasting right now, listening to that band."

"Da'ts de troof," he says. "Well, ef I lives twell night hit's gwine to be two bits mo dey takin out of town, da'ts sho."

"Then you're a fool," I says.

"Well," he says. "I dont spute dat neither. Ef dat uz a crime, all chain-gangs wouldn't be black."

Well, just about that time I happened to look up the alley and saw her. When I stepped back and looked at my watch I didn't notice at

---

57) begrudge.

the time who he was because I was looking at the watch. It was just two thirty, forty-five minutes before anybody but me expected her to be out. So when I looked around the door the first thing I saw was the red tie he had on and I was thinking what the hell kind of a man would wear a red tie. But she was sneaking along the alley, watching the door, so I wasn't thinking anything about him until they had gone past. I was wondering if she'd have so little respect for me that she'd not only play out of school when I told her not to, but would walk right past the store, daring me not to see her. Only she couldn't see into the door because the sun fell straight into it and it was like trying to see through an automobile searchlight, so I stood there and watched her go on past, with her face painted up like a dam clown's and her hair all gummed and twisted and a dress that if a woman had come out doors even on Gayoso or Beale street[58)] when I was a young fellow with no more than that to cover her legs and behind, she'd been thrown in jail. I'll be damned if they dont dress like they were trying to make every man they passed on the street want to reach out and clap his hand on it. And so I was thinking what kind of a dam man would wear a red tie when all of a sudden I knew he was one of those show folks well as if she'd told me. Well, I can stand a lot; if I couldn't dam if I wouldn't be in a hell of a fix, so when they turned the corner I jumped down and followed. Me, without any hat, in the middle of the afternoon, having to chase up and down back alleys because of my mother's good name. Like I say you cant do anything with a woman like that, if She's got it in her. If It's in her blood, you cant do anything with her. The only thing you can do is to get rid of her, let her go on and live with her own sort.

I went on to the street, but they were out of sight. And there I was, without any hat, looking like I was crazy too. Like a man would

---

58) Beale street는 멤피스에 있는 유흥가로, 나이트클럽들이 즐비하고 창녀들을 살 수 있는 유명한 거리이다.

naturally think, one of them is crazy and another one drowned himself and the other one was turned out into the street by her husband, what's the reason the rest of them are not crazy too. All the time I could see them watching me like a hawk, waiting for a chance to say Well I'm not surprised I expected it all the time the whole family's crazy. Selling land to send him to Harvard and paying taxes to support a state University all the time that I never saw except twice at a baseball game and not letting her daughter's name be spoken on the place until after a while Father wouldn't even come down town anymore but just sat there all day with the decanter I could see the bottom of his nightshirt and his bare legs and hear the decanter clinking until finally T. P. had to pour it for him and she says You have no respect for your Father's memory and I says I dont know why not it sure is preserved well enough to last only if I'm crazy too God knows what I'll do about it just to look at water makes me sick and I'd just as soon swallow gasoline as a glass of whiskey and Lorraine telling them he may not drink but if you dont believe he's a man I can tell you how to find out she says If I catch you fooling with any of these whores you know what I'll do she says I'll whip her grabbing at her I'll whip her as long as I can find her she says and I says if I dont drink that's my business but have you ever found me short[59)] I says I'll buy you enough beer to take a bath in if you want it because I've got every respect for a good honest whore because with Mother's health and the position I try to uphold to have her with no more respect for what I try to do for her than to make her name and my name and my Mother's name a byword in the town.

She had dodged out of sight somewhere. Saw me coming and dodged into another alley, running up and down the alleys with a dam show man in a red tie that everybody would look at and think what kind of a dam man would wear a red tie. Well, the boy kept

---

59) 제이슨은 자신의 남성성에 상당히 방어적임을 알 수 있다.

speaking to me and so I took the telegram without knowing I had taken it. I didn't realise what it was is until I was signing for it, and I tore it open without even caring much what it was. I knew all the time what it would be, I reckon. That was the only thing else that could happen, especially holding it up until I had already had the check entered on the pass book.

I dont see how a city no bigger than New York can hold enough people to take the money away from us country suckers. Work like hell all day every day, send them your money and get a little piece of paper back, Your account closed at 20.62. Teasing you along, letting you pile up a little paper profit, then bang! Your account closed at 20.62. And if that wasn't enough, paying ten dollars a month to somebody to tell you how to lose it fast, that either dont know anything about it or is in cahoots with the telegraph company. Well, I'm done with them. They've sucked me in for the last time. Any fool except a fellow that hasn't got any more sense than to take a jew's word for anything could tell the market was going up all the time, with the whole dam delta about to be flooded again and the cotton washed right out of the ground like it was last year. Let it wash a man's crop out of the ground year after year, and them up there in Washington spending fifty thousand dollars a day keeping an army in Nicarauga or some place. Of course it'll overflow again, and then cotton'll be worth thirty cents a pound. Well, I just want to hit them one time and get my money back. I dont want a killing; only these small town gamblers are out for that, I just want my money back that these dam jews have gotten with all their guaranteed inside dope. Then I'm through; they can kiss my foot for every other red cent of mine they get.

I went back to the store. It was half past three almost. Dam little time to do anything in, but then I am used to that. I never had to go to Harvard to learn that. The band had quit playing. Got them all inside now, and they wouldn't have to waste any more wind. Earl says,

"He found you, did he? He was in here with it a while ago. I thought you were out back somewhere."

"Yes," I says. "I got it. They couldn't keep it away from me all afternoon. The town's too small. I've got to go out home a minute," [60] I says. "You can dock me if it'll make you feel any better."

"Go ahead," he says, "I can handle it now. No bad news, I hope."

"You'll have to go to the telegraph office and find that out," I says. "They'll have time to tell you. I haven't."

"I just asked," he says. "Your mother knows she can depend on me."

"She'll appreciate it," I says. "I wont be gone any longer than I have to."

"Take your time," he says. "I can handle it now. You go ahead."

I got the car and went home. Once this morning, twice at noon, and now again, with her and having to chase all over town and having to beg them to let me eat a little of the food I am paying for. Sometimes I think what's the use of anything. With the precedent I've been set I must be crazy to keep on. And now I reckon I'll get home just in time to take a nice long drive after a basket of tomatoes or something and then have to go back to town smelling like a camphor factory so my head wont explode right on my shoulders. I keep telling her there's not a dam thing in that aspirin except flour and water for imaginary invalids. I says you dont know what a headache is. I says you think I'd fool with that dam car at all if it depended on me. I says I can get along without one I've learned to get along without lots of things but if you want to risk yourself in that old wornout surrey with a halfgrown nigger boy all right because I says God looks after Ben's kind, God knows He ought to do something for him but if you think I'm going to trust a thousand dollar's worth of

---

60) 앞서 언급되고 있듯이, 제이슨이 주식 투자에서 돈을 잃게 되자, 투자자의 주식거래 잔고가 투자하고자 하는 금액의 10%를 웃돌아야 하는 뉴욕의 증권거래 조건을 충족시키기 위해, 집으로 즉시 가서 돈을 가져와 뉴욕으로 보내려는 그의 의도를 읽을 수 있다.

delicate machinery to a halfgrown nigger or a grown one either, you'd better buy him one yourself because I says you like to ride in the car and you know you do.

Dilsey said she was in the house. I went on into the hall and listened, but I didn't hear anything. I went up stairs, but just as I passed her door she called me.

"I just wanted to know who it was," she says. "I'm here alone so much that I hear every sound."

"You dont have to stay here," I says. "You could spend the whole day visiting like other women, if you wanted to." She came to the door.

"I thought maybe you were sick," she says. "Having to hurry through your dinner like you did."

"Better luck next time," I says. "What do you want?"

"Is anything wrong?" she says.

"What could be?" I says. "Cant I come home in the middle of the afternoon without upsetting the whole house?"

"Have you seen Quentin?" she says.

"She's in school," I says.

"It's after three," she says. "I heard the clock strike at least a half an hour ago. She ought to be home by now."

"Ought she?" I says. "When have you ever seen her before dark?"

"She ought to be home," she says. "When I was a girl—"

"You had somebody to make you behave yourself," I says. "She hasn't."

"I cant do anything with her," she says. "I've tried and I've tried."

"And you wont let me, for some reason," I says. "So you ought to be satisfied." I went on to my room. I turned the key easy and stood there until the knob turned. Then she says,

"Jason."

"What," I says.

"I just thought something was wrong."

"Not in here," I says. "You've come to the wrong place."

"I dont mean to worry you," she says.

"I'm glad to hear that," I says. "I wasn't sure. I thought I might have been mistaken. Do you want anything?"

After a while she says, "No. Not any thing." Then she went away. I took the box down and counted out the money and hid the box again and unlocked the door and went out. I thought about the camphor, but it would be too late now, anyway. And I'd just have one more round trip. She was at her door, waiting.

"You want anything from town?" I says.

"No," she says. "I dont mean to meddle in your affairs. But I dont know what I'd do if anything happened to you, Jason."

"I'm all right," I says. "Just a headache."

"I wish you'd take some aspirin," she says. "I know you're not going to stop using the car."

"What's the car got to do with it?" I says. "How can a car give a man a headache?"

"You know gasoline always made you sick," she says. "Ever since you were a child. I wish you'd take some aspirin."

"Keep on wishing it," I says. "It wont hurt you."

I got in the car and started back to town. I had just turned onto the street when I saw a ford coming helling toward me. All of a sudden it stopped. I could here the wheels sliding and it slewed around and backed and whirled and just as I was thinking what the hell they were up to, I saw that red tie. Then I recognised her face looking back through the window. It whirled into the alley. I saw it turn again, but when I got to the back street it was just disappearing, running like hell.

I saw red. When I recognised that red tie, after all I had told her, I forgot about everything. I never thought about my head even until I came to the first forks and had to stop. Yet we spend money and spend money on roads and dam if it isn't like trying to drive over a sheet of corrugated iron roofing. I'd like to know how a man could be expected to keep up with even a wheelbarrow. I think too much of my car; I'm not going to hammer it to pieces like it was a ford. Chances were they had stolen it, anyway, so why should they give a dam. Like I say blood always tells. If you've got blood like that in you, you'll do anything. I says whatever claim you believe she has on you has already been discharged; I says from now on you have only yourself to blame because you know what any sensible person would do. I says if I've got to spend half my time being a dam detective, at least I'll go where I can get paid for it.

So I had to stop there at the forks. Then I remembered it. It felt like somebody was inside with a hammer, beating on it. I says I've tried to keep you from being worried by her; I says far as I'm concerned, let her go to hell as fast as she pleases and the sooner the better. I says what else do you expect except every dam drummer and cheap show that comes to town because even these town jellybeans give her the go-by now. You dont know what goes on I says, you dont hear the talk that I hear and you can just bet I shut them up too. I says my people owned slaves here when you all were running little shirt tail country stores and farming land no nigger would look at on shares.

If they ever farmed it. It's a good thing the Lord did something for this country; the folks that live on it never have. Friday afternoon, and from right here I could see three miles of land that hadn't even been broken,[61)] and every able bodied man in the county in town at that show. I might have been a stranger staving to death, and there wasn't a soul in sight to ask which way to town even. And she trying to get me to take aspirin. I says when I eat bread I'll do it at the table. I says you always talking about how much you give up for us when you could buy ten new dresses a year on the money you spend for those dam patent medicines. It's not something to cure it I need it's just a even break not to have to have them but as long as I have to

---

61) land that hadn' t been plowed for planting.

work ten hours a day to support a kitchen full of niggers in the style they're accustomed to and send them to the show where very other nigger in the county, only he was late already.[62] By the time he got there it would be over.

After a while he got up to the car and when I finally got it through his head if two people in a ford had passed him, he said yes. So I went on, and when I came to where the wagon road turned off I could see the tire tracks. Ab Russell was in his lot, but I didn't bother to ask him and I hadn't got out of sight of his barn hardly when I saw the ford. They had tried to hide it. Done about as well at it as she did at everything else she did. Like I say it's not that I object to so much; maybe she cant help that, it's because she hasn't even got enough consideration for her own family to have any discretion. I'm afraid all the time I'll run into them right in the middle of the street or under a wagon on the square, like a couple of dogs.

I parked and got out. And now I'd have to go way around and cross a plowed field, the only one I had seen since I left town, with every step like somebody was walking along behind me, hitting me on the head with a club. I kept thinking that when I got across the field at least I'd have something level to walk on, that wouldn't jolt me every step, but when I got into the woods it was full of underbrush and I had to twist around through it, and then I came to a ditch full of briers. I went along it for a while, but it got thicker and thicker, and all the time Earl probably telephoning home about where I was and getting Mother all upset again.

When I finally got through I had had to wind around so much that I had to stop and figure out just where the car would be. I knew they wouldn't be far from it, just under the closest bush, so I turned and worked back toward the road. Then I couldn't tell just how far I was,

62) he는 다음 문단에서 설명되는, 제이슨에게 미스 퀜틴과 남자친구에 대해 유용한 정보를 제공해 줄 수 있는 한 흑인남자.

so I'd have to stop and listen, and then with my legs not using so much blood, it all would go into my head like it would explode any minute, and the sun getting down just to where it could shine straight into my eyes and my ears ringing so I couldn't hear anything. I went on, trying to move quiet, then I heard a dog or something and I knew that when he scented me he'd have to come helling up, then it would be all off.

I had gotten beggar lice and twigs and stuff all over me, inside my clothes and shoes and all, and then I happened to look around and I had my hand right on a bunch of poison oak. The only thing I couldn't understand was why it was just poison oak and not a snake or something. So I didn't even bother to move it. I just stood there until the dog went away. Then I went on.

I didn't have any idea where the car was now. I couldn't think about anything except my head, and I'd just stand in one place and sort of wonder if I had really seen a ford even, and I didn't even care much whether I had or not. Like I say, let her lay out all day and all night with everything in town that wears pants, what do I care. I dont owe anything to anybody that has no more consideration for me, that wouldn't be a dam bit above planting that ford there and making me spend a whole afternoon and Earl taking her back there and showing her the books[63] just because he's too dam virtuous for this world. I says you'll have one hell of a time in heaven, without anybody's business to meddle in only dont you ever let me catch you at it I says, I close my eyes to it because of your grandmother, but just you let me catch you doing it one time on this place, where my mother lives. These dam little slick haired squirts, thinking they are raising so much hell, I'll show them something about hell I says, and you

63) 얼이 언젠가는 캄슨 부인을 데려와 그녀에게 장부, 즉 제이슨이 천 달러를 이미 다른 용도로 빼내갔다는 증거가 되는 그 장부를 그녀에게 보여주지는 않을까 하는 제이슨의 우려를 엿볼 수 있다.

too. I'll make him think that dam red tie is the latch string to hell, if he thinks he can run the woods with my niece.

With the sun and all in my eyes and my blood going so I kept thinking every time my head would go on and burst and get it over with, with briers and things grabbing at me, then I came onto the sand ditch where they had been and I recognised the tree where the car was, and just as I got out of the ditch and started running I heard the car start. It went off fast, blowing the horn. They kept on blowing it, like it was saying Yah. Yah: Yaaahhhhhhhh, going out of sight. I got to the road just in time to see it go out of sight.

By the time I got up to where my car was, they were clean out of sight, the horn still blowing. Well, I never thought anything about it except I was saying Run. Run back to town. Run home and try to convince Mother that I never saw you in that car. Try to make her believe that I dont know who he was. Try to make her believe that I didn't miss ten feet of catching you in that ditch. Try to make her believe you were standing up, too.

It kept on saying Yahhhhh, Yahhhhh, Yaaahhhhhhhhh, getting fainter and fainter. Then it quit, and I could hear a cow lowing up at Russell's barn. And still I never thought. I went up to the door and opened it and raised my foot. I kind of thought then that the car was leaning a little more than the slant of the road would be, but I never found it out until I got in and started off.

Well, I just sat there. It was getting on toward sundown, and town was about five miles. They never even had guts enough to puncture it, to jab a hole in it. They just let the air out. I just stood there for a while, thinking about that kitchen full of niggers and not one of them had time to lift a tire onto the rack and screw up a couple of bolts. It was kind of funny because even she couldn't have seen far enough ahead to take the pump out on purpose, unless she though about it while he was letting out the air maybe. But what it probably was was somebody took it out and gave it to Ben to play with for a squirt gun because they'd take the whole car to pieces if he wanted it and Dilsey says, Aint nobody teched yo car. What we want to fool with hit fer? and I says You're a nigger. You're lucky, do you know it? I says I'll swap with you any day because it takes a white man not to have anymore sense than to worry about what a little slut of a girl does.

I walked up to Russell's. He had a pump. That was just an oversight on their part, I reckon. Only I still couldn't believe she'd have had the nerve to. I kept thinking that. I dont know why it is I cant seem to learn that a woman'll do anything. I kept thinking, Let's forget for a while how I feel toward you and how you feel toward me: I just wouldn't do you this way. I wouldn't do you this way no matter what you had done to me. Because like I say blood is blood and you cant get around it. It's not playing a joke that any eight year old boy could have thought of, It's letting your own uncle be laughed at by a man that would wear a red tie. They come into town and call us all a bunch of hicks and think It's too small to hold them. Well he doesn't know just how right he is. And her too. If that's the way she feels about it, she'd better keep right on going and a dam good riddance.

I stopped and returned Russell's pump and drove on to town. I went to the drugstore and got a shot[64] and then I went to the telegraph office. It had closed at 20.21, forty points down. Forty times five dollars; buy something with that if you can, and she'll say, I've got to have it[65] I've just got to and I'll say that's too bad you'll

---

64) 대부분 미국의 약국은 식료품가게(대·소형 마트) 내에 위치하고 있으며, 여기 "shot"은 아마도 마약이나 주사를 맞았다기보다는 앞서 언급된 "dope"처럼 코카콜라를 의미할 확률이 높다.

65) 제이슨이 투자한 주식은 20.62로 시작하여 20.21로 장 마감을 함으로써 그 주는 40포인트가 떨어진 셈이며, 그는 200달러의 손실을 보았다. 그러면서 아까 가게에서 캐디가 보내준 돈이 꼭 필요하다고 조르던 조카 미스 퀸턴을 생각하며, 그 실랑이 끝에 겨우 5달러만 그녀에게 건네준 걸 떠올리며 자신의 주식투자 손실액은 그것의 40배라고 계산하는 부분이다.

have to try somebody else, I haven't got any money; I've been too busy to make any.

I just looked at him.

"I'll tell you some news," I says. "You'll be astonished to learn that I am interested in the cotton market," I says. "That never occurred to you, did it?"

"I did my best to deliver it," he says. " I tried the store twice and called up your house, but they didn't know where you were," he says, digging in the drawer.

"Deliver what?" I says. He handed me a telegram. "What time did this come?" I says.

"About half past three," he says.

"And now it's ten minutes past five," I says.

"I tried to deliver it," he says. "I couldn't find you."

"That's not my fault, is it?" I says. I opened it, just to see what kind of a lie they'd tell me this time. They must be in one hell of a shape if they've got to come all the way to Mississippi to steal ten dollars a month. Sell, it says. The market will be unstable, with a general downward tendency. Do not be alarmed following government report.

"How much would a message like this cost?" I says. He told me.

"They paid it," he says.

"Then I owe them that much," I says. "I already knew this. Send this collect," I says, taking a blank. Buy, I wrote, Market just on point of blowing its head off. Occasional flurries for purpose of hooking a few more country suckers who haven't got in to the telegraph office yet. Do not be alarmed. " Send that collect," I says.

He looked at the message, then he looked at the clock. "Market closed an hour ago," he says.

"Well," I says. "That's not my fault either. I didn't invent it; I just bought a little of it while under the impression that the telegraph company would keep me informed as to what it was doing."

"A report is posted whenever it comes in," he says.

"Yes," I says. "And in Memphis they have it on a blackboard every ten seconds," I says. "I was within sixty-seven miles of there once this afternoon."

He looked at the message. "You want to send this?" he says.

"I still haven't changed my mind," I says. I wrote the other one out and counted the money. "And this one too, if you're sure you can spell b-u-y."

I went back to the store. I could hear the band from down the street. Prohibition's a fine thing. Used to be they'd come in Saturday with just one pair of shoes in the family and him wearing them, and they'd go down to the express office and get his package; now they all go to the show barefooted, with the merchants in the door like a row of tigers or something in a cage, watching them pass. Earl says,

"I hope it wasn't anything serious."

"What?" I says. He looked t his watch. Then he went to the door and looked at the courthouse clock. "You ought to have a dollar watch," I says. "It wont cost you so much to believe it's lying each time."

"What?" he says.

"Nothing," I says. "Hope I haven't inconvenienced you."

"We were not busy much," he says. "They all went to the show. It's all right."

"If It's not all right," I says, "you know what you can do about it."

"I said it was all right," he says.

"I heard you," I says. "And if it's not all right, you know what you can do about it."

"Do you want to quit?" he says.

"It's not my business," I says. "My wishes dont matter. But dont get the idea that you are protecting me by keeping me."

"You'd be a good business man if you'd let yourself, Jason," he says.

"At least I can tend to my own business and let other people's alone," I says.

"I dont know why you are trying to make me fire you," he says. "You know you could quit anytime and there wouldn't be any hard feelings between us."

"Maybe that's why I dont quit," I says. "As long as I tend to my job, that's what you are paying me for." I went on to the back and got a drink of water and went on out to the back door. Job had the cultivators all set up at last. It was quiet there, and pretty soon my head got a little easier. I could hear them singing now, and then the band played again. Well, let them get every quarter and dime in the county; it was no skin off my back. I've done what I could; a man that can live as long as I have and not know when to quit is a fool. Especially as It's no business of mine. If it was my own daughter now it would be different, because she wouldn't have time to; she'd have to work some to feed a few invalids and idiots and niggers, because how could I have the face to bring anybody there. I've too much respect for anybody to do that. I'm a man, I can stand it, it's my own flesh and blood and I'd like to see the color of the man's eyes that would speak disrespectful of any woman that was my friend it's these dam good women that do it I'd like to see the good, church-going woman that's half as square as Lorraine, whore or no whore. Like I say if I was to get married you'd go up like a balloon and you know it and she says I want you to be happy to have a family of your own not to slave your life away for us. But I'll be gone soon and then you can take a wife but you'll never find a woman who is worthy of you and I says yes I could. You'd get right up out of your grave you know you would. I says no thank you I have all the woman I can take care of now if I married a wife she'd probably turn out to be a hophead or something. That's all we lack in this family, I says.

The sun was down beyond the Methodist church now, and the pigeons were flying back and forth around the steeple, and when the band stopped I could hear them cooing. It hadn't been four months since Christmas, and yet they were almost as thick as ever. I reckon Parson Walthall was getting a belly full of them now. You'd have thought we were shooting people, with him making speeches and even holding onto a man's gun when they came over. Talking about peace on earth good will toward all and not a sparrow can fall to earth. But what does he care how thick they get, he hasn't got anything to do: what does he care what time it is. He pays no taxes, he doesn't have to see his money going every year to have the courthouse clock cleaned to where it'll run. They had to pay a man forty-five dollars to clean it. I counted over a hundred half-hatched pigeons on the ground. You'd think they'd have sense enough to leave town. It's a good thing I dont have anymore ties than a pigeon, I'll say that.

The band was playing again, a loud fast tune, like they were breaking up. I reckon they'd be satisfied now. Maybe they'd have enough music to entertain them while they drove fourteen or fifteen miles home and unharnessed in the dark and fed the stock and milked. All they'd have to do would be to whistle the music and tell the jokes to the live stock in the barn, and then they could count up how much they'd made by not taking the stock to the show too. They could figure that if a man had five children and seven mules, he cleared a quarter by taking his family to the show. Just like that. Earl came back with a couple of packages.

"Here's some more stuff going out," he says. "Where's Uncle Job?"

"Gone to the show, I imagine," I says. "Unless you watched him."

"He doesn't slip off," he says. "I can depend on him."

"Meaning me by that," I says.

He went to the door and looked out, listening.

"That's a good band," he says. "It's about time they were breaking up, I'd say."

"Unless they're going to spend the night there," I says. "The swallows had begun, and I could hear the sparrows beginning to swarm in the trees in the courthouse yard. Every once in a while a bunch of them would come swirling around in sight above the roof, then go away. They are as big a nuisance as the pigeons, to my notion. You cant even sit in the courthouse yard for them. First thing you know, bing. Right on your hat. But it would take a millionaire to afford to shoot them at five cents a shot. If they'd just put a little poison out there in the square, they'd get rid of them in a day, because if a merchant cant keep his stock from running around the square, he'd better try to deal in something besides chickens, something that dont eat, like plows or onions. And if a man dont keep his dogs up, he either dont want it or he hasn't any business with one. Like I say if all the businesses in a town are run like country businesses, you're going to have a country town.

"It wont do you any good if they have broke up," I says. "They'll have to hitch up and take out to get home by midnight as it is."

"Well," he says. "They enjoy it. Let them spend a little money on a show now and then. A hill farmer works pretty hard and gets mighty little for it."

"There's no law making them farm in the hills," I says. "Or anywhere else."

"Where would you and me be, if it wasn't for the farmers?" he says.

"I'd be home right now," I says. "Lying down, with an ice pack on my head."

"You have these headaches too often," he says. "Why dont you have your teeth examined good? Did he go over them all this morning?"

"Did who?" I says.

"You said you went to the dentist this morning."

"Do you object to my having the headache on your time?" I says. "Is that it?" They were crossing the alley now, coming up from the show.

"There they come," he says. "I reckon I better get up front." He went on. It's a curious thing how, no matter what's wrong with you, a man'll tell you to have your teeth examined and a woman'll tell you to get married. It always takes a man that never made much at any thing to tell you how to run your business, though. Like these college professors without a whole pair of socks to his name, telling you how to make a million in ten years, and a woman that couldn't even get a husband can always tell you how to raise a family.

Old man Job came up with the wagon. After a while he got through wrapping the lines around the whip socket.

"Well," I says. "Was it a good show?"

"I aint been yit," he says. "But I kin be arrested in dat tent tonight, dough."

"Like hell you haven't," I says. "You've been away from here since three oclock. Mr Earl was just back here looking for you."

"I been tendin to my business," he says. "Mr Earl knows whar I been."

"You may can fool him," I says. "I wont tell on you."

"Den he's de onliest man here I'd try to fool," he says. "Whut I want to waste my time foolin a man whut I dont keer whether I sees him Sat'dy night er not? I wont try to fool you," he says. "You too smart fer me. Yes, suh," he says, looking busy as hell, putting five or six little packages into the wagon. "You's too smart fer me. Aint a man in dis town kin keep up wid you fer smartness. You fools a man whut so smart he cant even keep up wid hisself," he says, getting in the wagon and unwrapping the reins.

"Who's that?" I says.

"Dat's Mr Jason Compson," he says. "Git up dar, Dan!"

One of the wheels was just about to come off. I watched to see if he'd get out of the alley before it did. Just turn any vehicle over to a nigger, though. I says that old rattletrap's just an eyesore, yet you'll keep it standing there in the carriage house a hundred years just so that boy can ride to the cemetery once a week. I says he's not the first fellow that'll have to do things he doesn't want to. I'd make him ride in that car like a civilised man or stay at home. What does he know about where he goes or what he goes in, and us keeping a carriage and a horse so he can take a ride on Sunday afternoon.

A lot Job cared whether the wheel came off or not, long as he wouldn't have too far to walk back. Like I say the only place for them is in the field, where they'd have to work from sunup to sundown. They cant stand prosperity or an easy job. Let one stay around white people for a while and he's not worth killing. They get so they can outguess you about work before your very eyes, like Roskus the only mistake he ever made was he got careless one day and died. Shirking and stealing and giving you a little more lip and a little more lip until some day you have to lay them out with a scantling or something. Well, it's Earl's business. But I'd hate to have my business advertised over this town by an old doddering nigger and a wagon that you thought every time it turned a coner it would come all to pieces.

The sun was all high up in the air now, and inside it was beginning to get dark. I went up front. The square was empty. Earl was back closing the safe, and then the clock begun to strike.

"You lock the back door?" he says. I went back and locked it a came back. "I suppose you're going to the show tonight," he says. "I gave you those passes yesterday, didn't I?"

"Yes," I says. "You want them back?"

"No, no," he says. "I just forgot whether I gave them to you or not. No sense in wasting them."

He locked the door and said Goodnight and went on. The sparrows were still rattling away in the trees, but the square was empty except for a few cars. There was a ford in front of the drugstore, but I didn't even look at it. I know when I've had enough of anything. I dont mind trying to help her, but I know when I've had enough. I guess I could teach Luster to drive it, then they could chase her all day long if they wanted to, and I could stay home and play with Ben.

I went in and got a couple of cigars. Then I thought I'd have another headache shot for luck, and I stood and talked with them a while.

"Well," Mac says. "I reckon you've got your money on the Yankees this year."

"What for?" I says.

"The Pennant," he says. "Not anything in the league can beat them."

"Like hell there's not," I says. "They're shot," I says. "You think a team can be that lucky forever?"

"I dont call it luck," Mac says.

"I wouldn't bet on any team that fellow Ruth played on,"[66] I says. "Even if I knew it was going to win."

"Yes?" Mac says.

"I can name you a dozen men in either league who're more valuable than he is," I says.

"What have you got against Ruth?" Mac says.

"Nothing," I says. "I haven't got any thing against him. I dont even like to look at his picture." I went on out. The lights were coming on, and people going along the streets toward home. Sometimes the sparrows never got still until full dark. The night they turned on the new lights around the courthouse it waked them up and they were flying around and blundering into the lights all night long. They kept it up two or three nights, then one morning they were all gone. Then after about two months they all came back again.

I drove on home. There were no lights in the house yet, but they'd all be looking out the windows, and Dilsey jawing away in the kitchen like it was her own food she was having to keep hot until I

---

66) 제이슨이 여기 뉴욕 양키즈 팀(야구)이나 팀의 전설적인 투수 Babe Ruth에게 적대적인 이유가 확실하지 않다. 제이슨이 만약 양키즈 팀의 게임들에 돈을 걸고 있었다면, 당시 그 팀의 게임 전적이나 Babe Ruth의 화려한 활약상을 염두에 둘 때 그는 큰돈을 벌 수 있었기 때문이다. 아마 Ruth에 대한 제이슨의 적개심은 1920년대와 1930년대 후반까지 돌고 있던 소문, Ruth가 흑인의 피가 섞였다는 소문에 근거하고 있는지 모른다.

got there. You'd think to hear that there wasn't but one supper in the world, and that was the one she had to keep back a few minutes on my account. Well at least I could come home one time without finding Ben and that nigger hanging on the gate like a bear and a monkey in the same cage. Just let it come toward sundown and he'd head for the gate like a cow for the barn, hanging onto it and bobbing his head and sort of moaning to himself. That's a hog for punishment for you. If what had happened to him for fooling with open gates had happened to me, I never would want to see another one. I often wondered what he'd be thinking about, down there at the gate, watching the girls going home from school, trying to want something he couldn't even remember he didn't and couldn't want any longer. And what he'd think when they'd be undressing him, and he'd happen to take a look at himself and begin to cry like he'd do. But like I say they never did enough of that. I says I know what you need you need what they did to Ben then you'd behave. And if you dont know what that was I says, ask Dilsey to tell you.

There was a light in Mother's room. I put the car up and went on into the kitchen. Luster and Ben were there.

"Where's Dilsey?" I says. "Putting supper on?"

"She up stairs wid Miss Cahline," Luster says. "Dey been goin hit. Ever since Miss Quentin come home. Mammy up there keepin um fum fightin. Is dat show come, Mr Jason?"

"Yes," I says.

"I thought I heard de band," he says. "Wish I could go," he says. "I could ef I jes had a quarter."

Dilsey came in. "You come, is you?" she says. "Whut you been up to dis evenin? You knows how much work I got to do; whyn't you git here on time?"

"Maybe I went to the show," I says. "Is supper ready?"

"Wish I could go," Luster says. "I could ef I jus had a quarter."

"You aint got no bisiness at no show," Dilsey says. "You go on in de house and set down," she says. "Dont you go up stairs and git um started again, now."

"What's the matter?" I says.

"Quentin come in a while ago and says you been follerin her around all evenin and den Miss Cahline jumped on her. Whyn't you let her alone? Cant you live in de same house wid yo own blood niece widout quoilin?"

"I cant quarrel with her," I says, "because I haven't seen her since this morning. What does she say I've done now? made her go to school? That's pretty bad," I says.

"Well, you tend to yo business and let her lone," Dilsey says. "I'll take keer of her ef you'n Miss Cahline'll let me. Go on in dar now and behave yoself twell I git supper on."

"Ef I jes had a quarter," Luster says, "I could go to dat show."

"En ef you had wings you could fly to heaven," Dilsey says. "I dont want to hear another word about dat show."

"That reminds me," I says. "I've got a couple of tickets they gave me." I took them out of my coat.

"You fixin to use um?" Luster says.

"Not me," I says. "I wouldn't go to it for ten dollars."

"Gimme one of um, Mr Jason," he says.

"I'll sell you one," I says. "How about it?"

"I aint got no money," he says.

"that's too bad," I says. I made to go out.

"Gimme one of um, Mr Jason," he says. "You aint gwine need um bofe."

"Hush yo mouf," Dilsey says. "Dont you know he aint gwine give nothin away?"

"How much you want fer hit?" he says.

"Five cents," I says.

"I aint got dat much," he says.

"How much you got?" I says.

"I aint got nothin," he says.

"All right," I says. I went on.

"Mr Jason," he says.

"Whyn't you hush up?" Dilsey says. "He jes teasin you. He fixin to use dem tickets hisself. Go on, Jason, and let him lone."

"I dont want them," I says. I came back to the stove. "I came in here to burn them up. But if you want to buy one for a nickel?" I says, looking at him and opening the stove lid.

"I aint got dat much," he says.

"All right," I says. I dropped one of them in the stove.

"You, Jason," Dilsey says. "Aint you shamed?"

"Mr Jason," he says. "Please, suh. I'll fix dem tires ev' y day fer a mont."

"I need the cash," I says. "You can have it for a nickel."

"Hush, Luster," Dilsey says. "She jerked him back. "Go on," she says. "Drop hit in. Go on. Git hit over with."

"You can have it for a nickel," I says.

"Go on," Dilsey says. "He aint got no nickel. Go on. Drop hit in."

"All right," I says. I dropped it in and Dilsey shut the stove.

"A big growed man like you," she says. "Git on outen my kitchen. Hush," she says to Luster. "Dont you git Benjy started. I'll git you a quarter fum Frony tonight and you kin go tomorrow night. Hush up, now."

I went on into the living room. I couldn't hear anything from upstairs. I opened the paper. After a while Ben and Luster came in. Ben went to the dark place on the wall where the mirror used to be, rubbing his hands on it and slobbering and moaning. Luster began punching at the fire.

"What're you doing?" I says. "We dont need any fire tonight."

"I trying to keep him quiet," he says. "Hit always cold Easter," he says.

"Only this is not Easter," I says. "Let it alone."

He put the poker back and got the cushion out of Mother's chair and gave it to Ben, and he hunkered down in front of the fireplace and got quiet.

I read the paper. There hadn't been a sound from upstairs when Dilsey came in and sent Ben and Luster on to the kitchen and said supper was ready.

"All right," I says. She went out. I sat there, reading the paper. After a while I heard Dilsey looking in at the door.

"Whyn't you come on and eat?" she says.

"I'm waiting for supper," I says.

"Hit's on the table," she says. "I done told you."

"Is it?" I says. "Excuse me. I didn't hear anybody come down."

"They aint comin," she says. "You come on and eat, so I can take something up to them."

"Are they sick?" I says. "What did the doctor say it was? Not Smallpox, I hope."

"Come on here, Jason," she says. "So I kin git done."

"All right," I says, raising the paper again. "I'm waiting for supper now."

I could feel her watching me at the door. I read the paper.

"Whut you want to act like this fer?" she says. "When you knows how much bother I has anyway."

"If Mother is any sicker than she was when she came down to dinner, all right," I says. "But as long as I am buying food for people younger than I am, they'll have to come down to the table to eat it. Let me know when supper's ready," I says, reading the paper again. I heard her climbing the stairs, dragging her feet and grunting and groaning like they were straight up and three feet apart. I heard her at Mother's door, then I heard her calling Quentin, like the door was locked, then she went back to Mother's room and then Mother went and talked to Quentin. Then they came down stairs. I read the paper.

Dilsey came back to the door. "Come on," she says. "fo you kin think up some mo devilment. You just tryin yoself tonight."

I went to the diningroom. Quentin was sitting with her head bent.

She had painted her face again. Her nose looked like a porcelain insulator.

"I'm glad you feel well enough to come down," I says to Mother.

"It's little enough I can do for you, to come to the table," she says. "No matter how I feel. I realise that when a man works all day he likes to be surrounded by his family at the supper table. I want to please you. I only wish you and Quentin got along better. It would be easier for me."

"We get along all right," I says. "I dont mind her staying locked up in her room all day if she wants to. But I cant have all this whoop-de-do and sulking at mealtimes. I know that's a lot to ask her, but I'm that way in my own house. Your house, I meant to say."

"It's yours," Mother says. "You are the head of it now."

Quentin hadn't looked up. I helped the plates and she begun to eat.

"Did you get a good piece of meat?" I says. "If you didn't, I'll try to find you a better one."

She didn't say anything.

"I say, did you get a good piece of meat?" I says.

"What?" she says. "Yes. It's all right."

"Will you have some more rice?" I says.

"No," she says.

"Better let me give you some more," I says.

"I dont want any more," she says.

"Not at all," I says. "You're welcome."

"Is your headache gone?" Mother says.

"Headache?" I says.

"I was afraid you were developing one," she says. "When you came in this afternoon."

"Oh," I says. "No, it didn't show up. We stated so busy this afternoon I forgot about it."

"Was that why you were late?" Mother says. I could see Quentin listening. I looked at her. Her knife and fork were still going, but I caught her looking at me, then she looked at her plate again. I says,

"No. I loaned my car to a fellow about three oclock and I had to wait until he got back with it." I ate for a while.

"Who was it?" Mother says.

"It was one of those show men," I says. "It seems his sister's husband was out riding with some town woman, and he was chasing them."

Quentin sat perfectly still, chewing.

"You ought not to lend your car to people like that," Mother says. "You are too generous with it. That's why I never call on you for it if I can help it."

"I was beginning to think that myself, for a while," I says. "But he got back, all right. He says he found what he was looking for."

"Who was the woman?" Mother says.

"I'll tell you later," I says. "I dont like to talk about such things before Quentin."

Quentin had quit eating. Every once in a while she'd take a drink of water, then she'd sit there crumbling a biscuit up, her face bent over her plate.

"Yes," Mother says. "I suppose women who stay shut up like I do have no idea what goes on in this town."

"Yes," I says. "They dont."

"My life has been so different from that," Mother says. "Thank God I dont know about such wickedness. I dont even want to know about it. I'm not like most people."

I didn't say any more. Quentin sat there, crumbling the biscuit until I quit eating. Then she says,

"Can I go now?" without looking at anybody.

"What?" I says. "Sure, you can go. Were you waiting on us?"

She looked at me. She had crumpled all the bread, but her hands still went on like they were crumpling it yet and her eyes looked like they were cornered or something and then she started biting her mouth like it ought to have poisoned her, with all that red lead.

"Grandmother," she says. "Grandmother——"

"Did you want something else to eat?" I says.

"Why does he treat me like this, Grandmother?" she says. "I never hurt him."

"I want you all to get along with one another," Mother says. "You are all that's left now, and I do want you all to get along better."

"It's his fault," she says. "He wont let me alone, and I have to. If he doesn't want me here, why wont he let me go back to—"

"That's enough," I says. "Not another word."

"Then why wont he let me alone?" she says ." He—he just—"

"He is the nearest thing to a father you've ever had," Mother says. "It's his bread you and I eat. It's only right that he should expect obedience from you."

"It's his fault," she says. She jumped up. "He makes me do it. If he would just—" she looked at us, her eyes cornered, kind of jerking her arms against her sides.

"If I would just what?" I says.

"Whatever I do, it's your fault," she says. "If I'm bad, it's because I had to be. You made me. I wish I was dead. I wish we were all dead." Then she ran. We heard her run up the stairs. Then a door slammed.

"That's the first sensible thing she ever said," I says.

"She didn't go to school today," Mother says.

"How do you know?" I says. " Were you down town?"

"I just know," she says. "I wish you could be kinder to her."

"If I did that I'd have to arrange to see her more than once a day," I says. "You'll have to make her come to the table every meal. Then I could give her an extra piece of meat every time."

"There are little things you could do," she says.

"Like not paying any attention when you ask me to see that she goes to school?" I says.

"She didn't go to school today," she says. "I just know she didn't. She says she went for a car ride with one of the boys this afternoon and you followed her."

"How could I," I says, "when somebody had my car all afternoon? Whether or not she was in school today is already past," I says. "If you've got to worry about it, worry about next Monday."

"I wanted you and she to get along with one another," she says. "But she has inherited all of the headstrong traits. Quentin's too. I thought at the time, with the heritage she would already have, to give her that name, too. Sometimes I think she is the judgment of both of them upon me."[67)]

"Good Lord," I says. "You've got a fine mind. No wonder you keep yourself sick all the time."

"What ?" she says. "I dont understand."

"I hope not," I says. "A good woman misses a lot she's better off without knowing."

"They were both that way," she says. "They would make interest with your father against me when I tried to correct them. He was always saying they didn't need controlling, that they already knew what cleanliness and honesty were, which was all that anyone could hope to be taught. And now I hope he's satisfied."

"You've got Ben to depend on," I says. "Cheer up."

"They deliberately shut me out of their lives," she says. "It was always her and Quentin. They were always conspiring against me. Against you too, though you were too young to realise it. They always looked on you and me as outsiders, like they did your Uncle Maury. I always told your father that they were allowed too much freedom, to be together too much. When Quentin started to school we had to let her go the next year, so she could be with him. She couldn't bear for any of you to do anything she couldn't. It was vanity in her, vanity and false pride. And then when her troubles began I knew that Quentin would feel that he had to do something just as bad. But I didn't believe that he would have been so selfish as to — I didn't dream that he —"

"Maybe he knew it was going to be a girl," I says. "And that one

---

67) "she" = Miss Quentin, "them" = Quentin and Caddy.

more of them would be more than he could stand."

"He could have controlled her," she says. "He seemed to be the only person she had any consideration for. But that is a part of the judgment too, I suppose."

"Yes," I says. "Too bad it wasn't me instead of him. You'd be a lot better off."

"You say things like that to hurt me," she says. "I deserve it though. When they began to sell the land to send Quentin to Harvard I told your father that he must make an equal provision for you. Then when Herbert offered to take you into the bank I said, Jason is provided for now, and when all the expense began to pile up and I was forced to sell our furniture and the rest of the pasture, I wrote her at once because I said she will realise that she and Quentin have had their share and part of Jason's too and that it depends on her now to compensate him. I said she will do that out of respect for her father. I believed that, then. But I'm just a poor old woman; I was raised to believe that people would deny themselves for their own flesh and blood. It's my fault. You were right to reproach me."

"Do you think I need any man's help to stand on my feet?" I says. "Let alone a woman that cant name the father of her own child."

"Jason," she says.

"All right," I says. "I didn't mean that. Of course not."

"If I believed that were possible, after all my suffering."

"Of course it's not," I says. "I didn't mean it."

"I hope that at least is spared me," she says.

"Sure it is," I says. "She's too much like both of them to doubt that."

"I couldn't bear that," she says.

"Then quit thinking about it," I says. "Has she been worrying you any more about getting out at night?"

"No. I made her realise that it was for her own good and that she'd thank me for it some day. She takes her books with her and studies after I lock the door. I see the light on as late as eleven oclock some nights."

"How do you know she's studying?" I says.

"I dont know what else she'd do in there alone," she says." She never did read any."

"No," I says. "You wouldn't know. And you can thank your stars for that," I says. Only what would be the use in saying it aloud. It would just have her crying on me again.

I heard her go up stairs. Then she called Quentin and Quentin says What? through the door. "Goodnight," Mother says. Then I heard the key in the lock, and Mother went back to her room.

When I finished my cigar and went up, the light was still on. I could see the empty keyhole, but I couldn't hear a sound. She studied quiet. Maybe she learned that in school. I told Mother goodnight and went on to my room and got the box out and counted it again. I could hear the Great American Gelding snoring away like a planing mill.[68)] I read somewhere they'd fix men that way to give them women's voices. But maybe he didn't know what they'd done to him. I dont reckon he even knew what he had been trying to do, or why Mr Burgess knocked him out with the fence picket. And if they'd just sent him on to Jackson while he was under the ether, he'd never have known the difference. But that would have been too simple for a Compson to think of. Not half complex enough. Having to wait to do it at all until he broke out and tried to run a little girl down on the street with her own father looking at him. Well, like I say they never started soon enough with their cutting, and they quit too quick. I know at least two more that needed something like that,[69)] and one of them not over a mile away, either. But then I dont reckon even that would do any good. Like I say once a bitch always a bitch. And just

---

68) 거칠게 잘려진 목재를 사용 가능하도록 긁어내어 다듬는 기계.

69) 여기 제이슨은 벤지가 거세된 것처럼 캐디와 미스 퀸틴 둘 다 거세되었으면 하는 그의 욕망을 드러내고 있다.

let me have twenty-four hours without any dam New York jew to advise me what it's going to do. I dont want to make a killing; save that to suck in the smart gambles with. I just want an even chance to get my money back. And once I've done that they can bring all Beale street and all bedlam in here and two of them can sleep in my bed and another one can have my place at the table too.

April Eighth, 1928

The day dawned bleak and chill, a moving wall of gray light out of the northeast which, instead of dissolving into moisture, seemed to disintegrate into minute and venomous particles, like dust that, when Dilsey opened the door of the cabin and emerged, needled laterally into her flesh, precipitating not so much a moisture as a substance partaking of the quality of thin, not quite congealed oil. She wore a stiff black straw hat perched upon her turban, and a maroon velvet cape with a border of mangy and anonymous fur above a dress of purple silk, and she stood in the door for a while with her myriad and sunken face lifted to the weather, and one gaunt hand flac-soled as the belly of a fish,[1] then she moved the cape aside and examined the bosom of her gown.

The gown fell gauntly from her shoulders, across her fallen breasts, then tightened upon her paunch and fell again, ballooning a little above the nether garments which she would remove layer by layer as the spring accomplished and the warm days, in color regal and moribund.[2] She had been a big woman once but now her skeleton rose, draped loosely in unpadded skin that tightened again upon a paunch almost dropsical, as though muscle and tissue had

---

1) 딜시가 (물고기 뱃살 같은 하얀) 손바닥을 위로 보게 펴서 비가 오는지를 확인하는 모습.

2) "accomplished" = progressed. 딜시가 입고 있는 "자줏빛 실크" 드레스를 "color regal and moribund"로 묘사하는데, 자주색은 전통적으로 왕실의 색상이며, 그 드레스는 오래입어 낡은 상태이기에 "moribund"라는 말로 표현하고 있다.

been courage or fortitude which the days or the years had consumed until only the indomitable skeleton was left rising like a ruin or a landmark above the somnolent and impervious guts, and above that the collapsed face that gave the impression of the bones themselves being outside the flesh, lifted into the driving day with an expression at once fatalistic and of a child's astonished disappointment, until she turned and entered the house again and closed the door.

The earth immediately about the door was bare. It had a patina, as though from the soles of bare feet in generations, like old silver or the walls of Mexican houses which have been plastered by hand. Beside the house, shading it in summer, stood three mulberry trees, the fledged leaves that would later be broad and placid as the palms of hands streaming flatly undulant upon the driving air. A pair of jaybirds came up from nowhere, whirled up on the blast like gaudy scraps of cloth or paper and lodged in the mulberries, where they swung in raucous tilt and recover, screaming into the wind that ripped their harsh cries onward and away like scraps of paper or of cloth in turn. Then three more joined them and they swung and tilted in the wrung branches[3)] for a time, screaming. The door of the cabin opened and Dilsey emerged once more, this time in a man's felt hat and an army overcoat, beneath the frayed skirts of which her blue gingham dress fell in uneven balloonings, streaming too about her as she crossed the yard and mounted the steps to the kitchen door.

A moment later she emerged, carrying an open umbrella now, which she slanted ahead into the wind, and crossed to the woodpile and laid the umbrella down, still open. Immediately she caught at it and arrested it and held to it for a while, looking about her. Then she closed it and laid it down and stacked stovewood into her crooked arm, against her breast, and picked up the umbrella and got it open at

---

3) "wrung"은 단순히 "비틀어진"(twisted)의 의미도 될 수 있지만, 동시에 빗물에 젖은 나뭇가지를 새들이 꽉 잡아 물을 짜낸 듯한 가지들의 이미지도 상상할 수 있다.

last and returned to the steps and held the wood precariously balanced while she contrived to close the umbrella, which she propped in the corner just within the door. She dumped the wood into the box behind the stove. Then she removed the overcoat and hat and took a soiled apron down from the wall and put it on and built a fire in the stove. While she was doing so, rattling the grate bars and clattering the lids, Mrs compson began to call her from the head of the stairs.

She wore a dressing gown of quilted black satin, holding it close under her chin. In the other hand she held a red rubber hot water bottle and she stood at the head of the back stairway, calling "Dilsey" at steady and inflectionless intervals into the quiet stairwell that descended into complete darkness, then opened again where a gray window fell across it. "Dilsey," she called, without inflection or emphasis or haste, as though she were not listening for a reply at all. "Dilsey."

Dilsey answered and ceased clattering the stove, but before she could cross the kitchen Mrs Compson called her again, and before she crossed the diningroom and brought her head into relief against the gray splash of the window, still again.

"All right," Dilsey said. "All right, here I is. I'll fill hit soon ez I git some hot water." She gathered up her skirts and mounted the stairs, wholly blotting the gray light. "Put hit down dar en g'awn back to bed."

"I couldn't understand what was the matter," Mrs Compson said.

"I've been lying awake for an hour at least, without hearing a sound from the kitchen."

"You put hit down and g'awn back to bed," Dilsey said. She toiled painfully up the steps, shapeless, breathing heavily. "I'll have de fire gwine in a minute, en de water hot in two mo."

"I've been lying there for an hour, at least," Mrs Compson said. "I thought maybe you were waiting for me to come down and start the fire."

Dilsey reached the top of the stairs and took the water bottle. "I'll fix hit in a minute," she said. "Luster overslep dis mawnin, up half de night at dat show. I gwine build de fire myself. Go on now, so you wont wake de others twell[4] I ready."

"If you permit Luster to do things that interfere with his work, you'll have to suffer for it yourself," Mrs Compson said. "Jason wont like this if he hears about it. You know he wont."

" 'Twusn't none of jason's money he went on," Dilsey said. "Dat's one thing sho." She went on down the stairs. Mrs Compson returned to her room. As she got into bed again she could hear Dilsey yet descending the stairs with a sort of painful and terrific slowness that would have become maddening had it not presently ceased beyond the flapping diminishment of the pantry door.

She entered the kitchen and built up the fire and began to prepare breakfast. In the midst of this she ceased and went to the window and looked out toward her cabin, then she went to the door and opened it and shouted into the driving weather.

"Luster!" she shouted, standing to listen, tilting her face from the wind. "You, Luster!" She listened, then as she prepared to shout again Luster appeared around the corner of the kitchen.

"Ma'am?" he said innocently, so innocently that Dilsey looked down at him, for a moment motionless, with something more than mere surprise.

"Whar you at?" she said.

"Nowhere," he said. "Jes in de cellar."

"Whut you doin in de cellar?" she said. "Dont stand dar in de rain, fool." she said.

"Aint doin nothin," he said. He came up the steps.

"Dont you dare come in dis do widout a armful of wood," she said. "Here I done had to tote yo wood en build yo fire bofe. Didn't I tole you not to leaves dis place last night befo dat woodbox wus full to de

4) until.

top?"

"I did," Luster said." I filled hit."

" Whar hit gone to, den?"

"I dont know'm. I aint teched hit."

"Well, you git hit full up now," she said. "And git on up dar en see bout Benjy."

She shut the door. Luster went to the woodpile. The five jaybirds whirled over the house, screaming, and into the mulberries again. He watched them. He picked up a rock and threw it. "Whoo," he said. "Git on back to hell, whar you belong at. 'Taint Monday yit." [5)]

He loaded himself mountainously with stove wood. He could not see over it, and he staggered to the steps and up them and blundered crashing against the door, shedding billets. Then Dilsey came and opened the door for him and he blundered across the kitchen. "You, Luster!" she shouted, but he had already hurled the wood into the box with a thunderous crash. "Hah!" he said.

"Is you tryin to wake up de whole house?" Dilsey said. She hit him on the back of his head with the flat of her hand. "Go on up dar and git Benjy dressed, now."

"Yessum," he said. He went toward the outer door.

"Whar you gwine?" Dilsey said.

"I thought I better go round de house en in by de front, so I wont wake up Miss Cahline[6)] en dem."

---

5) 전설에 의하면 까마귓과에 속하는 어치(jaybird = bluejay)는 악마와 연계된 새로, 지옥으로부터 온 방문객 내지는 스파이로 간주되며, 일주일에 한번 악마/사탄에게 인간들의 죄를 보고하기 위해 금요일에 지옥을 향한다(혹자는 금요일에 들어가 지옥에서 월요일에 나온다고 말한다). 러스터는 새들을 향해 월요일까지는 지옥에서 머무르며 나타나지 말아야 한다고, 특히 그것도 부활절인 일요일에 나타나는 것은 매우 재수 없다고 인지한데서 하는 말이다.

6) 캐롤라인 캄슨, 캄슨 부인이며, 남부에서 특히 흑인들 사이에서 성이 아닌 이름에다 Miss 같은 호칭을 붙여 쓰곤 하였다.

"You go on up dem back stairs like I tole you en git Benjy's clothes on him," Dilsey said. "Go on, now."

"Yessum," Luster said. He returned and left by diningroom door. After a while it ceased to flap. Dilsey prepared to make biscuit. As she ground the sifter steadily above the bread board, she sang, to herself at first, something without particular tune or words, repetitive, mournful and plaintive, austere, as she ground a faint, steady snowing of flour onto the bread board. The stove had begun to heat the room and to fill it with murmurous minors of the fire, and presently she was singing louder, as if her voice too had been thawed out by the growing warmth, and then Mrs Compson called her name again from within the house. Dilsey raised her face as if her eyes could and did penetrate the walls and ceiling and saw the old woman in her quilted dressing gown at the head of the stairs, calling her name with machinelike regularity.

"Oh, Lawd," Dilsey said. She set the sifter down and swept up the hem of her apron and wiped her hands and caught up the bottle from the chair on which she had laid it and gathered her apron about the handle of the kettle which was now jetting faintly. "Jes a minute," she called. " De water jes dis minute got hot."

It was not the bottle which Mrs Compson wanted, however, and clutching it by the neck like a dead hen Dilsey went to the foot of the stairs and looked upward.

"Aint Luster up dar wid him?" she said.

"Luster hasn't been in the house. I've been lying here listening for him. I knew he would be late, but I did hope he'd come in time to keep Benjamin from disturbing Jason on Jason's one day in the week to sleep in the morning."

"I dont see how you expect anybody to sleep, wid you standin in de hall, holl'in at folks fum de crack of dawn," Dilsey said. She began to mount the stairs, toiling heavily. "I sont dat boy up dar half an hour ago."

Mrs Compson watched her, holding the dressing gown under her chin. "What are you going to do?" she said.

"Gwine git Benjy dressed en bring him down to de kitchen, whar he wont wake Jason en Quentin," Dilsey said.

"Haven't you started breakfast yet?"

"I'll tent to dat too," Dilsey said. "You better git back in bed twell Luster make yo fire. Hit cold dis mawnin."

"I know it," Mrs Compson said. "My feet are like ice. They were so cold they waked me up." She watched Dilsey mount the stairs. It took her a long while. "You know how it frets Jason when breakfast is late," Mrs Compson said.

"I cant do but one thing at a time," Dilsey said. "You git on back to bed, fo I has you on my hands dis mawnin too."

"If you're going to drop everything to dress Benjamin, I'd better come down and get breakfast. You know as well as I do how Jason acts when it's late."

"En who gwine eat yo messin?"[7)] Dilsey said. "Tell me dat. Go on now," she said, toiling upward. Mrs Compson stood watching her as she mounted, steadying herself against the wall with one hand, holding her skirts up with the other.

"Are you going to wake him up just to dress him?" she said.

Dilsey stopped. With her foot lifted to the next step she stood there, her hand against the wall and the gray splash of the window behind her, motionless and shapeless she loomed.

"He aint awake den?" she said.

"He wasn't when I looked in," Mrs Compson said. "But it's past his time. He never does sleep after half past seven. You know he doesn't."

Dilsey said nothing. She made no further move, but though she could not see her save as a blobby shape without depth, Mrs Compson knew that she had lowered her face a little and that she stood now like cows do in the rain, holding the empty water bottle by

---

7) 캄슨 부인이 음식솜씨가 형편없음을 딜시는 지적한다.

its neck.

"You're not the one who has to bear it," Mrs Compson said. "It's not your responsibility. You can go away. You dont have to bear the brunt of it day in and day out. You owe nothing to them, to Mr Compson's memory. I know you have never had any tenderness for Jason. You've never tried to conceal it."

Dilsey said nothing. She turned slowly and descended, lowering her body from step to step, as a small child does, her hand against the wall. "You go on and let him alone," she said. "Dont go in dar no mo, now. I'll send Luster up soon as I find him. Let him alone, now."

She returned to the kitchen. She looked into the stove, then she drew her apron over her head and donned the overcoat and opened the outer door and looked up and down the yard. The weather drove upon her flesh, harsh and minute, but the scene was empty of all else that moved. She descended the steps, gingerly, as if for silence, and went around the corner of the kitchen. As she did so Luster emerged quickly and innocently from the cellar door.

Dilsey stopped. "Whut you up to?" she said.

"Nothin," Luster said. "Mr Jason say fer me to find out whar dat water leak in de cellar fum."

"En when wus hit he say fer you to do dat?" Dilsey said. "Last New Year's day, wasn't hit?"

"I thought I jes be lookin whiles dey sleep," Luster said. Dilsey went to the cellar door. He stood aside and she peered down into the obscurity odorous of dank earth and mold and rubber.

"Huh," Dilsey said. She looked at Luster again. He met her gaze blandly, innocent and open. "I dont know whut you up to, but you aint got no business doin hit. You jes tryin me too dis mawnin cause de others is, aint you? You git on up dar en see to Benjy, you hear?"

"Yessum," Luster said. He went on toward the kitchen steps, swiftly.

"Here," Dilsey said. "You git me another armful of wood while I got you."

"Yessum," he said. He passed her on the steps and went to the woodpile. When he blundered again at the door a moment later, again invisible and blind within and beyond his wooden avatar, Dilsey opened the door and guided him across the kitchen with a firm hand.

"Jes thow hit at dat box again," she said. "Jes thow hit."

"I got to," Luster said, panting. "I cant put hit down no other way."

"Den you stand dar en hold hit a while," Dilsey said. She unloaded him a stick at a time. "Whut got into you dis mawnin? Here I sont you fer wood en you aint never brought mo'n six sticks at a time to save yo life twell today. Whut you fixin to ax me kin you do now? Aint dat show lef town yit?"

"Yessum. Hit done gone."

She put the last stick into the box. "Now you go on up dar wid Benjy, like I tole you befo," she said. "And I dont want nobody else yellin down dem stairs at me twell I rings de bell. You hear me."

"Yessum," Luster said. He vanished through the swing door. Dilsey put some more wood in the stove and returned to the bread board. Presently she began to sing again.

The room grew warmer. Soon Dilsey's skin had taken on a rich, lustrous quality as compared with that as of a faint dusting of wood ashes which both it and Luster's had worn as she moved about the kitchen, gathering about her the raw materials of food, coordinating the meal. On the wall above a cupboard, invisible save at night, by lamp light and even then evincing an enigmatic profundity because it had but one hand, a cabinet clock ticked, then with a preliminary sound as if it had cleared its throat, struck five times.

"Eight oclock,"[8)] Dilsey said. She ceased and tilted her head upward, listening. But there was no sound save the clock and the fire. She opened the oven and looked at the pan of bread, then stooping

---

8) 제시간에 맞춰 정확하게 종도 울리지 않는 부엌의 고장 난 시계를 딜시는 정확히 (5번 울리자 8시라고) 읽고 있다.

she paused while someone descended the stairs. She heard the feet cross the diningroom, then the swing door opened and Luster entered, followed by a big man who appeared to have been shaped of some substance whose particles would not or did not cohere to one another or the frame which supported it. His skin was dead looking and hairless; dropsical too, he moved with a shambling gait like a trained bear. His hair was pale and fine. It had been brushed smoothly down upon his brow like that of children in daguerrotypes. His eyes were clear, of the pale sweet blue of cornflowers, his thick mouth hung open, drooling a little.[9)]

"Is he cold?" Dilsey said. She wiped her hands on her apron and touched his hand.

"Ef he aint, I is," Luster said. "Always cold Easter. Aint never seen hit fail. Miss Cahilne say ef you aint got time to fix her hot water bottle to never mind about hit."

"Oh, Lawd," Dilsey said. She drew a chair into the corner between the woodbox and the stove. The man went obediently and sat in it. "Look in de dinin room and see whar I laid dat bottle down," Dilsey said. Luster fetched the bottle from the diningroom and Dilsey filled it and gave it to him. "Hurry up, now," she said. " See ef Jason wake now. Tell em hit's all ready."

Luster went out. Ben sat beside the stove. He sat loosely, utterly motionless save for his head, which made a continual bobbing sort of movement as he watched Dilsey with his sweet vague gaze as she moved about. Luster returned.

"He up," he said. "Miss Cahline say put hit on de table." He came to the stove and spread his hands palm down above the firebox. "He up, too," he said. "Gwine hit wid bofe feet dis mawnin." [10)]

---

9) 벤지의 모습이 처음으로 상세히 묘사되고 있다.

10) 오늘 아침 제이슨의 분위기가 심상치 않은, 분노로 발을 쾅쾅 구르며 소란을 피우는 그의 모습을 알 수 있다.

"Whut's de matter now?" Dilsey said. "Git away fum dar. How kin I do anything wid you standin over de stove?"

"I cold," Luster said.

"You ought to thought about dat whiles you wus down dar in dat cellar," Dilsey said. "Whut de matter wid Jason?"

"Sayin me en Benjy broke dat winder in his room." [11]

"Is dey one broke?" Dilsey said.

"Dat's whut he sayin," Luster said. "Say I broke hit."

"How could you, when he keep hit locked all day en night?"

"Say I broke hit chunkin rocks at hit," Luster said.

"En did you?"

"Nome," Luster said.

"Dont lie to me, boy," Dilsey said.

"I never done hit," Luster said. "Ask Benjy ef I did. I aint stud'in dat winder."

"Who could a broke hit, den?" Dilsey said. "He jes tryin hisself, to wake Quentin up," she said, taking the pan of biscuits out of the stove.

"Reckin so," Luster said. "Dese funny folks. Glad I aint none of em."

"Aint none of who?" Dilsey said. "Lemme tell you somethin, nigger boy, you got jes es much Compson devilment in you es any of em. Is you right sho you never broke dat window?"

"Whut I want to break hit fur?"

"Whut you do any of yo devilment fur?" Dilsey said. "Watch him now, so he cant burn his hand again twell I git de table set."

She went to the diningroom, where they heard her moving about, then she returned and set a plate at the kitchen table and set food

---

11) 제이슨이 자기 방 창문이 깨진 것을 두고 러스터와 벤지를 비난하는 부분인데, 사실 그 창문은, 곧 전모가 드러나듯, 미스 퀸틴이 돈을 '훔치기' 위해 제이슨 방을 침입하면서 생긴 일이다.

there. Ben watched her, slobbering, making a faint, eager sound.

"All right, honey," she said. "Here yo breakfast. Bring his chair, Luster." Luster moved the chair up and Ben sat down, whimpering and slobbering. Dilsey tied a cloth about his neck and wiped his mouth with the end of it. "And see kin you keep fum messin up his clothes one time," she said, handing Luster a spoon.

Ben ceased whimpering. He watched the spoon as it rose to his mouth. It was as if even eagerness were musclebound in him too, and hunger itself inarticulate, not knowing it is hunger. Luster fed him with skill and detachment. Now and then his attention would return long enough to enable him to feint the spoon and cause Ben to close his mouth upon the empty air, but it was apparent that Luster's mind was elsewhere. His other hand lay on the back of the chair and upon that dead surface it moved tentatively, delicately, as if he were picking an inaudible tune out of the dead void, and once he even forgot to tease Ben with the spoon while his fingers teased out of the slain wood a soundless and involved arpeggio until Ben recalled him by whimpering again.

In the diningroom Dilsey moved back and forth. Presently she rang a small clear bell, then in the kitchen Luster heard Mrs Compson and Jason descending, and Jason's voice, and he rolled his eyes whitely with listening.

"Sure, I know they didn't break it," Jason said. "Sure, I know that. Maybe the change of weather broke it."

"I dont see how it could have," Mrs Compson said. "Your room stays locked all day long, just as you leave it when you go to town. None of us ever go in there except Sunday, to clean it. I dont want you to think that I would go where I'm not wanted, or that I would permit anyone else to."

"I never said you broke it, did I?" Jason said.

"I dont want to go in your room," Mrs Compson said. "I respect anybody's private affairs. I wouldn't put my foot over the threshold, even if I had a key."

"Yes," Jason said. "I know your keys wont fit. That's why I had the lock changed. What I want to know is, how that window got broken."

"Luster say he didn't do hit," Dilsey said.

"I knew that without asking him," Jason said. "Where's Quentin?" he said.

"Where she is ev'y Sunday mawnin," Dilsey said. "Whut got into you de last few days, anyhow?"

"Well, we're going to change all that," Jason said. "Go up and tell her breakfast is ready."

"You leave her alone now, Jason," Dilsey said. "She gits up fer breakfast ev'y week mawnin, en Miss Cahline lets her stay in bed ev' y Sunday.

You knows dat."

"I cant keep a kitchen full of niggers to wait on her pleasure, much as I'd like to," Jason said. "Go and tell her to come down to breakfast."

"Aint nobody have to wait on her," Dilsey said. "I puts her breakfast in de warmer en she——"

"Did you hear me?" Jason said.

"I hears you," Dilsey said. "All I been hearin, when you in de house. Ef hit aint Quentin er yo maw, hit's Luster en Benjy. Whut you let him go on dat way fer, Miss Cahline?"

"You'd better do as he says," Mrs Compson said. "He's head of the house now. It's his right to require us to respect his wishes. I try to do it, and if I can, you can too."

" 'Taint no sense in him bein so bad tempered he got to make Quentin git up jes to suit him," Dilsey said. "Maybe you think she broke dat window."

"She would, if she happened to think of it," Jason said. "You go and do what I told you."

"En I wouldn't blame her none ef she did," Dilsey said, going toward the stairs. "Wid you naggin at her all de blessed time you in de house."

"Hush, Dilsey," Mrs Compson said. "It's neither your place nor mine to tell Jason what to do. Sometimes I think he is wrong, but I try to obey his wishes for you all's sakes. If I'm strong enough to come to the table, Quentin can too."

Dilsey went out. They heard her mounting the stairs. They heard her a long while on the stairs.

"You've got a prize set of servants," Jason said. He helped his mother and himself to food. "Did you ever have one that was worth killing? You must have had some before I was big enough to remember."

"I have to humor them," Mrs Compson said. "I have to depend on them so completely. It's not as if I were strong. I wish I were. I wish I could do all the house work myself. I could at least take that much off your shoulders."

"And a fine pigsty we'd live in, too," Jason said. "Hurry up, Dilsey," he shouted.

"I know you blame me," Mrs Compson said, "for letting them off to go to church today."

"Go where?" Jason said. "Hasn't that damn show left yet?"

"To church," Mrs Compson said. "The darkies are having a special Easter service. I promised Dilsey two weeks ago that they could get off."

"Which means we'll eat cold dinner," Jason said, "or none at all."

"I know it's my fault," Mrs Compson said. "I know you blame me."

"For what?" Jason said. "You never resurrected Christ, did you?"

They heard Dilsey mount the final stair, then her slow feet overhead.

"Quentin," she said. When she called the first time Jason laid his knife and fork down and he and his mother appeared to wait across the table from one another in identical attitudes; the one cold and shrewd, with close-thatched brown hair curled into two stubborn hooks, one on either side of his forehead like a bartender in caricature, and hazel eyes with black-ringed irises like marbles, the other cold and querulous, with perfectly white hair and eyes pouched and baffled and so dark as to appear to be all pupil or all iris.

"Quentin," Dilsey said." Get up, honey. Dey waitin breakfast on you."

"I cant understand how that window got broken," Mrs Compson said. "Are you sure it was done yesterday? It could have been like that a long time, with the warm weather. The upper sash, behind the shade like that."

"I've told you for the last time that it happened yesterday," Jason said. "Dont you reckon I know the room I live in? Do you reckon I could have lived in it a week with a hole in the window you could stick your hand···" his voice ceased, ebbed, left him staring at his mother with eyes that for an instant were quite empty of anything. It was as though his eyes were holding their breath, while his mother looked at him, het face flaccid and querulous, interminable, clairvoyant yet obtuse. As they sat so Dilsey said,

"Quentin. Dont play wid me, honey. Come on to breakfast, honey. Dey waitin fer you."

"I cant understand it," Mrs Compson said. "It's just as if somebody had tried to break into the house——" Jason sprang up. His chair crashed over backward. "What——" Mrs Compson said, staring at him as he ran past her and went jumping up the stairs, where he met Dilsey. His face was now in shadow, and Dilsey said,

"She sullin.[12] Yo maw aint unlocked——" But Jason ran on past her and along the corridor to a door. He didn't call. He grasped the knob and tried it, then he stood with the knob in his hand and his head bent a little, as if he were listening to something much further away than the dimensioned room beyond the door, and which he

---

12) sullen or sulking.

already heard. His attitude was that of one who goes through the motions of listening in order to deceive himself as to what he already hears. Behind him Mrs Compson mounted the stairs, calling his name. Then she saw Dilsey and she quit calling him and began to call Dilsey instead.

"I told you she aint unlocked dat do yit," Dilsey said.

When she spoke he turned and ran toward her, but his voice was quite, matter of fact." She carry the key with her?" he said. "Has she got it now, I mean, or will she have—"

"Dilsey," Mrs Compson said on the stairs.

"Is which?" Dilsey said. "Whn't you let—"

"The key," Jason said. "To that room. Does she carry it with her all the time. Mother." Then he saw Mrs Compson and he went down the stairs and met her. "Give me the key," he said. He fell to pawing at the pockets of the rusty black dressing sacque[13)] she wore. She resisted.

"Jason," she said. "Jason! Are you and Dilsey trying to put me to bed again?" she said, trying to fend him off. "Cant you even let me have Sunday in peace?"

"The key," Jason said, pawing at her. "Give it here." He looked back at the door, as if he expected it to fly open before he could get back to it with the key he did not yet have.

"You, Dilsey!" Mrs Compson said, clutching her sacque about her.

"Give me the key, you old fool!" Jason cried suddenly. From her pocket he tugged a huge bunch of rusted keys on an iron ring like a mediaeval jailer's and ran back up the hall with the two women behind him.

"You, Jason!" Mrs Compson said. "He will never find the right one," she said. "You know I never let anyone take my keys, Dilsey," she said. She began to wail.

---

13) 느슨하게 입는 가운.

"Hush." Dilsey said. "He aint gwine do nothin to her. I aint gwine let him."

"But on Sunday morning, in my own house," Mrs Compson said. "When I've tried so hard to raise them christians. Let me find the right key, Jason," she said. She put her hand on his arm. Then she began to struggle with him, but he flung her aside with a motion of his elbow and looked around at her for a moment, his eyes cold and harried, then he turned to the door again and the unwieldy keys.

"Hush," Dilsey said. "You, Jason!"

"Something terrible has happened," Mrs Compson said, wailing again. "I know it has. You, Jason," she said, grasping at him again. "He wont even let me find the key to a room in my own house!"

"Now, now," Dilsey said. "Whut kin happen? I right here. I aint gwine let him hurt her. Quentin," she said, raising her voice, "dont you be skeered, honey, I'se right here."

The door opened, swung inward. He stood in it for a moment, hiding the room, then he stepped aside. "Go in, "he said in a thick, light voice. They went in. It was not a girl's room. It was not anybody's room, and the faint scent of cheap cosmetics and the few feminine objects and the other evidences of crude and hopeless efforts to feminise it but added to its anonymity, giving it that dead and stereotyped transience of rooms in assignation houses. The bed had not been disturbed. On the floor lay a soiled undergarment of cheap silk a little too pink, from a half open bureau drawer dangled a single stocking. The window was open. A pear tree grew there, close against the house. It was in bloom and the branches scraped and rasped against the house and the myriad air, driving in the window, brought into the room the forlorn scent of the blossoms.

"Dar now," Dilsey said. "Didn't I told you she all right?"

"All right?" Mrs Compson said. Dilsey followed her into the room and touched her.

"You come on and lay down, now," she said. "I find her in ten minutes."

Mrs Compson shook her off. "Find the note," she said. "Quentin left a note when he did it." 14)

"All right," Dilsey said. "I'll find hit. You come on to yo room, now."

"I knew the minute they named her Quentin this would happen,"

Mrs Compson said. She went to the bureau and began to turn over the scattered object there—scent, bottles, a box of powder, a chewed pencil, a pair of scissors with one broken blade lying upon a darned scarf dusted with powder and stained with rouge. "Find the note," she said.

"I is," Dilsey said. "You come on, now. Me and Jason'll find hit. You come on to yo room."

"Jason," Mrs Compson said. "Where is he?" She went to the door. Dilsey followed her on down the hall, to another door. It was closed. "Jason," she called through the door. There was no answer. She tried the knob, then she called him again. But there was still no answer, for he was hurling things backward out of the closet, garments, shoes, a suitcase. Then he emerged carrying a sawn section of tongue-and-groove planking and laid it down and entered the closet again and emerged with a metal box. He set it on the bed and stood looking at the broken lock while he dug a keyring from his pocket and selected a key, and for a time longer he stood with the selected key in his hand, looking at the broken lock. Then he put the keys back in his pocket and carefully tilted the contents of the box out upon the bed. Still carefully he sorted the papers, taking them up one at a time and shaking them. Then he upended the box and shook it too and slowly replaced the papers and stood again, looking at the

---

14) 캄슨 부인은 손녀 미스 퀸턴이 없어진 걸 알자 자살하였을 것으로 생각하며, (아들 퀸턴의 경우를 떠 올리며) 그녀가 떠나면서 혹 자살편지라도 남겼는지 찾으라고 말하는 부분이다. 캄슨 부인의 이러한 확신은 곧이어 재확인된다("I knew the minute they named her Quentin this would happen").

broken lock, with the box in his hands and his head bent. Outside the window he heard some jaybirds swirl shrieking past and away, their cries whipping away along the wind, and an automobile passed somewhere and died away also. His mother spoke his name again beyond the door, but he didn't move. He heard Dilsey lead her away up the hall, and then a door closed. Then he replaced the box in the closet and flung the garments back into it and went down stairs to the tele-phone. While he stood there with the receiver to his ear waiting Dilsey came down the stairs. She looked at him, without stopping, and went on.

The wire opened. "This is Jason Compson," he said, his voice so harsh and thick that he had to repeat himself. "Jason Compson," he said, controlling his voice. "Have a car ready, with a deputy, if you cant go, in ten minutes. I'll be there——What?——Robbery. My house. I know who it——Robbery, I say. Have a car read——What? Aren't you a paid law enforcement——Yes, I'll be there in five minutes. Have that car ready to leave at once. If you dont, I'll report it to the governor."

He clapped the receiver back and crossed the diningroom, where the scarce broken meal lay cold now on the table, and entered the kitchen. Dilsey was filling the hot water bottle. Ben sat, tranquil and empty. Beside him Luster looked like a fice dog, brightly watchful. He was eating something. Jason went on across the kitchen.

"Aint you going to eat no breakfast?" Dilsey said. He paid her no attention. "Go on en eat yo breakfast, Jason." He went on. The outer door banged behind him. Luster rose and went to the window and looked out.

"Whoo," he said. "Whut happenin up dar? He been beatin Miss Quentin?"

"You hush yo mouf," Dilsey said. "You git Benjy started now en I beat yo head off. You keep him quiet es you kin twell I git back, now." She screwed the cap on the bottle and went out. They heard her go up the stairs, then they heard Jason pass the house in his car.

Then there was no sound in the kitchen save the simmering murmur of the kettle and the clock.

"You know whut I bet?" Luster said. "I bet he beat her. I bet he knock her in de head en now he gone fer de doctor. Dat's whut I bet." The clock tick-tocked, solemn and profound. It might have been the dry pulse of the decaying house itself, after a while it whirred and cleared its throat and struck six times. Ben looked up at it, then he looked at the bulletlike silhouette of Luster's head in the window and he begun to bob his head again, drooling. He whimpered.

"Hush up, looney," Luster said without turning. "Look like we aint gwine git to go to no church today." But Ben sat in the chair, his big soft hands dangling between his knees, moaning faintly. Suddenly he wept, a slow bellowing sound, meaningless and sustained. "Hush," Luster said. He turned and lifted his hand. "You want me to whup you?" But Ben looked at him, bellowing slowly with each expiration. Luster came and shook him. "You hush dis minute!" he shouted. "Here," he said. He hauled Ben out of the chair and dragged the chair around facing the stove and opened the door to the firebox and shoved Ben into the chair. They looked like a tug nudging at a clumsy tanker in a narrow dock. Ben sat down again facing the rosy door. He hushed. Then they heard the clock again, and Dilsey slow on the stairs. When she entered he began to whimper again. Then he lifted his voice.

"Whut you done to him," Dilsey said. "Why cant you let him lone dis mawnin, of all times?"

"I aint doin nothin to him," Luster said. " Mr Jason skeered him, dat's whut hit is. He aint kilt Miss Quentin, is he?"

"Hush, Benjy," Dilsey said. He hushed. She went to the window and looked out. "Is it quit rainin?" she said.

"Yessum," Luster said. "Quit long time ago."

"Den y'all go out do's a while," she said. "I jes got Miss Cahline quiet now."

"Is we gwine to church?" Luster said.

"I let you know bout dat when de time come. You keep him away fum de house twell I calls you."

"Kin we go to de pastuh?" Luster said.

"All right. Only you keep him away fum de house. I done stood all I kin."

"Yessum," Luster said. "Whar Mr Jason gone, mammy?"

"Dat's some mo of yo business, aint it?" Dilsey said. She began to clear the table. "Hush, Benjy. Luster gwine take you out to play."

"Whut he done to Miss Quentin, mammy?" Luster said.

"Aint done nothin to her. You all git on outen here."

"I bet she aint here," Luster said.

Dilsey looked at him. "How you know she aint here?"

"Me and Benjy seed her clamb out de window last night. Didn't us, Benjy?"

"You did?" Dilsey said, looking at him.

"We sees her doin hit ev'y night," Luster said. "Clamb right down dat pear tree."

"Dont you lie to me, nigger boy," Dilsey said.

"I aint lyin. Ask Benjy ef I is."

"Whyn't you say somethin about it, den?"

" 'Twarn't none o my business," Luster said. "I aint gwine git mixed up in white folks' business. Come on here, Benjy, les go out do's."

They went out. Dilsey stood for a while at the table, then she went and cleared the breakfast things from the diningroom and ate her break-fast and cleaned up the kitchen. Then she removed her apron and hung it up and went to the foot of the stairs and listened for a moment. There was no sound. She donned the overcoat and hat and went across to her cabin.

The rain had stopped. The air now drove out of the southeast, broken overhead into blue patches. Upon the crest of a hill beyond the trees and roofs and spires of town sunlight lay like a pale scrap of cloth, was blotted away. Upon the air a bell came, then as if at a signal, other bells took up the sound and repeated it.

The cabin door opened and Dilsey emerged, again in the maroon cape and the purple gown, and wearing soiled white elbow-length gloves and minus her headcloth now. She came into the yard and called Luster. She waited a while, then she went to the house and around it to the cellar door, moving close to the wall, and looked into the door. Ben sat on the steps. Before him Luster squatted on the damp floor. He held a saw in his left hand, the blade sprung a little by pressure of his hand, and he was in the act of striking the blade with the worn wooden mallet with which she had been making beaten biscuit for more than thirty years. The saw gave forth a single sluggish twang that ceased with lifeless alacrity, leaving the blade in a thin clean curve between Luster's hand and the floor. Still, inscrutable, it bellied.

"Dat's de way he done hit," Luster said. "I jes aint foun de right thing to hit it wid."

"Dat's whut you doin, is it?" Dilsey said. "Bring me dat mallet," she said.

"I aint hurt hit," Luster said.

"Bring hit here," Dilsey said. "Put dat saw whar you got hit first."

He put the saw away and brought the mallet to her. Then Ben wailed again, hopeless and prolonged. It was nothing. Just sound. It might have been all time and injustice and sorrow become vocal for an instant by a conjunction of planets.

"Listen at him," Luster said. "He been gwine on dat way ev'y since you sont us outen de house. I dont know whut got in to him dis mawnin."

"Bring him here," Dilsey said.

"Come on, Benjy," Luster said. He went back down the steps and took Ben's arm. He came obediently, wailing, that slow hoarse sound that ships make, that seems to begin before the sound itself has started, seems to cease before the sound itself has stopped.

"Run and git his cap," Dilsey said. "Dont make no noise Miss

Cahline kin hear. Hurry, now. We already late."

"She gwine hear him anyhow, ef you dont stop him," Luster said.

"He stop when we git off de place," Dilsey said. "He smellin hit. Dat's whut hit is."

"Smell whut, mammy?" Luster said.

"You go git dat cap," Dilsey said. Luster went on. They stood in the cellar door, Ben one step below her. The sky was broken now into scudding patches that dragged their swift shadows up out of the shabby garden, over the broken fence and across the yard. Dilsey stroked Ben's head, slowly and steadily, smoothing the bang upon his brow. He wailed quietly, unhurriedly. "Hush," Dilsey said. "Hush, now. We be gone in a minute. Hush, now." He wailed quietly and steadily.

Luster returned, wearing a stiff new straw hat with a colored band and carrying a cloth cap. The hat seemed to isolate Luster's skull in the beholder's eye as a spotlight would, in all its individual planes and angles. So peculiarly individual was its shape that at first glance the hat appeared to be on the head of someone standing immediately behind Luster. Dilsey looked at the hat.

"Whyn't you wear yo old hat?" she said.

"Couldn't find hit," Luster said.

"I bet you couldn't. I bet you fixed hit last night so you couldn't find hit. You fixin to ruin dat un."

"Aw, mammy," Luster said. "Hit aint gwine rain."

"How you know? You go git dat old hat en put dat new un away."

"Aw, mammy."

"Den you go git de umbreller."

"Aw, mammy."

"Take yo choice," Dilsey said. "Git yo old hat, er de umbreller. I dont keer which."

Luster went to the cabin. Ben wailed quietly.

"Come on," Dilsey said. "Dey kin ketch up wid us. We gwine to hear de singin." They went around the house, toward the gate.

"Hush," Dilsey said from time to time as they went down the drive. They reached the gate. Dilsey opened it. Luster was coming down the drive behind them, carrying the umbrella. A woman was with him. "Here dey come," Dilsey said. They passed out the gate. "Now, den," she said. Ben ceased. Luster and his mother overtook them. Frony wore a dress of bright blue silk and a flowered hat. She was a thin woman, with a flat, pleasant face.

"You got six weeks' work right dar on yo back," Dilsey said. "Whut you gwine do ef hit rain?"

"Git wet, I reckon," Frony said. "I aint never stopped no rain yit."

"Mammy always talkin bout hit gwine rain," Luster said.

"Ef I dont worry bout y'all, I dont know who is," Dilsey said. "Come on, we already late."

"Rev'un Shegog gwine preach today," Frony said.

"Is?" Dilsey said. "Who him?"

"He fum Saint Looey," Frony said. "Dat big preacher."

"Huh," Dilsey said. "Whut dey needs is a man kin put de fear of God into dese here triflin young niggers."

"Rev'un Shegog kin do dat," Frony said. "So dey tells."

They went on along the street. Along its quiet length white people in bright clumps moved churchward, under the windy bells, walking now and then in the random and tentative sun. The wind was gusty, out of the southeast, chill and after the warm days.

"I wish you wouldn't keep on bringin him to church, mammy," Frony said. "Folks talkin."

"Whut folks?" Dilsey said.

"I hears em," Frony said.

"And I knows whut kind of folks," Dilsey said. "Trash white folks. Dat's who it is. Thinks he aint good enough fer white church, but nigger church aint good enough fer him."

"Dey talks, jes de same," Frony said.

"Den you send um to me," Dilsey said. "Tell um de good Lawd dont keer whether he bright er not. Dont nobody but white trash keer dat."

A street turned off at right angles, descending, and became a dirt road. On either hand the land dropped more sharply; a broad flat dotted with small cabins whose weathered roofs were on a level with the crown of the road. They were set in small grassless plots littered with broken things, bricks, planks, crockery, things of a once utilitarian value. What growth there was consisted of rank weeds and the trees were mulberries and locusts and sycamores—trees that partook also of the foul desiccation which surrounded the houses; trees whose very burgeoning seemed to be the sad and stubborn remnant of September, as if even spring had passed them by, leaving them to feed upon the rich and unmistakable smell of negroes in which they grew.[15)]

From the doors negroes spoke to them as they passed, to Dilsey usually:

"Sis' Gibson! How you dis mawnin?"

"I'm well. Is you well?"

"I'm right well, I thank you."

They emerged from the cabins and struggled up the shaling levee to the road[16)]——men in staid, hard brown or black, with gold watch chains and now and then a stick; young men in cheap violent blues or stripes and swaggering hats; women a little stiffly sibilant, and children in garments bought second hand of white people, who looked at Ben with the covertness of nocturnal animals:

"I bet you wont go up en tech him."

---

15) 가난에 찌든 흑인들의 집 주변에 있는 나무들조차도 흑인 삶의 빈곤에 한몫을 하고 있음을 말하며, 여기 "흑인들의 냄새"는 인종차별적인 어법으로, 작가는 여기서 흑인들의 인종적 차별성 내지는 그들의 타자성을 확연히 드러내고 있다.

16) "shaling" = to break off in small and crumbling pieces. "levee"는 제방을 의미하지만, 여기서는 작은 오두막들이 점점이 박혀 있는 넓고 편편한 대지를 통과하는 고지에 난 길을 그렇게 표현하고 있다.

"How come I wont?"

"I bet you wont. I bet you skeered to."

"He wont hurt folks. He des a looney."

"How come a looney wont hurt folks?"

"Dat un wont. I teched him."

"I bet you wont now."

"Case Miss Dilsey lookin."

"You wont no ways."

"He dont hurt folks. He des a looney."

And steadily the older people speaking to Dilsey, though, unless they were quite old, Disey permitted Frony to respond.

"Mammy aint feelin well dis mawnin."

"Dat's too bad. But Rev'un Shegog'll kyo[17)] dat. He'll give her de comfort en de unburdenin."

The road rose again, to a scene like a painted backdrop. Notched into a cut of red clay crowned with oaks the road appeared to stop short off, like a cut ribbon. Beside it a weathered church lifted its crazy steeple like a painted church, and the whole scene was as flat and without perspective as a painted cardboard set upon the ultimate edge of the flat earth, against the windy sunlight of space and April and a midmorning filled with bells. Toward the church they thronged with slow sabbath deliberation, the women and children went on in, the men stopped outside and talked in quiet groups until the bell ceased ringing. Then they too entered.

The church had been decorated, with sparse flowers from kitchen gardens and hedgerows, and with streamers of colored crepe paper. Above the pulpit hung a battered Christmas bell, the accordion sort that collapses. The pulpit was empty, though the choir was already in place, fanning themselves although it was not warm.

Most of the women were gathered on one side of the room. They

---

17) cure.

were talking. Then the bell struck one time and they dispersed to their seats and the congregation sat for an instant, expectant. The bell struck again one time. The choir rose and began to sing and the congregation turned its head as one as six small children—four girls with tight pigtails bound with small scraps of cloth like butterflies, and two boys with close napped heads—entered and marched up the aisle, strung together in a harness of white ribbons and flowers, and followed by two men in single file. The second man was huge, of a light coffee color, imposing in a frock coat and white tie. His head was magisterial and profound, his neck rolled above his collar in rich folds. But he was familiar to them, and so the heads were still reverted when he had passed, and it was not until the choir ceased singing that they realised that the visiting clergyman had already entered, and when they saw the man who had preceded their minister enter the pulpit still ahead of him an indescribable sound went up, a sigh, a sound of astonishment and disappointment.

The visitor was undersized, in a shabby alpaca coat. He had a wizened black face like a small, aged monkey. And all the while that the choir sang again and while the six children rose and sang in thin, frightened, tuneless whispers, they watched the insignificant looking man sitting dwarfed and countrified by the minister's imposing bulk, with something like consternation. They were still looking at him with consternation and unbelief when the minister rose and introduced him in rich, rolling tones whose very unction served to increase the visitor's insignificance.

"En dey brung dat all de way fum Saint Looey," Frony whispered.

"I've knowed de Lawd to use cuiser tools dan dat," Dilsey said. "Hush, now," she said to Ben. "Dey fixin to sing again in a minute."

When the visitor rose to speak he sounded like a white man. His voice was level and cold. It sounded too big to have come from him and they listened at first through curiosity, as they would have to a monkey talking. They began to watch him as they would a man on a tight rope. They even forgot his insignificant appearance in the virtuosity with which he ran and poised and swooped upon the cold inflectionless wire of his voice, so that at last, when with a sort of swooping glide he came to rest again beside the reading desk with one arm resting upon it at shoulder height and his monkey body as reft of all motion as a mummy or an emptied vessel, the congregation sighed as if it waked from a collective dream and moved a little in its seats. Behind the pulpit the choir fanned steadily. Dilsey whispered, "Hush, now. Dey fixin to sing in a minute."

Then a voice said, "Brethren."

The preacher had not moved. His arm lay yet across the desk, and he still held that pose while the voice died in sonorous echoes between the walls. It was as different as day and dark from his former tone, with a sad, timbrous quality like an alto horn, sinking into their hearts and speaking there again when it had ceased in fading and cumulate echoes.

"Brethren and sisteren," it said again. The preacher removed his arm and he began to walk back and forth before the desk, his hands clasped behind him, a meagre figure, hunched over upon itself like that of one long immured in striving with the implacable earth, "I got the recollection and the blood of the Lamb!" He tramped steadily back and forth beneath the twisted paper and the Christmas bell, hunched, his hands clasped behind him. He was like a worn small rock whelmed by the successive waves of his voice. With his body he seemed to feed the voice that, succubus like, had fleshed its teeth in him.[18] And the congregation seemed to watch with its own eyes while the voice consumed him, until he was nothing and they were nothing and there was not even a voice but instead their hearts were

---

18) "whelmed" = submerged or overwhelmed. 작은 체구의 쉬고그 목사가 놀라울 정도의 강력한 목소리로 그의 몸을 소모하듯 전력을 다해 설교하고 있음을 알 수 있다. 하지만 작가가 여기서 목사의 목소리를 수면 중의 남성들과 성교하는 마녀("succubus")에 비유한 것은 조금 납득하기 힘든 부분이다.

speaking to one another in chanting measures beyond the need for words, so that when he came to rest against the reading desk, his monkey face lifted and his whole attitude that of a serene, tortured crucifix that transcended its shabbiness and insignificance and made it of no moment, a long moaning expulsion of breath rose from them, and a woman's single soprano: "Yes, Jesus!"

As the scudding day passed overhead the dingy windows glowed and faded in ghostly retrograde.[19] A car passed along the road outside, laboring in the sand, died away. Dilsey sat bolt upright, her hand on Ben's knee. Two tears slid down her fallen cheeks, in and out of the myriad coruscations of immolation and abnegation and time.[20]

"Brethren," the minister said in a harsh whisper, without moving.

"Yes, Jesus!" the woman's voice said, hushed yet.

"Breddren en sistuhn!" His voice rang again, with the horns. He removed his arm and stood erect and raised his hands. "I got de ricklickshun en de blood of de Lamb!"[21] They did not mark just when his intonation, his pronunciation, became negroid, they just sat swaying a little in their seats as the voice took them into itself.

"When de long, cold——Oh, I tells you, breddren, when de long, cold. . . . I sees de light en I sees de word,[22] po sinner! Dey passed away in Egypt, de swingin chariots; de generations passed away.[23] Wus a rich man: whar he now, O breddren? Wus a po man: whar he

---

19) 바람에 날리는 구름들("scud")이 간간히 해를 막는 모습이 교회 창문 위에 햇빛(해)과 그림자(구름)가 교대로 나타났다 유령같이 사라지는 모양이다.

20) 딜시의 얼굴에 진 주름들은 단순히 시간의 흐름만을 말해주는 것이 아니라, 그녀가 가족과 캄슨 집안을 위해 보여준 희생과 스스로를 버리는 극기의 세월을 말해준다.

21) 성경(Revelation 7.14). ricklickshun = recollection.

22) 성경(John 1.1-4).

23) 유대인들의 이집트 감금상태와 흑인영가 "Swing Low, Sweet Chariot"를 언급하고 있다(Genesis 50.22-6).

now, O sistuhn?[24] Oh I tells you, ef you aint got de milk en de dew of de old salvation when de long, cold years rolls away!"

"Yes, Jesus!"

"I tells you, breddren, en I tells you, sistuhn, dey'll come a time. Po sinner sayin Let me lay down wid de Lawd, lemme lay down my load. Den whut Jesus gwine say, O breddren? O sistuhn? Is you got de ricklickshun en de Blood of de Lamb? Case I aint gwine load down heaven!"

He fumbled in his coat and took out a handkerchief and mopped his face. A low concerted sound rose from the congregation: "Mmmmmmmmmmmmm!" The woman's voice said, "Yes, Jesus! Jesus!"

"Breddren! Look at dem little chillen settin dar. Jesus wus like dat once. He mammy suffered de glory en de pangs. Sometime maybe she helt him at de nightfall, whilst de angels singin him to sleep; maybe she look out de do en see de Roman police passin." He tramped back and forth, mopping his face. "Listen, breddren! I sees de day. Ma'y settin in de do wid Jesus on her lap, de little Jesus. Like dem chillen dar, de little Jesus. I hears de angels singin de peaceful songs en de glory; I sees de closin eyes; sees Mary jump up, sees de sojer face: We gwine to kill! We gwine to kill! We gwine to kill yo little Jesus! I hears de weepin en de lamentation of de po mammy widout de salvation en de word of God!"[25]

"Mmmmmmmmmmmmmmmm! Jesus! Little Jesus!" and another

---

24) Dives와 Lazarus의 우화(Luke 16.19-31) 언급: 이 세상에서 가난한 Dives는 잘사는 Lazarus에게 빵 한 조각을 구걸하지만, 이승에 가서는 지옥에 떨어진 Lazarus가 손을 물에 적시고 물 한 모금을 마시기 위해 천당에 있는 Dives에게 구걸하는 신세로 변한다는 우화.

25) 그리스도의 부모는 2세 이하의 아이들을 다 죽이라는 헤롯(Herod)의 명령으로부터 그를 구하기 위해 도망하는 부분과 헤롯의 명령에 의해 아이들을 잃은 어머니들의 비탄과 애도의 눈물을 언급한다(Matthews 2.16-8).

voice, rising:

"I sees, O Jesus! Oh I sees!" and still another, without words, like bubbles rising in water.

"I sees hit, breddren! I sees hit! Sees de blastin, blindin sight! I sees Calvary, wid de sacred trees, sees de thief en de murderer[26] en de least of dese; I hears de boastin en de braggin: Ef you be Jesus, lif up yo tree en walk![27] I hears de wailin of women en de evenin lamentations; I hears de weepin en de cryin en de turnt-away face of God: dey done kilt Jesus; dey done kilt my Son!"

"Mmmmmmmmmmmmm. Jesus! I sees, O Jesus!"

"O blind sinner! Breddren, I tells you; sistuhn, I says to you, when de Lawd did turn His mighty face, say, Aint gwine overload heaven! I can see de widowed[28] God shet His do; I sees de whelmin flood roll between; I sees de darkness en de death everlastin upon de generations. Den, lo! Breddren! Yes, breddren! Whut I see? Whut I see, O sinner? I sees de resurrection en de light; sees de meek Jesus sáyin Dey kilt me dat ye shall live again; I died dat dem whut sees en believes shall never die.[29] Breddren, O breddren! I sees de doom crack en de golden horns shoutin down de glory,[30] en de arisen dead whut got de blood en de ricklickshun of de Lamb!"

In the midst of the voices and the hands Ben sat, rapt in his sweet blue gaze. Dilsey sat bolt upright beside, crying rigidly and quietly in

---

26) 여기 도둑과 살인자는 그리스도와 함께 십자가에 못 박혀 죽은 자들이며, de least of dese는 그리스도이다.

27) Matthew(27.39-44)에서 그리스도의 죽음을 목격하고 있는 구경꾼들이 그리스도를 야유하며, "네가 진정 하느님의 아들이라면 십자가에서 내려와 네 스스로를 구해보라"고 소리친다.

28) "widowed"는 abandoned(버림받은)의 의미로 보는 게 바람직하다.

29) 성경(John 11.25-6).

30) Revelation(8.2)에서 신은 시간의 종말을 알리기 위해 7명의 천사들에게 7개의 트럼펫을 준다.

the annealment and the blood of the remembered Lamb.

As they walked through the bright noon, up the sandy road with the dispersing congregation talking easily again group to group, she continued to weep, unmindful of the talk.

"He sho a preacher, mon! He didn't look like much at first, but hush!"

"He seed de power en de glory." [31)]

"Yes, suh. He seed hit. Face to face he seed hit."

Dilsey made no sound, her face did not quiver as the tears took their sunken and devious courses,[32)] walking with her head up, making no effort to dry them away even.

"Whyn't you quit dat, mammy?" Frony said. "Wid all dese people lookin. We be passin white folks soon."

"I've seed de first en de last," [33)] Dilsey said. "Never you mind me."

"First en last whut?" Frony said.

"Never you mind," Dilsey said. "I seed de beginnin, en now I sees de endin."

Before they reached the street though she stopped and lifted her skirt and dried her eyes on the hem of her topmost underskirt. Then they went on. Ben shambled along beside Dilsey, watching Luster who anticked along ahead, the umbrella in his hand and his new

---

31) Matthew(6:13)에 나오는 그리스도의 기도문(the Lord's Prayer) 끝 부분: "For thine is the kingdom, and the power, and the glory, for ever."

32) as the tears took their sunken and devious courses 설교를 들은 딜시가 눈물을 흘리고 있다. "devious"라는 말이 부정적인 의미(도리에서 벗어난, 마음이 비뚤어진)를 함축하고 있지만, 여기서는 흐르는 눈물이 딜시의 야위고 주름진 얼굴에서 똑바로 흘러내리지 않고 있음을 말한다.

33) Revelation(22.13): "I am Alpha and Omega, the beginning and the end, the first and the last." 딜시가 반복하고 있는 "처음과 끝을 보았다" 이 말은 성경보다는 캄슨 집안사를 염두에 두고 한 말로 볼 수 있다.

straw hat slanted viciously in the sunlight, like a big foolish dog watching a small clever one. They reached the gate and entered. Immediately Ben began to whimper again, and for a while all of them looked up the drive at the square, paintless house with its rotting portico.

"Whut's gwine on up dar today?" Frony said. "Somethin is."

"Nothin," Dilsey said. "You tend to yo business en let de whitefolks tend to deir'n."

"Somethin is," Frony said. "I heard him first thing dis mawnin. 'Taint none of my business, dough."

"En I knows whut, too," Luster said.

"You knows mo den you got any use fer," Dilsey said. "Aint you jes heard Frony say hit aint none of yo business? You take Benjy on to de back and keep him quiet swell I put dinner on."

"I knows whar Miss Quentin is," Luster said.

"Den jes keep hit," Dilsey said. "Soon es Quentin need any of yo egvice,[34)] I'll let you know. Y'all g'awn en play in de back, now."

"You know whut gwine happen soon es dey start playin dat ball over yonder," Luster said.

"Dey wont start fer a while yit. By dat time T. P. be here to take him ridin. Here, you gimme dat new hat."

Luster gave her the hat and he and Ben went on across the back yard. Ben was still whimpering, though not loud. Dilsey and Frony went to the cabin. After a while Dilsey emerged, again in the faded calico dress, and went to the kitchen. The fire had died down. There was no sound in the house. She put on the apron and went up stairs. There was no sound anywhere. Quentin's room was as they had left it. She entered and picked up the undergarment and put the stocking back in the drawer and closed it. Mrs Compson's door was closed. Dilsey stood beside it for a moment, listening. Then she opened it

---

34) advice.

and entered, entered a pervading reek of camphor. The shades were drawn, the room in halflight, and the bed, so that at first she thought Mrs Compson was asleep and was about to close the door when the other spoke.

"Well?" she said. "What is it?"

"Hit's me," Dilsey said. "You want anything?"

Mrs Compson didn't answer. After a while, without moving her head at all, she said: "Where's Jason?"

"He aint come back yit," Dilsey said. "Whut you want?"

Mrs Compson said nothing. Like so many cold, weak people, when faced at last by the incontrovertible disaster she exhumed from somewhere a sort of fortitude, strength. In her case it was an unshakable conviction regarding the yet unplumbed event.[35] "Well," she said presently. "Did you find it?"

"Find whut? Whut you talkin about?"

"The note. At least she would have enough consideration to leave a note. Even Quentin did that."

"Whut you talkin about?" Dilsey said. "Dont you know she all right? I bet she be walkin right in dis do befo dark."

"Fiddlesticks," Mrs Compson said. "It's in the blood. Like uncle, like niece. Or mother. I dont know which would be worse. I dont seem to care."

"Whut you keep on talkin that way fur?" Dilsey said. "Whut she want to do anything like that fur?"

"I dont know. What reason did Quentin have? Under God's heaven what reason did he have? It cant be simply to flout and hurt me. Whoever God is, He would not permit that. I'm a lady. You might not believe that from my offspring, but I am."

"You des wait en see," Dilsey said. "She be here by night, right dar in her bed." Mrs Compson said nothing. The camphor soaked cloth

---

35) 캄슨 부인이 심중으로 확신하고 있는 손녀(미스 퀸턴)의 자살.

lay upon her brow. The black robe lay across the foot of the bed. Dilsey stood with her hand on the door knob.

"Well," Mrs Compson said. "What do you want? Are you going to fix some dinner for Jason and Benjamin, or not?"

"Jason aint come yit," Dilsey said. "I gwine fix somethin. You sho you dont want nothin? Yo bottle still hot enough?"

"You might hand me my bible."

"I give hit to you dis mawnin, befo I left."

"You laid it on the edge of the bed. How long did you expect it to stay there?" Dilsey crossed to the bed and groped among the shadows beneath the edge of it and found the bible, face down. She smoothed the bent pages and laid the book on the bed again. Mrs Compson didn't open her eyes. Her hair and the pillow were the same color, beneath the wimple of the medicated cloth she looked like an old nun praying. "Dont put it there again," she said, without opening her eyes. "That's where you put it before. Do you want me to have to get out of bed to pick it up?" Dilsey reached the book across her and laid it on the broad side of the bed. "You cant see to read, noways," she said. "You want me to raise de shade a little?" "No. Let them alone. Go on and fix Jason something to eat."

Dilsey went out. She closed the door and returned to the kitchen. The stove was almost cold. While she stood there the clock above the cupboard struck ten times. "One oclock," she said aloud. "Jason aint comin home. Ise seed de first en de last," she said, looking at the cold stove. "I seed de first en de last." She set out some cold food on a table. As she moved back and forth she sang, a hymn. She sang the first two lines over and over to the complete tune. She arranged the meal and went to the door and called Luster, and after a time Luster and Ben entered. Ben was still moaning a little, as to himself.

"He aint never quit," Luster said.

"Y'all come on en eat," Dilsey said. "Jason aint comin to dinner." They sat down at the table. Ben could manage solid food pretty well for himself, though even now, with cold food before him, Dilsey tied a cloth about his neck. He and Luster ate. Dilsey moved about the kitchen, singing the two lines of the hymn which she remembered. "Y'all kin g'awn en eat," she said. "Jason aint comin home."

He was twenty miles away at that time. When he left the house he drove rapidly to town, overreaching the slow sabbath groups and the peremptory bells along the broken air. He crossed the empty square and turned into a narrow street that was abruptly quieter even yet, and stopped before a frame house and went up the flower bordered walk to the porch.

Beyond the screen door people were talking. As he lifted his hand to knock he heard steps, so he withheld his hand until a big man in black broadcloth trousers and a stiff bosomed white shirt without collar opened the door. He had vigorous untidy iron-gray hair and his gray eyes were round and shiny like a little boy's. He took Jason's hand and drew him into the house, still shaking it.

"Come right in," he said. "Come right in."

"You ready to go now?" Jason said.

"Walk right in," the other said, propelling him by the elbow into a room where a man and a woman sat. "You know Myrtle's husband, dont you? Jason Compson, Vernon."

"Yes," Jason said. He did not even look at the man, and as the sheriff drew a chair across the room the man said,

"We'll go out so you can talk. Come on, Myrtle."

"No, no," the sheriff said. "You folks keep your seat. I reckon it aint that serious, Jason? Have a seat."

"I'll tell you as we go along," Jason said. "Get your hat and coat."

"We'll go out," the man said, rising.

"Keep your seat," the sheriff said. "Me and Jason will go out on the porch."

"You get your hat and coat," Jason said. "They've already got a twelve hour start." The sheriff led the way back to the porch. A man and a woman passing spoke to him. He responded with a hearty florid gesture. Bells were still ringing, from the direction of the section known as Nigger Hollow. "Get your hat, Sheriff," Jason said. The sheriff drew up two chairs.

"Have a seat and tell me what the trouble is."

"I told you over the phone," Jason said, standing. "I did that to save time. Am I going to have to go to law to compel you to do your sworn duty?"

"You sit down and tell me about it," the sheriff said. "I'll take care of you all right."

"Care, hell," Jason said. "Is this what you call taking care of me?"

"You're the one that's holding us up," the sheriff said. "You sit down and tell me about it."

Jason told him, his sense of injury and impotence feeding upon its own sound, so that after a time he forgot his haste in the violent cumulation of his self justification and his outrage. The sheriff watched him steadily with his cold shiny eyes.

"But you dont know they done it," he said. "You just think so."

"Dont know?" Jason said. "When I spent two damn days chasing her through alleys, trying to keep her away from him, after I told her what I'd do to her if I ever caught her with him, and you say I dont know that that little b——"

"Now, then," the sheriff said. "That'll do. That's enough of that." He looked out across the street, his hands in his pockets.

"And when I come to you, a commissioned officer of the law," Jason said.

"That show's in Mottson this week," the sheriff said.

"Yes," Jason said. "And if I could find a law officer that gave a solitary damn about protecting the people that elected him to office, I'd be there too by now." He repeated his story, harshly recapitulant, seeming to get an actual pleasure out of his outrage and impotence. The sheriff did not appear to be listening at all.

"Jason," he said. "What were you doing with three thousand dollars hid in the house?"

"What?" Jason said. "That's my business where I keep my money.

Your business is to help me get it back."

"Did your mother know you had that much on the place?"

"Look here," Jason said. "My house has been robbed. I know who did it and I know where they are. I come to you as the commissioned officer of the law, and I ask you once more, are you going to make any effort to recover my property, or not?"

"What do you aim to do with that girl, if you catch them?"

"Nothing," Jason said. "Not anything. I wouldn't lay my hand on her. The bitch that cost me a job, the one chance I ever had to get ahead, that killed my father and is shortening my mother's life every day and made my name a laughing stock in the town. I wont do anything to her," he said. "Not anything."

"You drove that girl into running off, Jason," the sheriff said.

"How I conduct my family is no business of yours," Jason said. "Are you going to help me or not?"

"You drove her away from home," the sheriff said. "And I have some suspicions about who that money belongs to that I dont reckon I'll ever know for certain."[36)]

Jason stood, slowly wringing the brim of his hat in his hands. He said quietly: "You're not going to make any effort to catch them for me?"

"That's not any of my business, Jason. If you had any actual proof, I'd have to act. But without that I dont figger it's any of my business."

"That's your answer, is it?" Jason said. "Think well, now."

"That's it, Jason."

"All right," Jason said. He put his hat on. "You'll regret this. I wont be helpless. This is not Russia, where just because he wears a little metal badge, a man is immune to law." He went down the steps and

---

36) 경찰의 이러한 발언은 마을사람들 또한 캄슨 집안에서 일어나고 있는 일들에 대해 알고 있음을 암시하는 부분이다.

got in his car and started the engine. The sheriff watched him drive away, turn, and rush past the house toward town.

The bells were ringing again, high in the scudding sunlight in bright disorderly tatters of sound. He stopped at a filling station and had his tires examined and the tank filled.

"Gwine on a trip, is you?" the negro asked him. He didn't answer. "Look like hit gwine fair off, after all," the negro said.

"Fair off, hell." Jason said. "It'll be raining like hell by twelve oclock." He looked at the sky, thinking about rain, about the slick clay roads, himself stalled somewhere miles from town. He thought about it with a sort of triumph, of the fact that he was going to miss dinner, that by starting now and so serving his compulsion of haste, he would be at the greatest possible distance from both towns when noon came. It seemed to him that in this circumstance was giving him a break, so he said to the negro:

"What the hell are you doing? Has somebody paid you to keep this car standing here as long as you can?"

"Dis here ti' aint got no air a-tall in hit," the negro said.

"Then get the hell away from there and let me have that tube," Jason said.

"Hit up now," the negro said, rising. "You kin ride now."

Jason got in and started the engine and drove off. He went into second gear, the engine spluttering and gasping, and he raced the engine, jamming the throttle down and snapping the choker in and out savagely. "It's going to rain," he said. "Get me half way there, and rain like hell." And he drove on out of the bells and out of town, thinking of himself slogging through the mud, hunting a team. "And every damn one of them will be at church." He thought of how he'd find a church at last and take a team and of the owner coming out, shoutin' at him and of himself striking the man down. "I'm Jason Compson. See if you can stop me. See if you can elect a man to office that can stop me," he said, thinking of himself entering the courthouse with a file of soldiers and dragging the sheriff out.

"Thinks he can sit with his hands folded and see me lose my job. I'll show him about jobs." Of his niece he did not think at all, nor of the arbitrary valuation of the money. Neither of them had had entity or individuality for him for ten years: together they merely symbolised the job in the bank of which he had been deprived before he ever got it.

The air brightened, the running shadow patches were now the obverse, and it seemed to him that the fact that the day was clearing was another cunning stroke on the part of the foe, the fresh battle toward which he was carrying ancient wounds. From time to time he passed churches, unpainted frame buildings with sheet iron steeples, surrounded by tethered teams and shabby motorcars, and it seemed to him that each of them was a picketpost where the rear guards of Circumstance peeped fleetingly back at him. "And damn You, too," he said. "See if You can stop me," thinking of himself, his file of soldiers with the manacled sheriff in the rear, dragging Omnipotence down from his throne, if necessary; of the embattled legions of both hell and heaven through which he tore his way and put his hands at last on his fleeing niece.

The wind was out of the southeast. It blew steadily upon his cheek. It seemed that he could feel the prolonged blow of it sinking through his skull, and suddenly with an old premonition he clapped the brakes on and stopped and sat perfectly still. Then he lifted his hand to his neck and began to curse, and sat there, cursing in a harsh whisper. When it was necessary for him to drive for any length of time he fortified himself with a handkerchief soaked in camphor, which he would tie about his throat when clear of town, thus inhaling the fumes, and he got out and lifted the seat cushion on the chance that there might be a forgotten one there. He looked beneath both seats and stood again for a while, cursing, seeing himself mocked by his own triumphing. He closed his eyes, leaning on the door. He could return and get the forgotten camphor, or he could go on. In either case, his head would be splitting, but at home he could be sure of finding camphor on Sunday, while if he went on he could not be sure. But if he went back, he would be an hour and a half later in reaching Mottson. "Maybe I can drive slow," he said. "Maybe I can drive slow, thinking of something else . . . ."

He got in and started. "I'll think of something else," he said, so he thought about Lorraine. He imagined himself in bed with her, only he was just lying beside her, pleading with her to help him,[37)] then he thought of the money again, and that he had been outwitted by a woman, a girl. If he could just believe it was the man who had robbed him. But to have been robbed of that which was to have compensated him for the lost job, which he had acquired through so much effort and risk, by the very symbol of the lost job itself, and worst of all, by a bitch of a girl. He drove on, shielding his face from the steady wind with the corner of his coat.

He could see the opposed forces of his destiny and his will drawing swiftly together now, toward a junction that would be irrevocable; he became cunning. I cant make a blunder, he told himself. There would be just one right thing, without alternatives: he must do that. He believed that both of them would know him on sight, while he'd have to trust to seeing her first, unless the man still wore the red tie. And the fact that he must depend on that red tie seemed to be the sum of the impending disaster; he could almost smell it, feel it above the throbbing of his head.

He crested the final hill. Smoke lay in the valley, and roofs, a spire or two above trees. He drove down the hill and into the town, slowing, telling himself again of the need for caution, to find where the tent was located first. He could not see very well now, and he knew that it was the disaster which kept telling him to go directly and get something for his head. At a filling station they told him that the tent was not up yet, but that the show cars were on a siding at the

---

37) 아마 제이슨이 로레인과 성관계를 갖는데 문제가 있음을 암시한다.

station. He drove there.

Two gaudily painted pullman cars stood on the track. He reconnoitred them before he got out. He was trying to breathe shallowly, so that the blood would not beat so in his skull. He got out and went along the station wall, watching the cars. A few garments hung out of the windows, limp and crinkled, as though they had been recently laundered. On the earth beside the steps of one sat three canvas chairs. But he saw no sign of life at all until a man in a dirty apron came to the door and emptied a pan of dishwater with a broad gesture, the sunlight glinting on the metal belly of the pan, then entered the car again.

Now I'll have to take him by surprise, before he can warn them, he thought. It never occurred to him that they might not be there, in the car. That they should not be there, that the whole result should not hinge on whether he saw them first or they saw him first, would be opposed to all nature and contrary to the whole rhythm of events. And more than that: he must see them first, get the money back, then what they did would be of no importance to him, while otherwise the whole world would know that he, Jason Compson, had been robbed by Quentin, his niece, a bitch.

He reconnoitred again. Then he went to the car and mounted the steps, swiftly and quietly, and paused at the door. The galley was dark, rank with stale food. The man was a white blur, singing in a cracked, shaky tenor. An old man, he thought, and not as big as I am. He entered the car as the man looked up.

"Hey?" the man said, stopping his song.

"Where are they?" Jason said. "Quick, now. In the sleeping car?"

"Where's who?" the man said.

"Dont lie to me," Jason said. He blundered on in the cluttered obscurity.

"What's that?" the other said. "Who you calling a liar?" and when Jason grasped his shoulder he exclaimed, "Look out, fellow!"

"Dont lie," Jason said. "Where are they?"

"Why, you bastard," the man said. His arm was frail and thin in Jason's grasp. He tried to wrench free, then he turned and fell to scrabbling on the littered table behind him.

"Come on," Jason said. "Where are they?"

"I'll tell you where they are," the man shrieked. "Lemme find my butcher knife."

"Here," Jason said, trying to hold the other. "I'm just asking you a question."

"You bastard," the other shrieked, scrabbling at the table. Jason tried to grasp him in both arms, trying to prison the puny fury of him. The man's body felt so old, so frail, yet so fatally singlepurposed that for the first time Jason saw clear and unshadowed the disaster toward which he rushed.

"Quit it!" he said. "Here. Here! I'll get out. Give me time, and I'll get out."

"Call me a liar," the other wailed. "Lemme go. Lemme go just one minute. I'll show you."

Jason glared wildly about, holding the other. Outside it was now bright and sunny, swift and bright and empty, and he thought of the people soon to be going quietly home to Sunday dinner, decorously festive, and of himself trying to hold the fatal, furious little old man whom he dared not release long enough to turn his back and run.

"Will you quit long enough for me to get out?" he said. "Will you?" But the other still struggled, and Jason freed one hand and struck him on the head. A clumsy, hurried blow, and not hard, but the other slumped immediately and slid clattering among pans and buckets to the floor. Jason stood above him, panting, listening. Then he turned and ran from the car. At the door he restrained himself and descended more slowly and stood there again. His breath made a hah hah hah sound and he stood there trying to repress it, darting his gaze this way and that, when at a scuffling sound behind him he turned in time to see the little old man leaping awkwardly and furiously from the vestibule, a rusty hatchet high in his hand.

He grasped at the hatchet, feeling no shock but knowing that he was falling, thinking So this is how it'll end, and he believed that he was about to die and when something crashed against the back of his head he thought How did he hit me there? Only maybe he hit me a long time ago, he thought, And I just now felt it, and he thought Hurry. Hurry. Get it over with, and then a furious desire not to die seized him and he struggled, hearing the old man wailing and cursing in his cracked voice.

He still struggled when they hauled him to his feet, but they held him and he ceased.

"Am I bleeding much?" he said. "The back of my head. Am I bleeding?" He was still saying that while he felt himself being propelled rapidly away, heard the old man's thin furious voice dying away behind him. "Look at my head," he said. "Wait, I'—"

"Wait, hell," the man who held him said. "That damn little wasp'll kill you. Keep going. You aint hurt."

"He hit me," Jason said. "Am I bleeding?"

"Keep going," the other said. He led Jason on around the corner of the station, to the empty platform where an express truck stood, where grass grew rigidly in a plot bordered with rigid flowers and a sign in electric lights: Keep your  on Mottson, the gap filled by a human eye with an electric pupil. The man released him.

"Now," he said. "You get on out of here and stay out. What were you trying to do? commit suicide?"

"I was looking for two people," Jason said. "I just asked him where they were."

"Who you looking for?"

"It's a girl," Jason said. "And a man. He had on a red tie in Jefferson yesterday. With this show. They robbed me."

"Oh," the man said. "You're the one, are you. Well, they aint here."

"I reckon so," Jason said. He leaned against the wall and put his hand to the back of his head and looked at his palm. "I thought I was bleeding," he said. "I thought he hit me with that hatchet."

"You hit your head on the rail," the man said. "You better go on. They aint here."

"Yes. He said they were not here. I thought he was lying."

"Do you think I'm lying?" the man said.

"No," Jason said. "I know they're not here."

"I told him to get the hell out of there, both of them," the man said. "I wont have nothing like that in my show. I run a respectable show, with a respectable troupe."

"Yes," Jason said. "You dont know where they went?"

"No. And I dont want to know. No member of my show can pull a stunt like that. You her . . . brother?"

"No," Jason said. "It dont matter. I just wanted to see them. You sure he didn't hit me? No blood, I mean."

"There would have been blood if I hadn't got there when I did. You stay away from here, now. That little bastard'll kill you. That your car yonder?"

"Yes."

"Well, you get in it and go back to Jefferson. If you find them, it wont be in my show. I run a respectable show. You say they robbed you?"

"No," Jason said. "It dont make any difference." He went to the car and got in. What is it I must do? he thought. Then he remembered. He started the engine and drove slowly up the street until he found a drugstore. The door was locked. He stood for a while with his hand on the knob and his head bent a little. Then he turned away and when a man came along after a while he asked if there was a drugstore open anywhere, but there was not. Then he asked when the northbound train ran, and the man told him at two thirty. He crossed the pavement and got in the car again and sat there. After a while two negro lads passed. He called to them.

"Can either of you boys drive a car?"

"Yes, suh."

"What'll you charge to drive me to Jefferson right away?"

They looked at one another, murmuring.

"I'll pay a dollar," Jason said.

They murmured again. "Couldn't go fer dat," one said.

"What will you go for?"

"Kin you go?" one said.

"I cant git off," the other said. "Whyn't you drive him up dar? You aint got nothin to do."

"Yes I is."

"Whut you got to do?"

They murmured again, laughing.

"I'll give you two dollars," Jason said. "Either of you." "I cant git away neither," the first said.

"All right," Jason said. "Go on."

He sat there for some time. He heard a clock strike the half hour, then people began to pass, in Sunday and easter clothes. Some looked at him as they passed, at the man sitting quietly behind the wheel of a small car, with his invisible life ravelled out about him like a wornout sock, and went on. After a while a negro in overalls came up.

"Is you de one wants to go to Jefferson?" he said.

"Yes," Jason said. "What'll you charge me?"

"Fo dollars."

"Give you two."

"Cant go fer no less'n fo." The man in the car sat quietly. He wasn't even looking at him. The negro said, "You want me er not?"

"All right," Jason said. "Get in."

He moved over and the negro took the wheel. Jason closed his eyes. I can get something for it at Jefferson, he told himself, easing himself to the jolting, I can get something there. They drove on, along the streets where people were turning peacefully into houses and Sunday dinners, and on out of town. He thought that. He wasn't thinking of home, where Ben and Luster were eating cold dinner at the kitchen table. Something—the absence of disaster, threat, in any constant evil—permitted him to forget Jefferson as any place which he had ever seen before, where his life must resume itself.

When Ben and Luster were done Dilsey sent them outdoors. "And see kin you let him alone twell fo oclock. T. P. be here den."

"Yessum," Luster said. They went out. Dilsey ate her dinner and cleared up the kitchen. Then she went to the foot of the stairs and listened, but there was no sound. She returned through the kitchen and out the outer door and stopped on the steps. Ben and Luster were not in sight, but while she stood there she heard another sluggish twang from the direction of the cellar door and she went to the door and looked down upon a repetition of the morning's scene.

"He done hit jes dat way," Luster said. He contemplated the motionless saw with a kind of hopeful dejection. "I aint got de right thing to hit it wid yit," he said.

"En you aint gwine find hit down here, neither," Dilsey said. "You take him on out in de sun. You bofe get pneumonia down here on dis wet flo."

She waited and watched them cross the yard toward a clump of cedar trees near the fence. Then she went on to her cabin.

"Now, dont you git started," Luster said. "I had enough trouble wid you today." There was a hammock made of barrel staves slatted into woven wires. Luster lay down in the swing, but Ben went on vaguely and purposelessly. He began to whimper again. "Hush, now," Luster said. "I fixin to whup you." He lay back in the swing. Ben had stopped moving, but Luster could hear him whimpering. "Is you gwine hush, er aint you?" Luster said. He got up and followed and came upon Ben squatting before a small mound of earth. At either end of it an empty bottle of blue glass that once contained poison was fixed in the ground. In one was a withered stalk of jimson weed. Ben squatted before it, moaning, a slow, inarticulate sound. Still moaning he sought vaguely about and found a twig and put it in the other bottle. "Whyn't you hush?" Luster said. "You want me to give you somethin to sho nough moan about? Sposin I does dis." He knelt and swept the bottle suddenly up and behind him. Ben ceased moaning. He squatted, looking at the small depression where the bottle had sat, then as he drew his lungs full Luster brought the bottle back into view. "Hush!" he hissed. "Dont you dast to beller! Dont you. Dar hit is. See? Here. You fixin to start ef you stays here. Come on, les go see ef dey started knockin ball yit." He took Ben's arm and drew him up and they went to the fence and stood side by side there, peering between the matted honeysuckle not yet in bloom.

"Dar," Luster said. "Dar come some. See um?"

They watched the foursome play onto the green and out, and move to the tee and drive. Ben watched, whimpering, slobbering. When the foursome went on he followed along the fence, bobbing and moaning. One said,

"Here, caddie. Bring the bag."

"Hush, Benjy," Luster said, but Ben went on at his shambling trot, clinging to the fence, wailing in his hoarse, hopeless voice. The man played and went on, Ben keeping pace with him until the fence turned at right angles, and he clung to the fence, watching the people move on and away.

"Will you hush now?" Luster said. "Will you hush now?" He shook Ben's arm. Ben clung to the fence, wailing steadily and hoarsely. "Aint you gwine stop?" Luster said. "Or is you?" Ben gazed through the fence. "All right, den," Luster said. "You want somethin to beller about?" He looked over his shoulder, toward the house. Then he whispered: "Caddy! Beller now. Caddy! Caddy! Caddy!"

A moment later, in the slow intervals of Ben's voice, Luster heard Dilsey calling. He took Ben by the arm and they crossed the yard toward her.

"I tole you he warnt gwine stay quiet," Luster said.

"You vilyun!" [38] Dilsey said. "Whut you done to him?"

---

38) villain.

"I aint done nothin. I tole you when dem folks start playin, he git started up." "You come on here," Dilsey said. "Hush, Benjy. Hush, now." But he wouldn't hush. They crossed the yard quickly and went to the cabin and entered. "Run git dat shoe," Dilsey said. "Dont you sturb Miss Cahline, now. Ef she say anything, tell her I got him. Go on, now; you kin sho do dat right, I reckon." Luster went out. Dilsey led Ben to the bed and drew him down beside her and she held him, rocking back and forth, wiping his drooling mouth upon the hem of her skirt. "Hush, now," she said, stroking his head. "Hush. Dilsey got you." But he bellowed slowly, abjectly, without tears; the grave hopeless sound of all voiceless misery under the sun. Luster returned, carrying a white satin slipper. It was yellow now, and cracked, and soiled, and when they gave it into Ben's hand he hushed for a while. But he still whimpered, and soon he lifted his voice again.

"You reckon you kin find T. P.?" Dilsey said.

"He say yistiddy he gwine out to St John's today. Say he be back at fo."

Dilsey rocked back and forth, stroking Ben's head.

"Dis long time, O Jesus," she said. "Dis long time."

"I kin drive dat surrey,[39] mammy," Luster said.

"You kill bofe y'all," Dilsey said. "You do hit fer devilment. I knows you got plenty sense to. But I cant trust you. Hush, now," she said. "Hush. Hush."

"Nome I wont," Luster said. "I drives wid T. P." Dilsey rocked back and forth, holding Ben. "Miss Cahline say ef you cant quiet him, she gwine git up en come down en do hit."

"Hush, honey," Dilsey said, stroking Ben's head. "Luster, honey," she said. "Will you think about yo ole mammy en drive dat surrey right?"

---

39) 바퀴가 4개이며 두 사람이 앉을 수 있는 작은 마차.

"Yessum," Luster said. "I drive hit jes like T. P."

Dilsey stroked Ben's head, rocking back and forth. "I does de tees I kin," she said. "Lewd knows dat. Go git it, den," she said, rising. Luster scuttled out. Ben held the slipper, crying. "Hush, now. Luster gone to git de surrey en take you to de graveyard. We aint gwine risk gittin yo cap," she said. She went to a closet contrived of a calico curtain hung across a corner of the room and got the felt hat she had worn. "We's down to worse'n dis, ef folks jes knowed," she said. "You's de Lawd's chile anyway. En I be His'n too, fo long, praise Jesus. Here." She put the hat on his head and buttoned his coat. He wailed steadily. She took the slipper from him and put it away and they went out. Luster came up, with an ancient white horse in a battered and lopsided surrey.

"You gwine be careful, Luster?" she said.

"Yessum," Luster said. She helped Ben into the back seat. He had ceased crying, but now he began to whimper again.

"Hit's his flower," Luster said. "Wait, I'll git him one."

"You set right dar," Dilsey said. She went and took the cheekstrap. "Now, hurry en git him one." Luster ran around the house, toward the garden. He came back with a single narcissus.

"Dat un broke," Dilsey said. "Whyn't you git him a good un?"

"Hit de onliest one I could find," Luster said, "Y'all took all of um Friday to dec'rate de church. Wait, I'll fix hit." So while Dilsey held the horse Luster put a splint on the flower stalk with a twig and two bits of string and gave it to Ben. Then he mounted and took the reins. Dilsey still held the bridle.

"You knows de way now?" she said. "Up de street, round de square, to de graveyard, den straight back home."

"Yessum," Luster said. "Hum up, Queenie."

"You gwine be careful, now?"

"Yessum." Dilsey released the bridle.

"Hum up, Queenie," Luster said.

"Here," Dilsey said. "You hen me dat whup."

"Aw, mammy," Luster said.

"Give hit here," Dilsey said, approaching the wheel. Luster gave it to her reluctantly.

"I wont never git Queenie started now."

"Never you mind about dat," Dilsey said. "Queenie know mo bout whar she gwine den you does. All you got to do es set dar en hold dem reins. You knows de way, now?"

"Yessum. Same way T. P. goes ev'y Sunday."

"Den you do de same thing dis Sunday."

"Cose I is. Aint I drove fer T. P. mo'n a hund'ed times?"

"Den do hit again," Dilsey said. "G'awn, now. En ef you hurts Benjy, nigger boy, I dont know whut I do. You bound fer de chain gang, but I'll send you dar fo even chain gang ready fer you."

"Yessum," Luster said. "Hum up, Queenie."

He flapped the lines on Queenie's broad back and the surrey lurched into motion.

"You, Luster!" Dilsey said.

"Hum up, dar!" Luster said. He flapped the lines again. With subterranean rumblings Queenie jogged slowly down the drive and turned into the street, where Luster exhorted her into a gait resembling a prolonged and suspended fall in a forward direction.

Ben quit whimpering. He sat in the middle of the seat, holding the repaired flower upright in his fist, his eyes serene and ineffable. Directly before him Luster's bullet head turned backward continually until the house passed from view, then he pulled to the side of the street and while Ben watched him he descended and broke a switch from a hedge. Queenie lowered her head and fell to cropping the grass until Luster mounted and hauled her head up and harried her into motion again, then he squared his elbows and with the switch and the reins held high he assumed a swaggering attitude out of all proportion to the sedate cropping of Queenie's hooves and the organlike basso of her internal accompaniment. Motors passed them, and pedestrians; once a group of half grown negroes:

"Dar Luster. Whar you gwine Luster? To de boneyard?"

"Hi," Luster said. "Aint de same boneyard y'all headed fen Hum up, elefump."

They approached the square, where the Confederate soldier gazed with empty eyes beneath his marble hand in wind and weather. Luster took still another notch in himself and gave the impervious Queenie a cut with the switch, casting his glance about the square. "Dar Mr Jason car," he said, then he spied another group of negroes. "Les show dem niggers how quality does, Benjy," he said.

"Whut you say?" He looked back. Ben sat, holding the flower in his fist, his gaze empty and untroubled. Luster hit Queenie again and swung her to the left at the monument.

For an instant Ben sat in an utter hiatus. Then he bellowed. Bellow on bellow, his voice mounted, with scarce interval for breath. There was more than astonishment in it, it was horror; shock; agony eyeless, tongueless; just sound, and Luster's eyes backrolling for a white instant. "Gret God," he said. "Hush! Hush! Gret God!" He whirled again and struck Queenie with the switch. It broke and he cast it away and with Ben's voice mounting toward its unbelievable crescendo Luster caught up the end of the reins and leaned forward as Jason came jumping across the square and onto the step.

With a backhanded blow he hurled Luster aside and caught the reins and sawed Queenie about and doubled the reins back and slashed her across the hips. He cut her again and again, into a plunging gallop, while Ben's hoarse agony roared about them, and swung her about to the right of the monument. Then he struck Luster over the head with his fist.

"Dont you know any better than to take him to the left?" he said. He reached back and struck Ben, breaking the flower stalk again. "Shut up!" he said. "Shut up!" He jerked Queenie back and jumped down. "Get to hell on home with him. If you ever cross that gate with him again, I'll kill you!"

"Yes, suh!" Luster said. He took the reins and hit Queenie with the end of them. "Git up! Git up, dar! Benjy, fer God's sake!"

Ben's voice roared and roared. Queenie moved again, her feet began to clop-clop steadily again, and at once Ben hushed. Luster looked quickly back over his shoulder, then he drove on. The broken flower drooped over Ben's fist and his eyes were empty and blue and serene again as cornice and façade flowed smoothly once more from left to right, post and tree, window and doorway and signboard each in its ordered place.

New York, N.Y.
October 1928

Appendix
Compson 1699–1945

• • • (중략) • • •

These were Compsons:

QUENTIN MACLACHAN. Son of a Glasgow printer, orphaned and raised by his mother's people in the Perth highlands. Fled to Carolina from Culloden Moor with a claymore and the tartan he wore by day and slept under by night, and little else. At eighty, having fought once against an English king and lost, he would not make that mistake twice and so fled again one night in 1779, with his infant grandson and the tartan(the claymore had vanished, along with his son, the grandson's father, from one of Tarleton's regiments on a Georgia battlefield about a year ago) into Kentucky, where a neighbor named Boon or Boone had already established a settlement.

CHARLES STUART. Attainted and proscribed by name and grade in his British regiment. Left for dead in a Georgia swamp by his own retreating army and then by the advancing American one, both of which were wrong. He still had claymore even when on his homemade wooden leg he finally overtook his father and son four years later at Harrodsburg, Kentucky, just in time to bury the father and enter upon a long period of being a split personality while still trying to be the schoolteacher which he believed he wanted to be, until he gave up at last and became the gambler he actually was and which no Compson seemed to realize they all were provided the gambit was desperate and the odds long enough. Succeeded at last in risking not only his neck but the security of his family and the very integrity of the name he would leave behind him, by joining the confederation headed by an acquaintance named Wilkinson (a man of considerable talent and influence and intellect and power) in a plot to secede the whole Mississippi Valley from the United States and join it to Spain. Fled in his turn when the bubble burst (as anyone except a Compson schoolteacher should have known it would), himself unique in being the only one of the plotters who had to flee the country: this not from the vengeance and retribution of the government which he had attempted to dismember, but from the furious revulsion of his late confederates now frantic for their own safety. He was not expelled from the United States, he talked himself countryless, his expulsion due not to the treason but to his having been so vocal and vociferant in the conduct of it, burning each bridge vocally behind him before he had even reached the place to build the next one: so that it was no provost marshal nor even a civic agency but his late coplotters themselves who put afoot the movement to evict him from Kentucky and the United States and, if they had caught him, probably from the world too. Fled by night, running true to family tradition, with his son and the old claymore and the tartan.

JASON LYCURGUS. Who, driven perhaps by the compulsion of the flamboyant name given him by the sardonic embittered woodenlegged indomitable father who perhaps still believed with his heart that what he wanted to be was a classicist schoolteacher, rode up the Natchez Trace one day in 1811 with a pair of fine pistols and one meagre saddlebag on a small lightwaisted but stronghocked mare which could do the first two furlongs in definitely under the halfminute and the next two in not appreciably more, though that was all. But it was enough: who reached the Chickasaw Agency at Okatoba (which in 1860 was still called Old Jefferson) and went no further. Who within six month was the Agent's clerk and within twelve his partner, officially still the clerk though actually halfowner of what was now a considerable store stocked with the mare's winnings in races against the horses of Ikkemotubbe's young men which he, Compson, was always careful to limit to a quarter or at most three furlongs; and in the next year it was Ikkemotubbe who owned the little mare and Compson owned the solid square mile of land which someday would be almost in the center of the town of Jefferson, forested then and still forested twenty years later though rather a park than a forest by that time, with its slavequarters and stables and kitchengardens and the for-mal lawns and promenades and pavilions laid out by the same architect who built the columned porticoed house furnished by steamboat from France and New Orleans, and still the square intact mile in 1840 (with not only the little white village called Jefferson beginning to enclose it but an entire white county about to surround it because in a few years now Ikkemotubbe's descendents and people would be gone, those remaining living not as warriors and hunters but as white men—as shiftless farmers or, here and there, the masters of what they too called plantations and the owners of shiftless slaves, a little dirtier than the white man, a little lazier, a little crueller—until at last even the wild blood itself would have vanished, to be seen only occasionally in the noseshape of a Negro on a cottonwagon or a white sawmill hand or trapper or locomotive fireman), known as the Compson Domain then, since now it was fit to breed princes, statesmen and generals and bishops, to avenge the dispossessed Compsons from Culloden and Carolina and Kentucky, then known as the Governor's house because sure enough in time it did produce or at least spawn a governor—Quentin MacLachan again, after the Culloden grandfather—and still known as the Old Governor's even after it had spawned (1861) a general—(called so by predetermined accord and agreement by the whole town and county, as though they knew even then and beforehand that the old governor was the last

Compson who would not fail at everything he touched save longevity or suicide)—the brigadier Jason Lycurgus II who failed at Shiloh in '62, and failed again though not so badly at Resaca in '64, who put the first mortgage on the still intact square mile to a New England carpetbagger in '66, after the old town had been burned by the Federal General Smith and the new little town, in time to be populated mainly by the descendent not of Compsons but of Snopeses, had begun to encroach and then nibble at and into it as the failed brigadier spent the next forty years selling fragments of it off to keep up the mortgage on the remainder: until one day in 1990 he died quietly on an army cot in the hunting and fishing camp in the Tallahatchie River bottom where he passed most of the end of his days.

And even the old governor was forgotten now; what was left of the old square mile was now known merely as the Compson place—the weed-choked traces of the old ruined lawns and promenades, the house which had needed painting too long already, the scaling columns of the portico where Jason III (bred for a lawyer and indeed he kept an office upstairs above the square, where entombed in dusty filingcases some of the oldest names in the county—Holston and Sutpen, Grenier and Beauchamp and Coldfield—faded year by year among the bottomless labyrinths of chancery: and who knows what dream in the perennial heart of his father, now completing the third of his three avatars—the one as son of a brilliant and gallant statesman, the second as battleleader of brave and gallant men, the third as a sort of privileged pseudo—Daniel Boone—Robinson Crusoe, who had not returned to juvenility because actually he had never left it—that that lawyer's office might again be the anteroom to the governor's mansion and the old splendor) sat all day long with a decanter of whisky and a little of dogeared Horaces and Livys and Catulluses, composing(it was said) caustic and satiric eulogies on both his dead and his living fellowtownsmen, who sold the last of the property, except that fragment containing the house and the kitchengarden and the collapsing stables and one servant's cabin in which Dilsey's family lived, to a golfclub for the ready money with which his daughter Candace could have her fine wedding in April and his son Quentin could finish one year at Harvard and commit suicide in the following June of 1910; already known as the Old Compson place even while Compson were still living in it on that spring dusk in 1928 when the old governor's doomed lost nameless seventeen-year-old greatgreat-granddaughter robbed her last remaining sane male relative (her uncle Jason IV) of his secret hoard of money and climbed down a rainpipe and ran off with a pitchman in a travelling streetshow, and still known as the Old Compson place long after all trace of Compsons were gone from it: after the widowed mother died and Jason IV, no longer needing to fear Dilsey now, committed his idiot brother, Benjamin, to the state Asylum in Jackson and sold the house to a countryman who operated it as a boarding house for juries and horse- and muletraders, and still known as the Old Compson place even after the boardinghouse (and presently the golfcourse too) had vanished and the old square mile was even intact again in row after row of small crowded jerrybuilt individuallyowned demiurban bungalows.

And these:

QUENTIN III. Who loved not his sister's body but some concept of Compson honor precariously and (he knew well) only temporarily supported by the minute fragile membrane of her maidenhead as a miniature replica of all the whole vast globy earth may be poised on the nose of a trained seal. Who loved not the idea of the incest which he would not commit, but some presbyterian concept of its eternal punishment: he, not God, could by that means cast himself and sister both into hell, where he could guard her forever and keep her forevermore intact amid the eternal fires. But who loved death above all, who loved only death, loved and lived in a deliberate and almost perverted anticipation of death as a lover loves and deliberately refrains from the waiting willing friendly tender incredible body of his beloved, until he can no longer bear not the refraining but the restraint and so flings, hurls himself, relinquishing, drowning. Committed suicide in Cambridge Massachusetts, June 1910, two months after his sister's wedding, waiting first to complete the current academic year and so get the full value of his paid-in-advance tuition, not because he had his old Culloden and Carolina and Kentucky grandfathers in him but because the remaining piece of the old Compson mile which had been sold to pay for his sister's wedding and his year at Harvard had been the one thing, excepting that same sister and the sight of an open fire, which his youngest brother, born an idiot, had loved.

CANDACE (CADDY). Doomed and knew it, accepted the doom without either seeking or fleeing it. Loved her brother despite him, loved not only him but loved in him that bitter prophet and inflexible corruptless judge of what he considered the family's honor and its doom, as he thought he loved but really hated in her what he considered the frail doomed vessel of its pride and the foul instrument of its disgrace; not only this, she loved him not only in spite of but because of the fact that he himself was incapable of love, accepting the fact that he must value above all not her but the virginity of which she was custodian and on which she placed no value whatever: the frail physical stricture which to her was no more than a hangnail would have been. Knew the brother loved death best of all and was not jealous, would (and perhaps in the calculation and deliberation of her marriage did) have handed him the hypothetical hemlock. Was two months pregnant with another man's child which regardless of what its sex would be she had already named Quentin after the brother whom they both (she and her brother) knew was already the same as dead, when she married (1910) and extremely eligible young Indianian she and her mother had met while vacationing at French Lick the summer before. Divorced by him 1911. Married 1920 to a minor movingpicture magnate, Hollywood California. Divorced by mutual agreement, Mexico 1925. Vanished in Paris with the German occupation, 1940, still beautiful and probably still wealthy too since she did not look within fifteen years of her actual fortyeight, and was not heard of again. Except there was a woman in Jefferson, the county librarian, a mousesized and colored woman who had never married, who had passed through the city schools in the same class with Candace Compson and then spent the rest of her life trying to keep *Forever Amber* in its orderly overlapping avatars and *Jurgen* and *Tom Jones* out of the hands of the highschool juniors and seniors who could reach them down without even having to tip-toe form the back shelves where she herself would have to stand on a box to hide them. One day in 1943, after a week of a distraction bordering on disintegration almost, during which those entering the library would find her always in the act of hurriedly closing her desk drawer and turning the key in it (so that the matrons, wives of the bankers and doctors and lawyers, some of whom had also been in that old highschool class, who came and went in the afternoons with the copies of the *Forever Ambers* and the volumes of Thorne Smith carefully wrapped from view in sheets of Memphis and Jackson newspapers, believed she was on the verge of illness or perhaps even loss of mind) she closed and locked the library in the middle of the afternoon and with her handbag clasped tightly under her arm and two feverish spots of determination in her ordinarily colorless cheeks, she entered the farmers' supply store where Jason IV had started as a clerk and where he now owned his own business as a buyer of and dealer in cotton, striding on through that gloomy cavern which only men ever entered—a cavern cluttered and walled and stalagmitehung with plows and discs and loops of tracechain and singletrees and mulecollars and sidemeat and cheap shoes and horselinament and flour and molasses, gloomy because the goods it contained were not shown but hidden rather since those who supplied Mississippi farmers or at least Negro Mississippi farmers for a share of the crop did not wish, until that crop was made and its value approximately computable, to show them what they could learn to want but only to supply them on specific demand with what they could not help but need—and strode on back to Jason's particular domain in the rear: a railed enclosure cluttered with shelves and pigeonholes bearing spiked dust-and-lintgathering gin receipts and ledgers and cottonsamples and rank with the blended smell of cheese and kerosene and harnessoil and the tremendous iron stove against which chewed tobacco had been spat for almost a hundred years, and up to the long high sloping counter behind which Jason stood and, not looking again at the overalled men who had quietly stopped talking and even chewing when she entered, with a kind of fainting desperation she opened the handbag and fumbled something out of it and laid it open on the counter and stood trembling and breathing rapidly while Jason looked down at it—a picture, a photograph in color clipped obviously from a slick magazine—a picture filled with luxury and money and sunlight—a Cannebière backdrop of mountains and palms and cypresses and the sea, an open powerful expensive chromiumtrimmed sports car, the woman's face hatless between a rich scarf and a seal coat, ageless and beautiful, cold serene and damned; beside her a handsome lean man of middleage in the ribbons and tabs of a German staffgeneral—and the mousesized mousecolored spinster trembling and aghast at her own temerity, staring across it at the childless bachelor in whom ended that long line of men who had had something in them of decency and pride even after they had begun to fail at the integrity and the pride had become mostly vanity and selfpity: from the expatriate who had to flee his native land with little else except his life yet who still refused to accept defeat, through the man who gambled his life and his good name twice and lost twice and declined to accept that either, and the one who with only a clever small quarterhorse for tool avenged his dispossessed father and grandfather and gained a principality, and the brilliant and gallant governor and the general who though he failed at leading in battle brave and gallant men at least risked his own life too in the failing, to the cultured dipsomaniac who sold the last of his patrimony not to buy drink but to give one of his descendants at least the best chance in life he could think of.

'It's Caddy!' the librarian whispered. 'We must save her!'

'It's Cad, all right,' Jason said. Then he began to laugh. He stood there laughing above the picture, above the cold beautiful face now creased and dogeared from its week's sojourn in the desk drawer and the handbag. And the librarian knew why he was laughing, who had not called him anything but Mr Compson for thirty-two years now, ever since the day in 1911 when Candace, cast off by her husband, had brought her infant daughter home and left the child and departed by the next train, to return no more, and not only the Negro cook, Dilsey, but the librarian too divined by simple instinct that Jason was somehow using the child's life and its illegitimacy both to blackmail the mother not only into stayingaway from Jefferson for the rest of her life but into appoint-ing him sole unchallengeable trustee of the money she would send for the child's maintenance, and had refused to speak to him at all since that day in 1928 when the daughter climbed down the rainpipe and ran away with the pitchman.

'Jason!' she cried. 'We must save her! Jason! Jason!' —and still crying it even when he took up the picture between thumb and finger and threw it back across the counter toward her.

'That Candace?' he said. 'Dont make me laugh. This bitch aint thirty yet. The other one's fifty now.'

And the library was still locked all the next day too when at three oclock in the afternoon, footsore and spent yet still unflagging and still clasping the handbag tightly under her arm, she turned into a neat small yard in the Negro residence section of Memphis and mounted the steps of the neat small house and rang the bell and the door opened and a black woman of about her own age looked quietly out at her. 'It's Frony, isn't it?' the librarian said. 'Dont you remember me—Melissa Meek, from Jefferson—'

'Yes,' the Negress said. 'Come in. You want to see Mama.' And she entered the room, the neat yet cluttered bedroom of an old Negro, rank with the smell of old people, old women, old Negroes, where the old woman herself sat in a rocker beside the hearth where even though it was June a fire smoldered—a big woman once, in faded clean calico and an immaculate turban wound round her head above the bleared and now apparently almost sightless eyes—and put the dogeared clipping into the black hands which, like the women of her race, were still as supple and delicately shaped as they had been when she was thirty or twenty or even seventeen.

'It's Caddy!' the librarian said. 'It is! Dilsey! Dilsey!'

'What did he say?' the old Negress said. And the librarian knew whom she meant by 'he', nor did the librarian marvel, not only that the old Negress would know that she (the librarian) would know whom she meant by the 'he', but that the old Negress would know at once that she had already shown the picture to Jason.

'Dont you know what he said?' she cried. 'When he realised she was in danger, he said it was her, even if I hadn't even had a picture to show him. But as soon as he realised that somebody, anybody, even just me, wanted to save her, would try to save her, he said it wasn't. But it is! Look at it!'

'Look at my eyes,' the old Negress said. 'How can I see that picture?'

'Call Frony!' the librarian cried. 'She will know her!' But already the old Negress was folding the clipping carefully back into its old creases, handing it back.

'My eyes aint good anymore,' she said. 'I cant see it.'

And that was all. At six oclock she fought her way though the crowded bus terminal, the bag clutched under one arm and the return half of her roundtrip ticket in the other hand, and was swept out onto the roaring platform on the diurnal tide of a few middleaged civilians but mostly soldiers and sailors enroute either to leave or to death and the homeless young women, their companions, who for two years now had lived from day to day in pullmans and hotels when they were lucky and in daycoaches and busses and stations and lobbies and public restrooms when not, pausing only long enough to drip their foals in charity wards or policestations and then move on again, and fought her way into the bus, smaller than any other there so that her feet touched the floor only occasionally until a shape (a man in khaki; she couldn't see him at all because she was already crying) rose and picked her up bodily and set her into a seat next the window, where still crying quietly she could look out upon the fleeing city as it streaked past and then was behind and presently now she would be home again, safe in Jefferson where life lived too with all its incomprehensible passion and turmoil and grief and fury and despair, but here at six oclock you could close the covers on it and even the weightless hand of a child could put it back among its unfeatured kindred on the quiet eternal shelves and turn the key upon it for the whole and dreamless night. *Yes* she thought, crying quietly *that was it she didn't want to see it know whether it was Caddy or not because she knows Caddy doesn't want to be saved hasn't anything anymore worth being saved for nothing worth being lost that she can lose.*

JASON IV. The first sane Compson since before Culloden and (a childless bachelor) hence the last. Logical rational contained and even a philosopher in the old stoic tradition: thinking nothing whatever of God one way or the other and simply considering the police and so fearing and respecting only the Negro woman, his sworn enemy since his birth and his mortal one since that day in 1911 when she too divined by simple clairvoyance that he was somehow using his infant niece's illegitimacy to blackmail its mother, who cooked the food he ate. Who not only fended off and held his own with Compsons but competed and held his own with the Snopeses who took over the little town following the turn of the century as the Compsons and Sartorises and their ilk faded from it (no Snopes, but Jason Compson himself who as soon as his mother died—the niece had already climbed down the rainpipe and vanished so Dilsey no longer had either of these clubs to hold over him—committed his idiot younger brother to the state and vacated the old house, first chopping up the vast oncesplendid rooms into what he called apartments and selling the whole thing to a countryman who opened a boardinghouse in it), though this was not difficult since to him all the rest of the town and the world and the human race too except himself were Compsons, inexplicable yet quite predictable in that they were in no sense whatever to be trusted. Who, all the money from the sale of the pasture having gone for his sister's wedding and his brother's course at Harvard, used his own niggard savings out of his meagre wages as a storeclerk to send himself to a Memphis school where he learned to class and grade cotton, and so established his own business with which, following his dipsomaniac father's death, he assumed the entire burden of the rotting family in the rotting house, supporting his idiot brother because of their mother, sacrificing what pleasures might have been the right and just due and even the necessity of a thirty-year-old bachelor, so that his mother's life might continue as nearly as possible to what it had been; this not because he loved her but (a sane man always) simply because he was afraid of the Negro cook whom he could not even force to leave, even when he tried to stop paying her weekly wages; and who despite all this, still managed to save almost three thousand dollars ($2840.50) as he reported it on the night his niece stole it; in niggard and agonised dimes and quarters and half dollars, which hoard he kept in no bank because to him a banker too was just one more Compson, but hid in a locked bureau drawer in his bedroom whose bed he made and changed himself since he kept the bedroom door locked all the time save when he was passing through it. Who, following a fumbling abortive attempt by his idiot brother on a passing female child, had himself appointed the idiot's guardian without letting heir mother know and so was able to have the creature castrated before the mother even knew it was out of the house, and who following the mother's death in 1933 was able to free himself forever not only from the idiot brother and the house but from the Negro woman too, moving into a pair of offices up a flight of stairs above the supplystore containing his cotton ledgers and samples, which he had converted into a bedroom-kitchen-bath, in and out of which on weekends there would be seen a big plain friendly brazen-haired pleasantfaced woman no longer very young, in round picture hats and (in its season) an imitation fur coat, the two of them, the middleaged cottonbuyer and the woman whom the town called, simply, his friend from Memphis, seen at the local picture show on Saturday night and on Sunday morning mounting the apartment stairs with paper bags from the grocer's containing loaves and eggs and oranges and cans of soup, domestic, uxorious, connubial, until the late afternoon bus carried her back to Memphis. He was emancipated now. He was free. 'In 1865,' he would say, 'Abe Lincoln freed the niggers from the Compsons. In 1933, Jason Compson freed the Compsons from the niggers.'

BENJAMIN. Born Maury, after his mother's only brother: a handsome flashing swaggering workless bachelor who borrowed money from almost anyone, even Dilsey although she was a Negro, explaining to her as he withdrew his hand from his pocket that she was not only in his eyes the same as a member of his sister's family, she would be considered a born lady anywhere in any eyes. Who, when at last even his mother realised what he was and insisted weeping that his name must be changed, was rechristened Benjamin by his brother Quentin (Benjamin, our lastborn, sold into Egypt). Who loved three thing: the pasture which was sold to pay for Candace's wedding and to send Quentin to Harvard, his sister Candace, firelight. Who lost none of them because he could not remember his sister but only the loss of her, and firelight was the same bright shape as going to sleep, and the pasture was even better sold than before because now he and TP could not only follow timeless along the fence the motions which it did not even matter to him were humanbeings swinging golfsticks, TP could lead them to clumps of grass or weeds where there would appear suddenly in TP's hand small white spherules which competed with and even conquered what he did not even know was gravity and all the immutable laws when released from the hand toward plank floor or smokehouse wall or concrete sidewalk. Gelded 1913. Committed to the State Asylum, Jackson 1933. Lost nothing then either because, as with his sister, he remembered not the pasture but only its loss, and firelight was still the same bright shape of sleep.

QUENTIN. The last. Candace's daughter. Fatherless nine months before her birth, nameless at birth and already doomed to be unwed from the instant the dividing egg determined its sex. Who at seventeen, on the one thousand eight hundred ninetyfifty anniversary of the day before the resurrection of Our Lord, swung herself by a rainpipe form the window of the room in which her uncle had locked her at noon, to the locked window of his own locked and empty bedroom and broke a pane and entered the window and with the uncle's firepoker burst open the locked bureau drawer and took the money (it was not $2840.50 either, it was almost seven thousand dollars and this was Jason's rage, the red unbearable fury which on that night and at intervals recurring with little or no diminishment for the next five years, made him seriously believe would at some unwarned instant destroy him, kill him as instantaneously dead as a bullet or a lightningbolt: that although he had been robbed not of a mere petty three thousand dollars but of almost seven thousand he couldn't even tell anybody; because he had been robbed of seven thousand dollars instead of just three he could not only never receive justification—he did not want sympathy—from other men unlucky enough to have one bitch for a sister and another for a niece, he couldn't even go to the police; because he had lost four thousand dollars which did not belong to him he couldn't even recover the three thousand which did since those first four thousand dollars were not only the legal property of his niece as a part of the money supplied for her support and maintenance by her mother over the last sixteen years, they did not exist at all, having been officially recorded as expended and consumed in the annual reports he submitted to the district Chancellor, as required of him as guardian and trustee by his bondsmen: so that he had been robbed not only of his thievings but his savings too, and by his own victim; he had been robbed not only of the four thousand dollars which he had risked jail to acquire but of the three thousand which he had hoarded at the price of sacrifice and denial, almost a nickel and a dime at a time, over a period of almost twenty years: and this not only by his own victim but by a child who did it at one blow, without premeditation or plan, not even knowing or even caring how much she would find when she broke the drawer open; and now eh couldn't even go to the police for help: he who had considered the police always, never given them an trouble, had paid the taxes for years which supported them in parasitic and sadistic idleness; not only that, he didn't dare pursue the girl himself because he might catch her and she would talk, so that his only recourse was a vain dream which kept him tossing and sweating on nights two and three and even four years after the event, when he should have forgotten about it: of catching her without warning, springing on her out of the dark, before she had spent all the money, and murder her before she had time to open her mouth) and climbed down the same rainpipe in the dusk ran away with the pitchman who was already under sentence for bigamy. And so vanished; whatever occupation overtook her would have arrived in no chromium Mercedes; whatever snapshot would have contained no general of staff.

And that was all. These others were not Compsons. They were black:

TP. Who wore on Memphis's Beale Street the fine bright cheap intransigent clothes manufactured specifically for him by the owners of Chicago and New York sweatshops.

FRONY. Who married a pullman porter and went to St Louis to live and later moved back to Memphis to make a home for her mother since Dilsey refused to go further than that.

LUSTER. A man, aged 14. Who was not only capable of the complete care and security of an idiot twice his age and three times his size, but could keep him entertained.

DILSEY.

They endured.

포크너 연보

1897년 9월 25일, 윌리엄 C. 포크너 미시시피주 뉴 알바니에서 탄생.

1898년 12월, 가족은 미시시피주 리플리로 이사.

1902년 9월 22일, 가족은 옥스퍼드로 이사.

1905년 9월 25일, 8세가 된 포크너 초등학교 입학. 이듬해 2학년 월반.

1910년 10월 4일, 할아버지 존 W. T. 포크너는 옥스퍼드에 "제일국민은행" 설립.

1911년 9월, 포크너 8학년이 됨. 학교 공부에 점점 싫증내며 수업을 빠지기 시작.

1914년 6월, 시를 쓰기 시작하며 필 스톤과의 우정이 시작됨. 9월, 그는 11학년이 되지만 12월에 자퇴. 그 후 그는 축구팀에 가입하기 위해 학교를 다시 들어가지만 다음 해 가을 다시 학교를 그만둠.

1915년 훗날 아내가 될 에스텔과 '단짝' 이 됨.

1916년 겨울, 할아버지 은행에서 잠시 동안 일함. 에스텔에게 가끔 자신이 쓴 시들을 보여주면서 시작 활동 계속.

1917년 최초의 작품이라고 할 수 있는 그림 한 장이 미시시피대학 연보에 실림.

1918년 봄, 체격이 왜소하다는 이유로 공군에 입대 거절, 뉴 헤이번으로 가서 점원으로 일함. 4월 18일, 에스텔과 코넬 프랭클린 결혼. 7월 9일, 영국 공군에 입대하기 옥스퍼드로 귀향.

1919년 8월 6일, *New Republic*에서 그의 시 "L'Apres-Midi d'une Faune"가 최초로 선보임. 9월, 그는 선과생으로 대학에서 불어, 스페인어, 문학을 수강하며, 학교 신문에 시들과 산문 스케치 등을 선보임.

1920년 가을, 다시 선과생으로 대학에 등록하여 교내 연극서클에 들어 활동하면서 "The Marionettes"(단막극)을 씀.

1921년 여름, 사랑을 주제로 한 시집인 *Vision in Spring*을 완성하며 극동지방에서 잠시 친정에 돌아와 쉬고 있는, 이미 한 아이(빅토리아)의 어머니가 된 에스텔에게 그 시집 바침. 그해 가을, 포크너는 뉴욕의 한 책방에서 점원으로 잠시 일하다 12월에 옥스퍼드로 돌아와 대학 우체국에서 일함.

1923년 꾸준히 시와 단편들을 썼으며, "Adolescence"와 "Love" 출판.

1924년 여름, 우체국에서 과음 문제로 해고당함. 11월, 뉴올리언스에서 셔우드 앤더슨 만남. 12월 15일, *The Marble Faun*이 출판되며 모친에게 그 책을 바치고 필 스톤이 서문을 씀.

1925년 1월 초, 뉴올리언스로 다시 돌아와 잡지들에 작품들 기고. 최초의 소설이 될 *Soldiers Pay*를 쓰기 시작. 6월, 다음 해 완성될 시집 *Helen: A Courtship*을 위해 시작 활동 계속. 이 시집을 헬렌 베어드에게 바침. 7월, 첫 소설 *Soldiers'Pay* 선금으로 받은 200달러를 가지고 유럽(이탈리아와 파리) 여행. 12월에 옥스퍼드로 귀향.

1927년 스놉스 삼부작의 전신이 될 “Father Abraham” 집필 시작. 2월, 에스텔의 딸 빅토리아를 위해 동화 “The Wishing Tree” 씀(사후 출판). 4월, *Mosquitoes*를 출판.

1928년 봄, *The Sound and the Fury*의 작업 시작.

1929년 *Flags in the Dust*가 *Sartoris*라는 제목으로 수정되어 출판. 4월, 두 아이(빅토리아와 말콤)를 둔 에스텔 이혼. 5월 25일, *The Sound and the Fury*는 완성되지만 Harcourt 출판사에게 거절, *Sanctuary*의 원고도 완성. 6월 20일, 에스텔과 결혼, 신혼 여행지에서 에스텔 익사 자살 시도. 10월 7일, Cape & Smith 출판사에 의해 *The Sound and the Fury* 출판. 10월에서 12월 사이, *As I Lay Dying* 원고 작업.

1930년 남북전쟁 이전 약 1844년경에 건축된 로원 오크(Rowan Oak)를 그들이 살 집으로 구매. 4월 말, *Forum*에 그의 최초의 단편작 “A Rose for Emily” 출판. 10월, *As I Lay Dying* 출판. 내용이 도덕적 물의를 빚고 있는 *Sanctuary*를 출판물 검열에 적절히 맞추기 위해 수정 작업.

1931년 1월 11일, 첫 아이(Alabama)가 태어나지만 생후 9일이 지난 후 사망. 2월 9일, Cape & Smith 출판사가 수정된 *Sanctuary* 출판. 9월 말, 그의 최초의 단편 선집인 *These 13* 출판. 8월부터 *Light in August* 작업 시작.

1932년 10월, *Light in August* 출판.

1933년 2월, 조종사 면허증을 취득한 후 개인 비행기 소유. 6월 24일, 포크너의 유일한 생존 혈육인 질(Jill)이 탄생.

1934년 4월, *Doctor Martino and Other Stories* 출판. 7월 할리우드의 유니버설 영화사와 주당 1,000달러를 받고 일함.

1935년 3월, *Pylon* 출판. *Absalom, Absalom*! 작업 시작. 11월 10일, 막내 동생 딘이 임신한 아내를 남긴 채 비행기 사고로 사망하자 그 가족을 포크너가 책임짐. 12월, 다시 할리우드로 돌아와 20세기 폭스사와 일함. 이때 각본 일을 보고 있던 메타 카펜터와 만나며 그들의 오랜 관계 시작.

1936년 1월 말, *Absalom, Absalom!*의 원고를 완성한 후, 알코올 속에 묻혀 살던 그의 몸이 극도로 악화되자 병원에 입원할 지경에 이르며, 일단 건강을 회복한 후 집에서 몸조리를 계속. 2월 말과 7월 중순 사이 할리우드를 다녀옴. 10월 26일 *Absalom, Absalom!* 출판.

1937년 겨울, 계속 할리우드에서 일함. 9월 중순에 Rowan Oaks로 돌아와 *The Unvanquished* 출판. 11월, 스놉스 삼부작의 첫 소설인 *The Hamlet* 집필 시작.

1940년 1월 말, 평생 포크너 집안을 헌신적으로 돌보아 온 흑인 보모 캐롤라인 바(매미 캘리)의 사망. 그녀는 *The Sound and the Fury*에서 딜시의 전형이 되며, 후에 포크너는 *Go Down, Moses*를 그녀에게 바침. 4월, *The Hamlet* 출판.

1942년 *Go Down, Moses and Other Stories* 출판. 이 책은 제2판 출간 시 *Go Down, Moses*로 명함. 7월, 캘리포니아 버뱅크에 도착, 워너 브러더스 영화사와 주당 300달러라는 적은 보수를 받으면서 7년간 계속될 계약 체결.

1943년 1월 중순경, 할리우드로 다시 돌아와 7개월 동안 여러 각본들 작업. 그 후 몇 년간은 많은 시간을 할리우드에서 보내게 되며, 1950년 초까지 계속 됨.

1946년 4월 말, 작가로서 새롭게 명성을 안겨 주게 될 *The Portable*

*Faulkner*가 말콤 카울리에 의해 편집되어 바이킹 출판사에서 출판. 12월 말경 *The Sound and the Fury* 그리고 *As Iay Dying*이 "Compson Appendix"와 함께 1권으로 편집되어 Modern Library에서 출판.

1947년 4월 중순, 미시시피 대학에서 강의.

1948년 7월, MGM사가 *Intruder in the Dust*의 영화 제작권으로 5만 달러 지불.

1949년 11월, 탐정 소설집인 *Knight's Gambit* 출판.

1950년 2월 초, 뉴욕 방문, 여기서 조안 윌리엄스를 만나며 *Requiem for a Nun*을 그녀와 함께 집필할 것을 계획(30세 아래인 조안과도 로맨틱한 관계). 5월, "American Academy of Arts and Letters"로부터 "Howells Medal" 수상. 8월 말, 단편집 *Collected Stories* 출판. 11월 10일, "1949년 노벨 문학상" 수상.

1951년 2월 초에서 3월 초까지 할리우드로 돌아와 주당 2천 달러를 받으면서 다시 일 시작. 3월, *Collected Stories* 로 "National Book Award" 수상. 9월 말, *Requiem for a Nun* 출판. 10월 말, 뉴올리언스에서 프랑스 영사로부터 "Legion of Honor" 수상.

1952년 5월, 한 달 동안 유럽 여행, 프랑스 국회에서 "문화의 자유"라는 주제로 연설.

1953년 뉴욕을 오가면서 많은 시간을 그곳에서 보냄. 이 해 알코올 중독과 신경증 증세로 병원에 입원하기도 하며 잠시 동안 정신과 병동을 드나들기도 함. 12월 초, 영화 *Land of the Pharaohs*의 제작 답사를 위하여 이집트와 이탈리아를 여행. 크리스마스이브, 당시 유럽에서 활약하던 젊은 미국인 저널

리스트 진 스타인을 만나며 그녀와 친분 관계 형성. 이즈음 조안과의 관계는 이미 종식됨.

1954년 1월, 영국·프랑스·이태리·카이로 등지를 여행하며 카이로에서 입원. 4월 초, *The Faulkner Reader* 출판. 파리에서 병원 입원. 8월 초, *A Fable* 출판. 8월 21일 딸 질과 웨스트 포인트 출신인 폴 서머즈(Paul D. Summers, Jr.)와 결혼.

1955년 1월, *A Fable*로 "National Book Award"와 픽션 부분에 "퓰리처 상" 수상. 7월 말, 국방성 후원으로 일본에서 3주일간 체류. 일본에서 엄청난 환영을 받으며 후에도 일본 방문을 요청받는다. 의붓딸 빅토리아와 그녀의 남편과 함께 마닐라에서 이틀간 체류. 10월 중순, 사냥 얘기들을 담고 있는 "Big Woods" 출판.

1956년 가을까지 뉴욕, 옥스퍼드, 샬롯스빌(딸 질이 거주하던 도시)을 오가면서 생활. *Paris Review*를 위해 진 스타인과 인터뷰. *The Town* 집필 중. 9월, 공산권 국가들에게 미국문화를 촉진시키기 위한 "People-to-People Program"에 참여.

1957년 2월에서 6월까지 버지니아 대학에서 거주, 작가로서 주로 질의응답 형식으로 강의. 3월 중순, 국방성 후원으로 2주 동안 그리스 방문, 아테네 아카데미에서 은메달 수상. 5월, *The Town* 출판. 5월 10일에서 8월 30일까지 제임스 메리웨더(James B. Meriwether)가 주선하여 프린스턴 대학 도서관에서 "포크너 작가 경력"(The Literary Career of William Faulkner) 전시회 가짐.

1958년 버지니아 대학 거주 작가로서 두 번째 학기 강의를 계속하지만, 그의 인종관 때문에 영구 교수직은 대학 총장에 의해 거절당함. *The Mansion* 집필.

1959년 1월 30일, *Requiem for a Nun* 뉴욕에서 첫 공연. 봄, 버지니아에서 대부분의 시간을 보내며, 8월 샬롯스빌에 주택 구매. *The Mansion* 출판.

1960년 10월 16일, 모친 모드 포크너 사망. 그해 말 자신의 모든 작품 원고들을 윌리엄 포크너 재단(William Faulkner Foundation)에 기증.

1961년 4월 초, 국방성 후원으로 베네수엘라에 도착, 2주 동안 외교 사절로서 임무 수행. 마지막 소설인 *The Reivers* 집필 시작.

1962년 1월, 낙마 사고로 병원 입원. 5월 말, 웰티(Eudora Welty)가 "American Academy of Arts and Letters"를 대신하여 픽션 부분에서 그에게 금메달 수여. 6월 초, *The Reivers* 출판. 또 한 차례의 낙마 사고. 7월 5일, 병원 입원. 다음날 심장마비로 사망.

001
Kyung Moon
Reading Classic

The Sound and the Fury
지은이 William Faulkner
편저자 강 희
펴낸이 박문규
펴낸곳 경문사
펴낸날 2007년 2월 28일 1판 1쇄
2013년 3월 5일 1판 2쇄
등 록 1979년 11월 9일 제313-1979-23호
주 소 121-818, 서울특별시 마포구 와우산로 174
전 화 (02) 332-2004 팩스 (02) 336-5193
이메일 kyungmoon@kyungmoon.com

값 16,000원

ISBN 89-7282-935-8
ISBN 978-89-6105-156-9 (세트)